Agape and Personhood

POSTMODERN ETHICS SERIES

Postmodernism and deconstruction are usually associated with a destruction of ethical values. The volumes in the Postmodern Ethics series demonstrate that such views are mistaken because they ignore the religious element that is at the heart of existential-postmodern philosophy. This series aims to provide a space for thinking about questions of ethics in our times. When many voices are speaking together from unlimited perspectives within the postmodern labyrinth, what sort of ethics can there be for those who believe there is a way through the dark night of technology and nihilism beyond exclusively humanistic offerings? The series invites any careful exploration of the postmodern and the ethical.

Series Editors:
Marko Zlomislić (Conestoga College)
David Goicoechea (Brock University)

Other Volumes in the Series:
Cross and Khôra: Deconstruction and Christianity in the Work of John D. Caputo edited by Neal DeRoo and Marko Zlomislić

Future Volumes:
David Goicoechea is producing "Millennial Meditations on 2000 Years of Christian Love: A Postmodern Summa—*Agape* as Reconciliation," of which the present volume is the first of nine.

I   Agape *and Personhood with Kierkegaard, Mother, and Paul (A Logic of Reconciliation from the Shamans to Today)*
II Agape *and the Four Loves with Nietzsche, Father, and Q (A Physiology of Reconciliation from the Greeks to Today)*
III Agape *and Ahav-Hesed with Levinas-Derrida and Matthew, at Mt. Angel-St. Thomas (A Doxology of Reconciliation from Moses and David to Today)*
IV Agape *and Bhakti with Bataille and Mark, at Loyola-St. Francis (A Mysticology of Reconciliation based on Hindu Karma from Arjuna to Augustine)*
V   Agape *and Karuna with Foucault and Luke, at Brock Philosophy Department (A Therapeutology of Reconciliation based on Buddhist No-Self from Buddha to Francis)*
VI Agape *and Rahim with Deleuze, Brock Philosophy Society, and John (An Atheology of Reconciliation based on Islamic Sharia from Muhammad to Luther)*
VII Agape *and Zen with Kristeva, Wilhelmina, and Catholic School (A Semiology of Reconciliation based on Japanese No-Drama from Nishida to John XXIII)*
VIII Agape *and Jen with Cixous, Carolyn, and Pauline School (A Phenomenology of Reconciliation based on the Confucianist Family from Tu Wei-Ming to John Paul II)*
IX Agape *and Tao with Irigaray, Johanna, and the Johannine School (An Eschatology of Reconciliation based on Taoist Gendering from Moeller to Benedict XVI)*

Agape and Personhood

with Kierkegaard, Mother, and Paul
(A Logic of Reconciliation from the Shamans to Today)

DAVID L. GOICOECHEA

POSTMODERN ETHICS SERIES

☙PICKWICK *Publications* · Eugene, Oregon

AGAPE AND PERSONHOOD
with Kierkegaard, Mother, and Paul (A Logic of Reconciliation from the Shamans to Today)

Postmodern Ethics Series 2

Copyright © 2011 David L. Goicoechea. All rights reserved. Except for brief quotations in critical publications or reviews, no part of this book may be reproduced in any manner without prior written permission from the publisher. Write: Permissions, Wipf and Stock Publishers, 199 W. 8th Ave., Suite 3, Eugene, OR 97401.

Pickwick Publications
An Imprint of Wipf and Stock Publishers
199 W. 8th Ave., Suite 3
Eugene, OR 97401

www.wipfandstock.com

ISBN 13: 978-1-60899-794-7

Cataloguing-in-Publication data:

Goicoechea, David

Agape and personhood : with Kierkegaard, mother, and Paul (a logic of reconciliation from the shamans to today) / David L. Goicoechea.

xxii + 358 p. ; 23 cm. Includes bibliographical references.

Postmodern Ethics Series 2

ISBN 13: 978-1-60899-794-7

1. Kierkegaard, Søren, 1813–1855. 2. Paul, the Apostle, Saint. 3. Motherhood. 4. Reconciliation—Religious aspects. I. Title. II. Series.

BL410 G65 2011

Manufactured in the U.S.A.

For my mother dear

with whom I still love

to pray the Rosary each morning.

"Mother at about the time she started praying her daily rosary"

Contents

List of Images / viii

Acknowledgments / ix

Detailed Line of Argument / x

Introduction / 1

Part One: Joyful Beginnings
Mother / 20
Søren Kierkegaard / 47
St. Paul / 74
Personhood / 102

Part Two: Sorrowful Proceedings
Mother / 134
Søren Kierkegaard / 161
St. Paul / 188
Personhood / 216

Part Three: Glorious Finishings
Mother / 248
Søren Kierkegaard / 275
St. Paul / 302
Personhood / 329

Bibliography / 357

Images

Mother at about the time she started praying her daily rosary / v
The Seven Chakras / 101
Gramma Coats at the time of her marriage / 129
Mother with her Mother up Iron Mine / 129
Mother's Anglican Mother / 129
Mother's Mormon Father / 130
Uncle El with Gramma and Grampa Coates / 130
Myself and Mother with Grandpa Coates and his Father / 130
Mother with her Catholic husband and me / 131
Myself and our sheepcamp up Dollarhyde Summit / 131
Myself with Dixie and her puppy, Penny / 131
Mother's five children / 132
Myself and Aunt Sadie / 132
Bette Jo and Bob come home after their wedding / 244
Mother with her first grandson, Joseph Robert / 244
Mother and her children at Cliff's wedding / 244
The Coates family reunion / 245
Mother and Daddy with Grandma Coates / 245
Mother's five children at the time of Daddy's death / 245
The Grandchildren at the time of Grandpa's death / 246
Mother at eighty / 246
Mother's Rebecca Lodge friends / 246

Acknowledgments

In getting out this first volume I owe a debt of great gratitude to my wife, Dr. Johanna M. Tito, who has helped me so much in so many ways. Secondly, I want to thank all those at Pickwick Publications and especially Chris Spinks and Kristen Bareman with whom it has been such a delight to work and who have done such a terrific job in getting the book ready for publication. Thirdly, I want to thank Dr. Marko Zlomislic who has helped me so much over the past 20 years. Thanks also to my good friend Ms. Dorothy Korchok for patiently helping me with proofreading the entire book.

Detailed Line of Argument

Part One: Joyful Beginnings

I. Mother

I.1 With Her Anglican Mother
I.1.1 Identification in Mother-Daughter Bonding
I.1.2 In the Attitude of Complacent *Agape*
I.1.3 In the Mood of Concerned *Agape*
I.1.4 In the Sense of Proactive Sensitivity
I.1.5 In the Passion of Positive Emotions
I.1.6 In the Logic of True Thoughts
I.1.7 In the Intonation of Incantational Words
I.1.8 In the Peace of a Gentle Touch
I.1.9 In the Construction of Upbuilding Deeds

I.2 With Her Mormon Father
I.2.1 In the Logic of the Triad
I.2.2 In the Logic of the Quadrad
I.2.3 In the Logic of the Quadratic Weaning
I.2.4 In the First Deceptive Weaning
I.2.5 In the Third Weaning of Mutual Mourning
I.2.6 In the Fourth Weaning or Providing Sustenance
I.2.7 Pauline Universalism—Johannine Exclusivism
I.2.8 Dyadic Johannine Glory
I.2.9 Pauline Triadic Glory

I.3 With Her Catholic Husband

I.3.1 The Holy Ideal and the Justice of Peace

I.3.2 Holy Child

I.3.3 Sacred Priest—Sacred Baptism—Sacred Matrimony

I.3.4 The Holy, the Sacred, and the Profane

I.3.5 Holy War—Holy Pregnancy—Holy Daughter

I.3.6 The Holy and the Sacred

I.3.7 Paul and John Becoming Mark

I.3.8 Communicating in Sacred Silence

I.3.9 Third Holy Child and Sacred Community

II. Søren Kierkegaard

II.1 Reconciling the God-Man and Socrates
II.1.1 The Paradoxical Logic of Erotic Inspiration
II.1.2 The Logic of Socratic Irony
II.1.3 The Logic of Skeptical Irony
II.1.4 The Logic of Agapeic Reconciliation
II.1.5 The Logic of Personal Growth
II.1.6 The Logic of The Both-And
II.1.7 Loving Socrates as More Important
II.1.8 The Noble Socratic Return
II.1.9 Loving the God-Man as More Important

II.2 Reconciling the God-Man and Abraham
II.2.1 The Absurd Contingency of the Single Individual
II.2.2 The Absurd Contingency of Postmodern Doubting
II.2.3 The Absurd Contingency of Unlimited Voices
II.2.4 The Absurd Contingency of Abraham's Faith in the Promise
II.2.5 The Absurd Contingency of Double Movement Leaping
II.2.6 The Absurdity of Ethically Suspending the Teleological
II.2.7 Loving Abraham as More Important
II.2.8 The Abrahamic Blessing for All Peoples
II.2.9 Loving the God-Man as More Important

II.3 Reconciling the God-Man and Job
II.3.1 Repetition's Reconciliation Is the Only Happy Love
II.3.2 Beyond Platonic Recollection to a New Future
II.3.3 Beyond Hegelian Mediation to a New Past
II.3.4 Repetition as the Ethical Task of Freedom
II.3.5 Metaphysic's Interest on Which Metaphysics Founders
II.3.6 The Single Individual and the Posthorn
II.3.7 Loving Job as More Important
II.3.8 Job's Faithful Love That Justifies the Exception
II.3.9 Loving the God-Man as More Important

III. St. Paul

III.1 Conversion to Reconciliation
III.1.1 The New *Agape*
III.1.2 The New Personal *Agape*
III.1.3 The New Universal *Agape*
III.1.4 A New Apocalyptic Universalism
III.1.5 The New Agapeic Logic of Suffering
III.1.6 Paul's Logic of Mixed Opposites
III.1.7 The New Logic of the Body of Christ
III.1.8 The Logic of the Communal Person
III.1.9 The Logic of Individual Persons

III.2 Paul's Love Letter to the Thessalonians
III.2.1 Motivating Thessalonians to Universal Love
III.2.2 Bonds Them in Familial Affection
III.2.3 So That He Constantly Loves Them in Prayer
III.2.4 To the Father, Son, and Holy Spirit
III.2.5 But There Is the Problem Of Death
III.2.6 Set in the Context of Christ's Resurrection
III.2.7 And His Second Coming in Our Lifetime
III.2.8 Which Gives Urgency to our Ethical Task
III.2.9 As We Abide in the Grace, Peace, and Joy of Jesus

III.3 Paul's Love Letter to the Corinthians
III.3.1 No Gift of Worth but Love
III.3.2 Which Gives Worth to Suffering
III.3.3 And to God's Foolishness and Ours
III.3.4 And to God's Weakness and Ours
III.3.5 In a Logic of the Cross
III.3.6 That Can Reconcile Factions
III.3.7 As well as Marital Alienation
III.3.8 In the Lord's Supper
III.3.9 Of Christ's Resurrected Body

IV. Personhood

IV.1 From Shamanic Humans in Relation
IV.1.1 Shamanic Humans
IV.1.2 Pelvis Healers and Porter Physicians
IV.1.3 Erotic Artists and Lector Teachers
IV.1.4 Liver Cleansers and Exorcist Deliverers
IV.1.5 From Sorcerer Heart to Acolyte Heart
IV.1.6 From Prophetic Mediums to Sub-Deacons
IV.1.7 Sixth Sense Diviner Leaders
IV.1.8 The Head Shaman as Integrator
IV.1.9 From Shamanic Bishops and Abbots to Modernity

IV.2 To Classical Soul and Spirit
IV.2.1 From Shamans to Pre-Socratics
IV.2.2 From Pre-Socratics to Sophists
IV.2.3 From Sophists to Socrates
IV.2.4 From Socrates to Plato
IV.2.5 From Plato to Aristotle
IV.2.6 Stoic *Recta Ratio*
IV.2.7 Matter Matters in Epicurean Friendship
IV.2.8 Non-Judgmental and Serene Skeptics
IV.2.9 The Neo-Platonic Synthesis.

IV.3 To the Chosen People's Nine Revelations against Gnosticism
IV.3.1 *The Law* and Creation Stories against Gnostic Origins
IV.3.2 Mosaic Redemption Stories against Gnostic Determinism
IV.3.3 Davidic Promise Stories against Gnostic Fatalism
IV.3.4 *The Prophets* and Elijah against Gnostic Orgies
IV.3.5 The Minor Prophets against Gnostic Immorality
IV.3.6 The Major Prophets against Gnostic Disaster
IV.3.7 *The Writings* and Prayers Replacing Gnostic Non-Prayer
IV.3.8 Lady Sophia's Joyful Wisdom against Gnostic Nihilism
IV.3.9 Apocalyptic Progression against Gnostic Regression

Part II: Sorrowful Proceedings

I. Mother

I.4 With Her Son, David, and Father Dougherty
I.4.1 Cultivating the Holy with the Sacred Heart of Jesus
I.4.2 Cultivating Holy Health with the Sacred *Sacerdos*
I.4.3 Cultivating Holy Happiness with Sacred Sacrifice
I.4.4 Cultivating Holy Wisdom with the Sacred Sacrament
I.4.5 Cultivating Holy Work with the Sacred Consecration
I.4.6 Cultivating Holy Forgiving with Q's Jesus
I.4.7 Offering All in the Dark Night
I.4.8 Offering Her Son to the Seed Bed
I.4.9 With the 'Jesus' of the Hail Mary

I.5 With Her Daughter, Bette Jo, and Father Heeren
I.5.1 The Holy Communion Covenant with the Sacred Heart
I.5.2 Dear Father's Affliction and Holy Communion Code
I.5.3 Loss of Father Heeren and Holy Communion Cult
I.5.4 The Mary-Like Crusading and Holy Communion Canon
I.5.5 Dear Husband's Addictions and Holy Communion Creed
I.5.6 Cultivating Petrine Authority with Matthew's Jesus
I.5.7 Obedience: Sacred Vertical and Holy Horizontal
I.5.8 Chastity: Sacred Vertical and Holy Horizontal
I.5.9 Poverty: Sacred Vertical and Holy Horizontal

I.6 With Her Son, Bobby Brian, and Father O'Connor
I.6.1 How Sacred Communion Graced Her with Holy Love
I.6.2 How Sacred Confession Graced Her with Holy Peace
I.6.3 How Sacred Matrimony Graced Her with Holy Joy
I.6.4 How Sacred Baptism Graced Her with Holy Hope
I.6.5 How Sacred Extreme Unction Graced Her with Holy Promise
I.6.6 Cultivating Freedom with the Jesus of Luke's Gospel
I.6.7 How Sacred Confirmation Graced Their Physical Exercises
I.6.8 How Sacred Holy Orders Graced Their Intellectual Exercises
I.6.9 How Sacred Sacraments Graced Their Spiritual Exercises

II. Søren Kierkegaard

II.4 Reconciling the God-Man and Plato
II.4.1 By Preserving Plato's Paradoxes in the Incarnational Leap
II.4.2 By Preserving the Learning Paradox in the Incarnation
II.4.3 By Preserving the Love Paradox in the Incarnation
II.4.4 By Preserving the Typhonic Paradox in the Incarnation
II.4.5 Preserving the Absolute Paradox in the Incarnation
II.4.6 By Not Taking Offense at the Paradox in the Incarnation
II.4.7 By Loving His Platonic Readers as More Important
II.4.8 Plato's Transition from *The Symposium* to *The Phaedrus*
II.4.9 That They Might Love the God-Man as More Important

II.5 Reconciling the God-Man and Hegel
II.5.1 In the Truth of the Existential Dialectic
II.5.2 In the Objective Uncertainty of the Historical Process
II.5.3 In Holding Fast to the Uncertainty of the Single Individual
II.5.4 By Living in Fragments instead of the System
II.5.5 In the Appropriation Process of a Postscript
II.5.6 In the Inwardness of a Double Movement Leap
II.5.7 Loving Hegel as More Important with Climacus
II.5.8 Hegel's History of Love and Personhood
II.5.9 Loving the God-Man in the Most Passionate Inwardness

II.6 Reconciling the God-Man and Adam and Eve
II.6.1 Adam and Eve's Leap out of Anxiety into Original Sin
II.6.2 Hereditary Sin's Quantitative Build-up of Anxiety
II.6.3 Anxiety and the Leap of Faith into Actual Sins
II.6.4 Anxious Leaping into the Inclosing Reserve or Repose
II.6.5 That Discloses Itself All of a Sudden or is Open to Disclosure
II.6.6 Out of Boredom or in Faith's Most Passionate Inwardness
II.6.7 Loving Adam and Eve as More Important in Atonement
II.6.8 Anxiety through Faith is Absolutely Educative
II.6.9 Loving the God-Man in Body, Soul, and Spirit

III. St. Paul

III.4 Paul's Second Love Letter to the Corinthians
III.4.1 It Was God Who Reconciled Us
III.4.2 To Himself through Christ
III.4.3 And Gives Us the Work
III.4.4 Of Handing on This Reconciliation
III.4.5 Not According to Standards of the Flesh
III.4.6 And Not in Accord with Christ in the Flesh
III.4.7(a) But We Have Been Reconciled (Part One)
III.4.7(b) But We Have Been Reconciled (Part Two)
III.4.8 As Different Members of Christ's Body
III.4.9 That We Should Love Our Enemies

III.5 Paul's Love Letter to the Galatians
III.5.1 Paul's Ethics of Reconciliation
III.5.2 Is Based on the Standards of Love
III.5.3 Which Believes That We Have Been Freed
III.5.4 From the Law and Self Indulgence
III.5.5 In Order to Serve All Others
III.5.6 Greeks as Well as Jews
III.5.7 Women as Well as Men
III.5.8 Slaves as Well as Masters
III.5.9 While We Prepare for the Lord's Coming

III.6 Paul's Love Letter to the Romans
III.6.1 Paul's Anthropology of Reconciliation
III.6.2 Bridges the Gap between God and Humans
III.6.3 Through a Gift of Faith Like Abraham's
III.6.4 Which Believes That Christ Died for Us Sinners
III.6.5 Which Proves That God Loves Us
III.6.6 Since before We Were Reconciled to God
III.6.7 By the Death of the Son
III.6.8 We Were Still Enemies
III.6.9 And Our Joyful Trust Is Proof of Our Salvation

IV. Personhood

IV.4 To Defining Personhood as Three Persons in One God
IV.4.1 The Person of the Father beyond Judaism and Neo-Gnosticism
IV.4.2 The Work of the Father beyond Judaism and Neo-Gnosticism
IV.4.3 The Person of the Son beyond Judaism and Neo-Gnosticism
IV.4.4 The Work of the Son beyond Judaism and Neo-Gnosticism
IV.4.5 The Person of the Spirit beyond Judaism and Neo-Gnosticism
IV.4.6 The Work of the Spirit beyond Judaism and Neo-Gnosticism
IV.4.7 Incarnational Origins beyond Judaism and Neo-Gnosticism
IV.4.8 Incarnational Religion beyond Judaism and Neo-Gnosticism
IV.4.9 Incarnational Eschatology beyond Judaism and Neo-Gnosticism

IV.5 To Defining Personhood as Two Natures in One Person
IV.5.1 The Son is Fully Divine against Arian Subordination
IV.5.2 For the Three Persons Share One Nature (*Homoousios*)
IV.5.3 And the Son has Two Natures (Hypostatic Union)
IV.5.4 His Divine Nature is Absolutely Perfect
IV.5.5 His Human Nature Suffers, Dies, and Rises
IV.5.6 Same Person before and after Incarnation
IV.5.7 The Western Contribution from Tertullian to Leo
IV.5.8 From Leo's Summary of the West to Chalcedon
IV.5.9 Chalcedon's Unique, Equal, Relational Persons

IV.6 To Boethius and Defining Human Personhood
IV.6.1 An Individual Substance of a Rational Nature
IV.6.2 Defining Individuals (beyond Plato and Eutyches)
IV.6.3 Distinguishing Substance (beyond Plotinus and Cyril)
IV.6.4 Knowing Rational Souls (beyond Epicurus and Cyril)
IV.6.5 A Natural History of Nature (beyond Stoics and Nestorius)
IV.6.6 Autonomy of Natural Sciences (*The Consolation of Philosophy*)
IV.6.7 Beyond Gnosticism (The *Consolation of Philosophy*)
IV.6.8 Beyond Aristotle and Arius (with Lady Philosophia)
IV.6.9 The Suffering Servant's Serene, Peaceful Gentleness

Detailed Line of Argument xix

Part Three: Glorious Finishings

I. Mother

I.7 With Her Son, Clifford Scott, and Father Waldman
I.7.1 Christmas is Everyday in Joyful Mystery Love
I.7.2 In the Annunciation and the *Hail Mary*'s Five Parts
I.7.3 In the Visitation and the Mystery's Five Parts
I.7.4 In the Nativity and Her Intention's Five Parts
I.7.5 In the Presentation and Her World's Five Parts
I.7.6 In the Temple Finding and God's World's Five Parts
I.7.7 In the Johannine School's Incarnational Joy
I.7.8 In the Holy Joy of the Sacred Liturgy of the Word
I.7.9 In the Holy Joy of the Sacred Liturgy of the Eucharist

I.8 With Her Son, Tommy Joe, and Father Denardis
I.8.1 Especially on Good Friday in Sorrowful Mystery Love
I.8.2 In the Garden Agony and the *Hail Mary*'s Five Parts
I.8.3 In the Pillar Scourging and the Mystery's Five Parts
I.8.4 In the Thorn Crowning and Her Intention's Five Parts
I.8.5 In the Cross Carrying and Her World's Five Parts
I.8.6 In the Crucifixion and God's World's Five Parts
I.8.7 In the Catholic School's Love That Cancels Sin
I.8.8 In the Holy Sorrow of the Sacred Liturgy of the Word
I.8.9 In the Holy Sorrow of the Sacred Liturgy of the Eucharist

I.9 With Her Grandchildren
I.9.1 In the Glorious Mystery of the Resurrection
I.9.2 In the Resurrection and the *Hail Mary*'s Five Parts
I.9.3 In the Ascension and the Mystery's Five Parts
I.9.4 The Descent of the Holy Spirit and Her Intention's Five Parts
I.9.5 In the Assumption and Her World's Five Parts
I.9.6 In the Coronation and God's World's Five Parts
I.9.7 In the Pauline School's Glorious Battle
I.9.8 In the Holy Glory of the Sacred Liturgy of the Word
I.9.9 In the Holy Glory of the Sacred Liturgy of the Eucharist

II. Søren Kierkegaard

II.7 Reconciling the God-Man and Luther
II.7.1 In the Agapeic Synthesis of Faith and Works
II.7.2 In the Agapeic Synthesis of Scripture and Tradition
II.7.3 In the Agapeic Synthesis of Law and Gospel
II.7.4 In the Agapeic Synthesis of the Universal Community
II.7.5 In the Synthesis of *Eros* and *Agape*
II.7.6 In the Synthesis of Affection and *Agape*
II.7.7 In the Synthesis of Friendship and *Agape*
II.7.8 In the Synthesis of Incarnation and Atonement
II.7.9 By Loving Lutherans as More Important

II.8 Reconciling the God-Man and the Desperado
II.8.1 By Giving Spirit to Those Ignorant of Being in Despair
II.8.2 By Giving Hope to Desperados of Finitude with Infinitude
II.8.3 By Giving Hope to Desperados of Infinitude with Finitude
II.8.4 By Giving Hope to Desperados Not Willing to Be Themselves
II.8.5 By Giving Hope to Desperados Who Will to Be Themselves
II.8.6 By Giving Hope to Desperados Who Are Sinners
II.8.7 By Loving Desperados as More Important with Anti-Climacus
II.8.8 Hope for Desperados Despairing over Their Sin
II.8.9 Loving the God-Man in Faith, Hope and *Agape*

II.9 Reconciling the God-Man and Our Modern Age
II.9.1 By Loving Those Who Are Guilty of Taking Offense
II.9.2 At This Actual Incarnate God-Man
II.9.3 In His Lowly Temporality
II.9.4 Or in His Lofty Power And Wisdom
II.9.5 By Loving the God-Man as Our Contemporary
II.9.6 By Loving Him as That Unique Single Individual
II.9.7 By Praising the Love in Our Modern Contempories
II.9.8 By Praying for Their Blessed Dead When They Do Not
II.9.9 By Loving Modernists as More Important than Ourselves

III. St. Paul

III.7 Paul's Love Letter to Philemon
III.7.1 Paul's Politics of Reconciliation
III.7.2 Begins with Affection and *Agape*
III.7.3 For the Slave Boy, Onesimus
III.7.4 Whom Paul Is Sending Back to His Master
III.7.5 With an Appeal to Philemon's *Agape*
III.7.6 That he will Treat him as a Dear Brother
III.7.7 And with a Guarantee That Paul Will Pay
III.7.8 For Anything Owed to the Master by the Slave
III.7.9 And Thus Is a Politics of Love for All

III.8 Paul's Love Letter to the Philippians
III.8.1 Paul's Logic of Reconciliation Bases All
III.8.2 On Giving Preference to Others as Did Jesus
III.8.3 Who as God Emptied Himself
III.8.4 By Taking the Form of a Slave
III.8.5 And by Accepting Death
III.8.6 So That All Beings Should Bend the Knee
III.8.7 At the Name of Jesus
III.8.8 Who Will Transfigure Our Wretched Body
III.8.9 Into the Mould of His Glorious Body

III.9 Paul's New Evidence for the New Love
III.9.1 From Mere Facts to Seven New Kings of Evidence
III.9.2 The New Historical Evidence of 1 Thessalonians
III.9.3 The New Exemplary Evidence of 1 Corinthians
III.9.4 The New Emotional Cognition of 2 Corinthains
III.9.5 The New Evidence of Comparative Ethics in Galatians
III.9.6 The New Evidence of Comparative Psychology in *Romans*
III.9.7 The New Evidence of Comparative Politics in *Philemon*
III.9.8 The New Evidence of Comparative Logic in *Philippians*
III.9.9 It Is Self-Evident That We Should Love *Agape*

IV. Personhood

IV.7 To Love and Personhood from Augustine to Aquinas
IV.7.1 The *Caritas* Synthesis (Grace and Freedom)
IV.7.2 *Uti et Frui* (The Problem of Evil and Loving Suffering)
IV.7.3 Two Loves Have Built Two Cities (Christian History)
IV.7.4 From St. Benedict to St. Anselm of Canterbury
IV.7.5 From Pseudo-Dionysius to St. Bernard
IV.7.6 From John the Scot to Abelard
IV.7.7 Charity is a Habit Created in the Human Soul
IV.7.8 Charity is the Most Powerful Virtue
IV.7.9 Charity is Complacency and Concern

IV.8 To Love and Personhood with the Franciscans
IV.8.1 Francis' Love for Wolf and *Sultan*
IV.8.2 Joachim of Fiore's Unlimited Scriptural Seeds
IV.8.3 Bonaventure's New Universalism of *Multiformes Theoriae*
IV.8.4 Bonaventure's History and the Worth of the Temporal Order
IV.8.5 Scotus's Move from *Multiformes Theoriae* to *Haecceity*
IV.8.6 Scotus' New Personhood of *Haecceity*
IV.8.7 From *Multiformes Theoriae* to Ockham's Nominalism
IV.8.8 From Okham's Nominalism to Luthor's Modernity
IV.8.9 From Ockham to Postmodern Nominalism

IV.9 From Love to Justice for Modern Individuals
IV.9.1 From Calvin's TULIP to Hobbes' *Homo Homini Lupus*
IV.9.2 From Luther's Faith Alone to Hume's Experience Alone
IV.9.3 From Henry VIII's Anglicans to Locke's Democracy
IV.9.4 From Descartes' Cogito to Leibnitz' Monad
IV.9.5 From Wesley's Evangelicals to Smith's *Wealth of Nations*
IV.9.6 From Rousseau's Gratitude Alone to Kant's Reason Alone
IV.9.7 From Kant's Persons to Hegel's Persons in Relation
IV.9.8 From Pentecostal Spirit to Equity Feminism
IV.9.9 From Pope's Total Goodness to Martin Luther King's Dream

Introduction

Two thousand years ago Jesus introduced
his new teaching and practice of *agape*
which commands us to love one another
as he loved us in self denial and sacrifice.
Each new age has emphasized a special aspect
of loving God with our whole heart, mind, and soul,
and of loving our neighbor as our self.
In our postmodern age at this millennial turn
the new emphasis is upon *agape* as reconciliation.
Jesus gives us the command:

> *If you are offering your gift at the altar*
> *and there remember that your brother*
> *has something against you*
> *leave your gift there before the altar*
> *and go and be reconciled with your brother*
> *and then come and offer your gift.* (Matt 5:23–24)

Of course, reconciliation has always been important
but given the new communication technology
of our global village it will here be argued that
it has become the focal point of our postmodern times.
In this first volume of our millennial meditations
I will reflect on how I learned faith, hope, and love
from my mother's reconciling life as she went through
her eighty-one years of personal growth through love.
Second, I will explain how the strategy of reconciliation
is at the heart of Kierkegaard's philosophy of loving persons.
Third, I will show how the gift and task of reconciliation
is the main theme of Paul's seven authentic letters.
Fourth, I will examine the history of *agape* and personhood
in the West from the perspective of agapeic reconciliation.
The point is to let the four perspectives enlighten each other.

Mother

Dear David, Oct 13, 1995

*Sorry I'm so late in answering your letter.
I pray the Rosary three times a day.
I offer the Joyful Mysteries for myself:
The Annunciation for humility,
The Visitation that I can help people
come closer to the love of God,
The Nativity to help me realize
my dependence on God for everything,
The Presentation for perfect obedience,
and The Finding in the Temple for a more
perfect understanding of God's Holy will.*

*I offer the Sorrowful Mysteries for my family:
The Agony in the Garden that each one in my family
be truly sorry for their sins,
The Scourging that each in my family obtain the purity
that they need and the graces to love and serve God,
The Crowning with Thorns that each one ban
all impure thoughts, suspicious thoughts,
and uncharitable thoughts and get rid of
their pride and selfishness;
The Carrying of the Cross that they will
be patient in their trials and sufferings,
and The Crucifixion that it will not be
in vain for anyone in my family.*

*The Glorious Mysteries:
The Resurrection I offer for you for the faith you need
and for true sorrow for your sins.
The Ascension I offer for my grandchildren*

for the graces, helps and protection and faith that each one needs.
The Descent of the Holy Spirit I offer for my Godchildren
for the love and charity, the faith and protection
and graces that each one needs.
The Assumption I offer for my brothers and sister
and their families and for my relatives and In-Laws
for the faith and help that each one needs.
The Coronation I offer for our Parish,
for the faith, love and protection that each one of us needs.

We had a real cold night. It was 28 degrees this morning.
Looks like we're going to have an early and cold winter.
I really enjoyed your visit and hope you can come more often.
Bette Jo and Bob are moving to Hagerman in November.
It will be nice to have them close.
Tell Josje "Hello." I'm glad he is taking some
more courses in college.

Love and Prayers
your mother

Mother identified with the sorrow of her mother whose mother died when she was but eight and with the sorrow of her father whose mother died when he was but five and she identified with their identification with each other for shamans often do lose a parent when they are children and thereby learn of the spirit world. From her mother, mother learned to pray the *Our Father* and from her father's Mormon community mother learned that our Heavenly Father loves us and is with us especially in sorrow. Then from her husband who lost his father when he was but five mother learned how to pray the *Hail Mary* and the *Angel of God*. Mother grew as her prayer took her into the five dimensional universe.

Mother lived most closely throughout her whole life with three
prodigal sons for her father was a prodigal son, her husband
was a prodigal son, and her own first son was a prodigal son.
And yet unlike the elder brother she never for a moment needed
to reconcile with them for each of them knew how she loved them
and from her they even knew how God would always love them.
For surely God's love would have to be as affirmative as was hers.
Her father dear became the town drunk and began squandering
the family fortune so that her mother had to divorce him even
though she proudly loved him and her father sobbed when he saw
his wonderful daughter, Sissy, and even though he could not change
and died in an insane asylum he always knew how loved he was.
Her husband dear who was a proud and gifted gambler was shot
in the ankle when hunting and became an alcoholic garbage man.
But with her help he knew that he was cleaning up the town
and unlike so many punk-kid adults he kept the faith,
put all his children through college and with her constant love
eventually quit smoking and drinking and was shamanic right
to the end as he taught his children how to love their mother
just as she taught them to love him forever more and more.
Her first son became the worst sinner of all for he was both
an habitual adulterer and an hypocrite who professed to be
religious and yet hurt his wives and children more than did
her father or her husband who never broke the commandments
but drank, perhaps, to fill the void of their dead lost parents.
But her son who had the best of educations and even prayed
with the various women he loved forced his wives to leave him.
And their children suffered so much to see their mothers so hurt
and to be separated from their father for living ghosts can be
harder to live with than dead ones who do not haunt you so.
Her first son knew his mother's love who saw all so clearly
and it let him feel like King David after whom she named him.

Mother's four noble truths

I   Mother as a person in relation suffered the sorrows
of those with whom she was most closely bonded

II   and her greatest sorrow of all was losing her loved ones
for love wants to be present with those whom we love.

III   But mother's Rosary and Mass taught her that Christmas
can be every day especially on Good Friday because of Easter
Sunday.

IV   And this became real for mother as she journeyed
on the nine-fold path of her life with

  (1) her Anglican mother from whom she learned of
joyful service not only for family but also for community

  (2) her Mormon father with whom she learned hard work and for whom
she always prayed as he became her broken, sobbing dad

  (3) her Catholic husband who knew she was the perfect wife and mother
and who was the alpha male for and with his alpha female

  (4) her son, David, who still prays with and for her every day and
Father Dougherty who taught her of the sacred heart of Jesus

  (5) her daughter, Bette Jo, who still identifies with her in all
of her mothering and Father Heeren, her spiritual director

  (6) her son, Robert Brian, who has her gentle heart and
Father O'Connor, her Irish priest with his sense of humor

  (7) her son, Clifford Scott, who like her daughter is like her
husband and Father Waldman, that true Idaho priest

  (8) her son, Tommy Joe, who like his two namesakes is
wise and strong and Father DeNardis, that saintly priest

  (9) her grandchildren and great grandchildren for whom she
still prays everyday and the new priests of Post Vatican Two.

And so mother is there now with Father, Son, and Holy Spirit
and with the Blessed Mother of God and with all of the Angels
and with all of the Saints and she is praying for and interceding
for all of us here now just as she did when she was here.
Since she lived in these five dimensions in her prayer
for her last fifty years she must still be living as she lived.

Kierkegaard

> *The greatest good, after all, which can be done*
> *for a being . . . is to make it free.*
> *In order to do just that Omnipotence is required.*
> *This seems strange, since it is precisely Omnipotence*
> *that supposedly would make (a being) dependent.*
> *But if one will reflect on Omnipotence, he will see*
> *that it also must contain the unique qualification*
> *of being able to withdraw itself again*
> *in a manifestation of Omnipotence in such a way*
> *that precisely for this reason that which has been*
> *originated through Omnipotence can be independent.*
> *That is why one human being cannot*
> *make another person wholly free . . .*
> *only Omnipotence can withdraw itself*
> *at the same time it gives itself away, and*
> *his relationship is the very independence of the receiver.*
> *(Journals and Papers 2.1252)*

The entirety of Kierkegaard's existential thinking could be interpreted as reflecting on this Omnipotence that stands back in order to let the other be free.
In the last three chapters of his *Works of Love* Kierkegaard explains the agapeic strategy for accomplishing reconciliation.[NL1-3]
(1) We need to love the other as more important than ourselves that he or she might be graced to love others as more important.
(2) We need to recollect the dead in praying for them and in asking them to pray for us that we might see a context that is big enough in time and space to let this impossible task happen.
(3) We need to praise Love which is God that we might praise all others as members of his Incarnate Body.
In humility Jesus taught us how God stands back to free others and thus sacrifices his omnipotence for the potency of others.

In part two, chapter eight, of *Works of Love: The Victory of the Conciliatory Spirit in Love, Which Wins the One Overcome*, Kierkegaard poses the problem clearly when he writes:

> *Let us suppose that the prodigal son's brother*
> *had been willing to do everything for his brother-yet*
> *one thing he could never have gotten into his head*
> *that the prodigal should be more important.* (338)

If the prodigal goes to the altar to thank God he will be
commanded by the Gospel to go to his elder brother and
to seek reconciliation in accord with Matt 5:23–24.
When the prodigal came home after squandering his money
his brother took offense at him and was resentful because his father
threw a party to welcome home the prodigal and did not seem
in the elder brother's eyes to see him as important as the prodigal.
It was as if the father thought the prodigal to be more important.
So for the prodigal to properly love the elder brother he has to
not only forgive him but to go and be reconciled with him.
That might be no easy task for the prodigal would have to treat
the elder brother as more important and the elder brother would
have to think of the prodigal as more important if there is
to be true reconciliation according to the model of *agape*.
The point of Kierkegaard's authorship is to show how the brother
can be brought to love the prodigal as more important than himself.
How will the elder brother stop taking offense and being resentful?
It is the task of the prodigal to be like Stephen for Paul.
He has to stand back in self denial to free his brother.
In resentment the brother may not want to become freed
from his taking offense that he might be reconciled.
So the prodigal has to have faith that it will happen
in his brother's and in God's good time and even if
it doesn't happen in this life time the prodigal must not
despair, but he must pray always even for the blessed dead.

In the middle of his chapter on *Praising Love* Kierkegaard gives a summary of how reconciliation can be achieved:

> *This is inwardly the condition or model*
> *in which praising love must be done.*
> *To carry it out has, of course,*
> *its intrinsic reward, although in addition*
> *by praising love in so far as one is able,*
> *it also has the purpose to win people to it,*
> *to make them properly aware of what*
> *in a conciliatory spirit is granted*
> *to every human being-that is, the highest.*
> *The one who praises art and science still*
> *shows dissention between the gifted and ungifted.*
> *But the one who praises love reconciles all,*
> *not in common poverty nor in a common*
> *mediocrity, but in the community of the highest.* (365)

For Kierkegaard the prodigal might remain an aesthete for whom the beauty of the party immediately pleases "me", but if so he will come to the common poverty of me-centered prodigals. Or the prodigal might become ethical and reflect upon "my self" but in simply avoiding the dire consequences of prodigality with gifted insight he might be just as mediocre as his brother. The prodigal might go beyond the common poverty of the pre-aesthetic me and the common mediocrity of the reflectively ethical myself and become the "I" who is thankful to his father and to God. But, this "me," "myself" and "I" can become other centered in a praising love that lets even aesthetic petition, ethical repentance and religious gratitude become praising. This is the seven step logic of reconciliation that is demanded of the prodigal and which is the core of Kierkegaard's philosophy. We will now examine how Kierkegaard applied this logic throughout his authorship in reconciling older brothers and Jesus.

Kierkegaard's four noble truths

I   We humans bring each other into the suffering of boredom and fear and trembling

II   through the sin of taking offence at God's existence in anxiety and despair

III   from which we can be creatively freed by following the God-man's loving self-denial and self-sacrifice

IV   along the nine-fold path of his conciliatory love that recollects the dead in the praising love of humankind's highest affirmation by moving

(1) from the irony of Socratic skepticism in which love is a matter of conscience

(2) to Abraham's knight of faith who follows his duty to love the people we see

(3) to love's renewing repetition that is a duty to remain in love's debt to one another for Job and to Regina

(4) and from Plato to accepting truth's paradox

(5) and from Hegel to holding fast to objective uncertainty in a true love that believes all things and yet is never deceived

(6) and from Adam and Eve's anxiety to a love that hopes in all things and yet is never put to shame

(7) to the *Works of Love* that do not seek their own in the wisdom of the logic of the like for like

(8) and which delivers us from the *Sickness Unto Death* by leading us through the journey of self reconciliation which lets us live on all three floors of our house

(9) and by the *Training in Christianity* that lets us abide in the love that never takes offence at any offence.

Kierkegaard clarifies this with nine key definitions of (1) love, (2) person, (3) the stages on life's way, (4) the double movement leap, (5) repetition, (6) truth, (7) sin, (8) despair, and (9) taking offence.

St. Paul

> *For Christ did not send me to baptize*
> *but to preach the Good News*
> *and not to preach that in terms of philosophy*
> *in which the crucifixion of Christ cannot be expressed.*
> *The language of the Cross may be illogical*
> *to those who are not on the way to salvation*
> *but those of us who are on the way*
> *see it as God's power to save . . .*
> *While the Jews demand miracles*
> *and the Greeks look for wisdom*
> *here we are preaching a crucified Christ;*
> *to the Jews an obstacle that they cannot get over*
> *to the pagans madness*
> *but to those who have been called*
> *whether they are Jews or Greeks*
> *a Christ who is the wisdom and power of God.*
> *For God's foolishness is wiser than human wisdom*
> *and god's weakness is stronger than human strength.*
> (1 Cor 1: 17–25)

So the Good News of agapeic reconciliation is contrary
to any human philosophy and works with the logic of the Cross
which in order to reconcile with other logics is contrary to them.
Kierkegaard's existential philosophy in treating the absurd logic
of the incarnation, crucifixion, resurrection, ascension, and pentecost
goes beyond the old logics of the categorical syllogism,
the disjunctive syllogism and the hypothetical syllogism
to the modal logic of contingency and freedom that has been
revealed by the Cross of Christ in the power of sacrificial love.
Paul shows how the problem of evil can be the mystery of suffering
for when we offer our suffering with the suffering of the God-man
the evil of suffering paradoxically becomes God's loving suffering.

Logic for the Greeks is related to the verb *legein* which means
to gather the parts into an orderly pattern and reasonable whole.
Logos is translated into Latin as *ratio* and into English as reason.
Logic in its basic meaning is related to theology because it is based
upon the necessary law that something cannot come from nothing.
What we call collecting in English is in Greek a syllogism.
It is the gathering of the logos of *legein* together or into
a collection of parts with each other into a coherent unit.
Logicians arrange their reasoning into syllogistic forms
based on three kinds of whole part meaning or relation.
An example of a categorical syllogism is: (1) Whatever is
caused is caused by another. (2) St. Paul is caused.
(3) Therefore, he is caused by another. An example of
a disjunctive syllogism is: (1) Either St. Paul is caused
or not caused, but not both. (2) But St. Paul is caused.
(3) Therefore, he is not not caused. An example of a conditional
syllogism is: (1) If St. Paul is caused, then he is caused by another.
(2) But he is caused. (3) Therefore, he is caused by another.
The Greeks thought that everything is held together in necessary
relationships based on whole part relations and logic makes
clear the necessary order of Being (ontology), of the world
(cosmology), of God (theology), of the living thing (psychology),
and of knowledge (epistemology). The faith of the Hebrew people
believed in a God that defied this logic of necessity by
deifying the Divine Will that could freely bring something
into existence out of the nothingness of a formless void.
But, when that omnipotent creator absurdly became a creature
and was both all powerful and all weak at once, that defied
both Greek logic and the Hebrew faith and when Paul experienced
the weakness of God that is more powerful than the power of men
he had to make sense of both the Greek and the Hebrew irrational.

The basic miracle in which the Hebrews believed had to do with
The Mosaic Covenant and The Davidic Promise by which
they were delivered from slavery in Egypt and as God's
chosen people given a law that continued to save them, and
by which they were promised a land flowing with milk and honey
and that they would be a nation more numerous than the stars of the sky
and that they would be a blessing to all the peoples of the earth.
The Mosaic Covenant gave them their meaning from the past
and The Davidic Promise gave them their meaning for the future.
Abraham, their father, kept his faith as he was tried over
and over again with threats to all three parts of the promise.
But then came the worst when God seemed to contradict himself
and demand that he sacrifice Isaac in an absurd move which
would keep God from keeping his promise if Isaac through whom
the promise was to be fulfilled would be cruelly taken away.
But Abraham had faith and God came through and put an end
to child sacrifice at least for his chosen family of Abraham.
However, what Paul witnessed is that God sacrificed his
only Son in an absurdity that was without visible miracles.
The mystery of love was such that Paul actually witnessed
in Stephen no visibly resurrected Christ, but instead
a look of love on Stephen's face that made more sense to him
than any logical meaning and it could fulfill The Davidic Promise.
Besides the look of love there was a voice so loving that it
called Paul to go forth and be a blessing to all the peoples.
In Paul's *Second Letter to the Corinthians*, chapter five, he
put it all very simply: "For anyone who is in Christ, there is
a new creation; the old creation has gone, and now the new
one is here. It is all God's work. It was God who
reconciled us to himself through Christ, and gave us the work
of handing on this reconciliation." It was now Paul's work
by suffering in love with Stephen and Jesus to reconcile all.

St. Paul's four noble truths

I   All sentient beings suffer including God in the God-man.

II   So the problem of evil becomes the mystery of suffering which should be embraced.

III For loving suffering not only builds character
but also in a reconciliation process saves others
with self denying sacrifice that loves them as more important

IV as St. Paul found along the nine-fold path
of his journey of reconciling love

(1) which began when he was touched by the loving face
of Stephen revealing the loving face of Jesus' Mystical Body

(2) and along which he progressed for his beloved Thessalonians
by teaching them how *agape* is increasing love for the whole
human race

(3) and for his beloved Corinthians by teaching them that
agape is the love feast and the Lord's Supper

(4) and again for his Corinthians by showing them how
agape is the suffering which consoles others

(5) and for his beloved Galatians by showing them how
agape is the freedom to serve one another

(6) and for the Romans by teaching them how
agape is the love of God made visible in Jesus Christ

(7) and for Philemon by teaching him how
agape loves the slave as a brother

(8) and for the Philippians whom he taught how
agape is the love that prepares us for greater glory

(9) and all the while pondering more deeply with the Romans
that what proves that God loves us is that Christ
died for us while we were still sinners. Having died
to make us righteous, is it likely that he would now
fail to save us from God's anger? Now that we have
been reconciled, surely we may count on being saved.

The history of personhood

> *Shamanism can be defined as a group of techniques*
> *by which the practitioners enter the 'spirit world',*
> *purportedly attaining information that is used to help*
> *and to heal members of their social group.*
> *The shamans' way of knowing depended on deliberately*
> *altering their conscious state and/or heightening*
> *their perception to contact spiritual entities*
> *in 'upper worlds', 'lower worlds', and 'middle earth'.*
> *For the shaman the totality of inner and outer reality*
> *was fundamentally an immense signal system,*
> *and shamanic states of consciousness were the first steps*
> *towards deciphering this signal system.*
> *Homo Sapiens Sapiens was probably unique*
> *among early humans in the ability to symbolize,*
> *mythologize, and, eventually, to shamanize.*
>
> *Although the term 'shaman' is of uncertain derivation,*
> *it is often traced to the language of the Tungus*
> *reindeer herders of Siberia where the word 'shaman'*
> *translates into "one who is excited, moved or raised".*
> *An alternative translation for the Tungus word is*
> *"inner heat," and an alternative etymology*
> *is the Sanskrit word 'saman' or 'song.'*
> Stanley Krippner[1]

For the first fifteen hundred years of Christian history the paradigm of persons in relation was worked out in progressive stages. But 500 years ago when modernity began with Luther, Calvin and Henry VIII and then with Descartes, Hobbes and up to Hegel the new paradigm of rugged individualism went through its stages. Now with the postmodernists there is a return to persons in relation with a communal emphasis as with the shamans.

The history of personhood in the West might be thought of
in its simplest form in the following three stages of three:

I   Praeparatio Evangelica
    1) with hunter-gatherer and agricultural shamans
    2) with Greek vegetative, animal and rational souls
    3) with Mosaic and Davidic tribal spirit

II Guiding definitions
    1) with three persons in one God
    2) with two natures in one person
    3) with an individual substance of a rational nature

III Three traditions of agape and personhood
    1) with the tradition from Augustine to Aquinas
    2) with the tradition from Francis to Luther
    3) with the tradition from Descartes to Kierkegaard

Agape is the gift and the task of a love for all persons
who as the brothers and sisters of Jesus, the Son of God,
are believed to have unique singularity and equal worth.
Agape is a universal love that is not based on equality
at the level the lowest common denominator, for even though
particularity does imply an exclusivity that destroys universalism,
the singularity of the incarnation is able to have a logic that
unlike particularity is able to go out affirming all differences.
When the Son of God became flesh we received the gift:
"That all flesh shall see the salvation of the Lord." (Luke 3:6)
The task of this gift is that we spend our lives promoting
the highest and the best in all persons and even all flesh.
Agape can affirm all other attempts at reconciliation
and all other ways of love and models of subjectivity.
The point of studying the history of love and personhood
is to see how the model of *agape* goes out to all others
and learns from them the worth of their different ways and
in loving service of them promotes individualizing differences.

Western culture with its own special religion, law, politics
and economics has developed out of the theory and practice
of *agape* and personhood which today is being everywhere considered.
Even if Chinese, Indian, Islamic and Eastern Orthodox cultures
do not embrace the *agape* of the West with its view that all persons
are equal under the law and even if they do not embrace
the implied democracy from the election of the Pope on down
they all want to get in on the technological and economic success.
Once they begin pursuing the economic fruit they do slowly
come to see the implied political blossoms and then the
legal branches and then the trunk of personhood and then finally
the roots of *agape* or the three persons in the one true God.
In this first set of meditations we shall examine the history
of the notion of personhood in the West as it grew out of
the new reality and concept of *agape* which Jesus introduced.
We shall not yet focus on the legal theory and practice
that developed with it but we might notice two systems
of the theory and practice of law which developed in the West.
There was the code law of the Continent with Justinian
and with Canon Law which gave rise to rational science
and there was the Case Law of England and its empirical method.
Already with Jesus and with Paul the new universal *agape*
for all persons was bringing forth a new approach to the law.
Of course, the Ten Commandments were still of utmost importance
but the practice of Jesus towards foreigners and sinners
and his Sermon on the Mount and many of his parables
extended the love of Jesus to all with the Good Samaritan.
Paul saw immediately that in Christ Jesus there is
no longer Greek nor Jew, master nor slave, male nor
female for they are now all persons equal under the law.
In these meditations we shall ponder together how *agape*
and person developed during their first two thousand years.

Each loving creature's four noble truths

I   Each person and each loving creature suffers and will die

II and will weep and wonder why for that is a mystery
    which none of us can understand unless we believe

III in that Divine love that so loves us that it became flesh
    and died and rose again from the dead that there
    can be hope for all loving creatures who belong
    to the Mystical Body of Jesus.

IV And the Holy Spirit of the Risen Lord Jesus has
    revealed to us a nine-fold path toward the salvation
    for all flesh, both for persons and loving creatures

   (1) for hunter-gatherer shamans across the face of the earth
       knew of persons and creatures in relation in spirit form
   (2) for the five Greek and Roman schools debated the plight
       of all souls and spirit: vegetative, animal, human, Divine
   (3) for Hebrew Hesed which became Christian *Agape* promised
       an everlasting Kingdom, for love is stronger than death
   (4) for God is the love between the three Divine persons
       which was revealed for all persons in the incarnation
   (5) for Jesus is one person equal to the other two
       and unique in his Divine and human nature
   (6) for in accord with the idea of Divine persons humans
       were seen as individual substances of a rational nature
   (7) for from Augustine to Aquinas the *Caritas* Synthesis
       embraced and learned from all persons of *eros*, affection,
       friendship
   (8) for with the Franciscans all loving creatures, and
       all do love, were the brothers an sister of Francis
   (9) for from Luther and Descartes to Kant and Hegel
       the human rights of all persons became law.

By meditating on this nine stage history of personhood
we will bring ourselves up to the brink of postmodernity
and be ready to appreciate Kierkegaard's love and personhood.

NOTES:

1. Stanley Krippner, "The Epistemology and Technologies of Shamanic Sates of Consciousness," *Journal of Consciousness Studies* 7 (2000) 93.

Part One

Joyful Beginnings

I. Mother

I.1 With Her Anglican mother

I.1.1 Identification in Mother-Daughter Bonding

Mother was born on September 6, 1917, at that time
of late summer when the sheep are brought down from
Rocky Mountain Highlands to greener lowland pastures
and when ewes are grouped with best bucks for breeding.
Mother was born into the passion of her mother,
Leona Hart-Abbott, and of her father, Levaur Paul Coates.
Gramma Coates had lost her mother when she was but eight
and Grandpa Coates lost his mother when he was only five.
They both grew up in the constant presence of their lost mothers.
When they met and told their stories to each other and ate
a meal together they knew that they were meant for each other.
And it was as if Levaur sensed his lost mother in Leona.
And in Levaur's lost mother in him, Leona seemed to find her own.
With her many strong Anglican relatives Leona Mae went
through the mourning process in a very successful way.
The beloved presence of her absent mother, Martha Mae, opened her
in sympathy to the sorrows of others and she was robust
and happy and she wanted to bring others into her graced joy.
Already in the womb mother identified with the very feelings,
moods and attitude of her upbeat, strong, pioneering mother.
The very hormones and nervous system of Leona Mae
were identified with by Joneva Mae as the mother's blood
and lymph system and mucosity became also the daughter's.
Leona Mae's preconscious feelings and passions and moods
and her unconscious attitude which evaluated and motivated
all of her conscious thoughts, words and deeds became also
the very fabric of little Joneva Mae and when she was born
and nursed through that first year at her mother's breast
they bonded in a special dream and vision that would let
little Joneva Mae live out the life that Martha Mae lost.
Martha Mae, Leona Mae and Joneva Mae were one in Mae-love.

I.1.2 In the Attitude of Complacent Agape

Leona and Levaur came together in very positive times.
The First World War was ending and the Roaring Twenties
were already beginning their expansive and manic build up.
The Republican Party made life good for American farmers.
They had claimed their free land and the banking system
helped them get a herd of sheep and a pick-up truck and
all they needed to make the whole wonderful outfit work.
As a young girl between five and eight Gramma went through
very difficult times that would strengthen her throughout life.
In her memoirs Gramma Coates writes: "Father and mother
had misunderstandings so mother took me to Montana with her
where we lived for a year. Later father came out and got me
and I lived with his sister, Ida Blair, near Bellevue.
My mother passed away from a heart attack." Gramma's
mother was only seventeen when she married and all
of her trials must have been damaging to her immune system.
For her eight years of grade school Gramma grew up
in Bellevue, right there in the center of Blaine County, Idaho,
in a thriving mining town which was the State's third largest city.
Already as a child Gramma loved her school and her church.
Two of her relatives from back in Kentucky were Bible scholars.
She loved reading and writing and listening and speaking and
those liberal arts opened her in her dreaming and thinking to
a desire for ever further learning, knowing and understanding.
The Anglican Church was very community minded and
searched out ways to be of service to any who were in need.
She learned the *Our Father* and it became her favorite prayer.
It helped form her inner-most attitude in a spirit of loving
forgiveness as she prayed each morn and each night: "Forgive
us our trespasses as we forgive those who trespass against us."
Baby Joneva Mae identified with Leona Mae's forgiving heart.

I.1.3 In the Mood of Concerned Agape

During her first and second year mother had her mother
all to herself but within eighteen months Gramma
was already carrying Aunt Mid and mother was weaned.
Even though as a young mother in her early twenties
Gramma Coates had a fundamental attitude of complacency,
literally, of being pleased with all of existence, she was still
a person of great concern for not only was she anxious
about having lost her mother but she had identified with
her young mother's anxiety that brought her to run away
with her baby and then saw her baby taken away from her.
After becoming settled in Bellevue her father then up rooted
her again and sent her to relatives in Spokane, Washington,
a city of much greater opportunity for her high school study.
Out of anxious concern her complacency was built up
just as it was out of the World War that the great jubilation
of the Twenties came frolicking forth all happy and free.
Gramma Coates' mood of complacent concern was
a preference for some values over others in an hierarchy.
She learned of intellectual and spiritual values and in
her mood she felt and preferred them over physical and
vital values which could perish and pass away as did
her physical mother and the physical town of Bellevue
even though spiritually they could be vitally present within.
Just as mother as an infant totally identified with her
mother's mood so she became a child concerned about
things that might remain and not be taken away.
And complacency and concern balanced each other
in a logic of mixed opposites that did not let
good complacency become bad, satisfied complacency or
let concern become worried and consuming concern.

I.1.4 In the Sense of Proactive Sensitivity

As a young girl Gramma Coates learned to control
her reactions so that she did not at once fall into
negativity out of the force of habit that increases habit.
In Spokane Leona identified with Aunt Sadie who was
only ten years older than herself and the good Episcopalians
taught the young ladies many proverbs to build character
such as: "Count to ten before you get angry." And Leona
reflected upon and worked upon affirmative proactive responses
instead of negative reactions which could taint everything.
St. Paul clearly saw that the good I intended to do I do not
but the evil that I resolve against, that I often do.
St. Paul was given the grace to be free to serve others
and the Anglicans taught their young to pray for that grace.
And even at the age of four mother began to care for
baby bum lambs who lost their mothers in late winter.
Her love for them taught her patience and peaceful positivity.
She became concerned about their welfare and their lives
and she was glad to feed them with the baby bottle
with all her mother's and father's gladness for
those sweet, bleating, darling little orphaned lambs.
And they told her about the Good Shepherd who left
the ninety-nine and went out to find the one lost sheep.
And Leona Mae and Levaur Paul identified with the lost
sheep who had been found and mother identified with them.
Mother felt secure in herself and with others
in the affection which her parents showered upon her.
And when mother was four her new baby brother,
Robert Abbott Coates, was born and mother was already
helping her mother as a "little mother" with a sensitivity
that learned the sweet voice and the gentle touch that could
aid a baby boy as well as bum lambs when they were discontent.

I.1.5 In the Passion of Positive Emotions

Gramma Coates had a real feeling for intellectual values.
Many around her were artists of pleasure who had a feel
for physical values and many were heroic types,
full of vitality, who ventured Westward seeking fortune
much like Abraham who wandered into the unknown.
But Leona identified with Aunt Sadie's love of books.
She subscribed to *Lady's Home Journal* and *Parent* magazines.
Mother loved hearing Gramma Coates tell and read stories.
By the time she was five she had her own *Bible Story Book*
and her own *Mother Goose Nursery Rhyme Book* and she
quickly learned many of the rhymes by heart and she
loved the picture of Jesus the Good Shepherd most of all.
She pondered stories of folly and wisdom, of love and hate,
of joy and sorrow and of fear and courage and she saw
a network of positive emotions and of negative emotions.
And if there was love and joy the network was positive.
And if there was hate and sorrow the network was negative.
She was impressed by heroes, wise men and saints
but most of all she loved the saints because their love
of the holy was a passion for love and joy that let
her also love the truth of the wise, the good of the heroes,
and the beauty of the artists in a network of affirmation.
Of course, as a child she was not aware of all this
but she did identify with it in the value system
of her young and buoyant mother who in great joy
with her young family could love all her sorrow
and even be confident in the face of any threats.
By identifying with her mother's belief in joy and of
turning sorrow into joy even though it remained sorrow
mother as a child already began practicing the Stoic ethic
that flowed into St. Paul and St. Francis and the Anglicans.

I.1.6 In the Logic of True Thoughts

When she was six mother finally got to go to school
in a little one-room school house on the Fish Creek Flats.
Through the summer high up the Iron Mine Canyon
she was already learning to read in her two books.
The anticipation increased through late August
and they took the sheep down and they moved into
their fall-winter ranch house and mother's birthday
finally arrived and her father drove her to school.
Already at six mother began practicing the liberal arts
of reading, writing, speaking and listening in orderly silence.
She had to learn to concentrate and not be distracted
as she practiced in her books and notebooks while
the teacher was talking to others in that same little room.
She began to reflect on words as she heard new voices.
She started making the transition into the age of reason.
Toward the end of that school year she began to lose
her baby teeth and to get the teeth one by one that
would lead her along toward the next stage of puberty.
And she was educated into the very first steps of
grammar, rhetoric and logic and the age of reason
into which she took her first steps was the age of logic.
And she began to learn to connect the dots into
an orderly whole as she moved from the immediacy
of emotional identification into reflection on words
and ideas that began to initiate her in self reflection.
And her teacher brought a very new voice into her life
and she would go home and eagerly tell her mother
about her school work and they already began to do
homework together as mother moved from the realm
of preconscious attitude, moods and feelings into
the realm of conscious thoughts, words and deeds.

I.1.7 In the Intonation of Incantational Words

As a little girl mother identified with her mother's speech
and its clearly articulated, sweet melodious tone.
The muscles and nerves of mother's lips, tongue and throat
were formed just as were her mother's as they spoke together
and worked more and more together doing dishes,
cleaning house, cooking and baking, washing and ironing.
Mother wanted to do all with her mother and though mother
had a child's voice it was moving ever closer to being exactly
like her mother's with its world making song and magic.
The sing-song reciting of nursery rhymes was almost
a dance that played forth out of joy and back into joy.
Leona's shamanic spiritual exercises that converted
absence into presence let her become a reader and speaker
of the word that had a cheering and helping power for any
who heard the near incantational rhythms of her voice.
Mother identified with her mother's power of speech
which could put a halo of magic around each spoken thing.
There would be bacon, eggs and toast with choke-cherry jelly.
They would look so good and smell and taste so good.
But, if Gramma said: "bacon, eggs, toast and jelly"
in her sweet, prolonged, intoned, musical way they
would become unforgettably lovely in your memory forever.
Mother took on her mother's lovely and playful tones
and her speech had something of a prayer that deified things.
Already in the second grade the discipline of her school work
was taking mother into a logic that was on the alert for
any mistakes or any self-deceit that might hinder truth.
The teacher gave her spelling exercises and checked each letter
and began to develop in mother a careful precision that tried
to get everything on the map of life and in the book of life just right.
And mother's attitude guided her words in style, form and content.

I.1.8 In the Peace of a Gentle Touch

From her mother and her practice mother learned how
to comfort a lamb, or cat, or dog in distress and to hold
and rock her baby brother in the way of soothing peace.
In her concern for the troubled other she could take
an hysterical animal or a panicking child and quickly
bring him or her into the complacency of a pleasant peace.
The joy of her agapeic attitude and affirmative mood
reached out into the healing caress of her fingers and
with their touch into her words so that she was a peace maker.
Her touch spoke volumes and her thoughts and words touched so
that anyone who came into her presence was touched by an angel.
Gramma Coates had something of a fun play in her voice,
a near devilish twinkling in her dancing brown eyes
and a healing power that could calm the devilish in her touch.
But Gramma Coates as an only child had a sprite's breeziness
while mother as a first child who learned to mother young
was a more serious and efficient calmer of troubled waters.
The Episcopalian ladies of Spokane became daughters of
the Rebecca Lodge and in their service club they volunteered
like their counterparts in the Masonic Lodge and had good fun
as they built small communities with their work together.
Gramma Coates was an expert of extroversion in her sociality
and conviviality and mother followed her example, but not quite,
for as more introverted and tranquility orientated mother took time
with the laying on of her hands whether she was teaching her
children to comb their hair, tie their ties, or brush their teeth.
Her common sense from childhood on that aimed at excellence
was more hands on and inner-world serious in its care.
In the third grade mother was riding to school on horse back
with her six year old sister, Mildred, holding on behind her.
And mother was a natural teacher and she helped the teacher
teach the first graders their reading, writing and arithmetic.

I.1.9 In the Construction of Upbuilding Deeds

Gramma Coates knew that our deeds as works of love
are all important and she knew how significant her example was
for her children and everyone just as Aunt Sadie's had been.
Mother believed with her mother in performing good deeds
and she also sensed that good intentions are not enough.
Gramma Coates had allowed grace to heal her heart and she
prayed: "Father, forgive them for they know not what they do."
We do not know what we do for our deeds are motivated by
preconscious forces in the attitudinal moods of our very bodies.
In order to upbuild our loved ones and ourselves we have
to cultivate totally constructive creeds with positive canons
and codes of behavior that are not negative and judgmental.
Because of the complexities of our relationships, as we see
in the case of Gramma Coates and mother, we are very limited
in our knowledge and in the logic of our thoughts, words and deeds
but we trust in goodness despite the evils that threaten us.
We can cultivate becoming the-glass-is-half-full persons
and by putting ourselves in healthy relations stop giving in
to being the-glass-is-half-empty persons or born losers.
As Mother identified with her mother's agapeic heart
and her truth pursuing mind and her spirit's quest
for excellence and her body's habit of constructing
a healthy immune system, Mother was already in the habit
of performing deeds that would cultivate the soil of a good heart
that could bring forth rich fruit from trees in the good earth.
That proverb: "By their fruits you shall know them"
pragmatically guided mother's mother and thus Mother
who as a nine year old girl was like St. Paul freed
from self-indulgence to perform the works of love
that could serve others in cultivating love, joy, peace,
patience, gentleness and all those fruits of the spirit.
In the mother-daughter bonding mother received a loving faith.

I.2 With Her Mormon Father

I.2.1 In the Logic of the Triad

Levaur Paul Coates was as proud as could be when his little daughter, Joneva Mae Coates, was born in Hailey, Idaho, on September 6, 1917. What a relief it was that everything went so well, for as soon as Leona had her first rhythmic cramps they got in their Ford Pick-Up and quickly drove the thirty five miles to Hailey, and Dr. Fox and his nurse at once took care of the anxious, soon to-be mother. Levaur checked in to a near-by hotel and from there kept watch. The next morning Leona introduced him to his daughter and she was well formed and healthy and normal and everything was alright. And the daughter did identify with the mother in all the deep down and important ways and was well mothered in her young, joyful mother's land of milk and honey and she grew up secure in herself. Her father was always there too as he worked hard with the sheep and the whole outfit, as he would say, that kept them all going. By the time Mother was ten she was secure in herself and with others for her father was doing well and she was as proud of him as he was of her and she was well protected from the mere mother-daughter dyad that would never freely and fully wean the child and give her security with others. Without the mother-father-child triad the mother and child can get locked into a bi-polar relation so that the child feels like an abject throw-away rather than a strong subject. If the mother is abandoned or abandons the father then the child will identify with the mother's abandonment and go through life aggressive with mother and sullen with others. In Levaur's strong, traditional, Mormon community of Carey that did not happen and the father would say: "She learns so quickly!" And the father would love the mother in the daughter and the mother would love the daughter in the father and all of his, and relationality was built up and Joneva was relating independently at ten. The triad by opening beyond the dyad became an open quadrad.

I.2.2 In the Logic of the Quadrad

By the time she was eleven mother and her family had moved
from their summer home up Iron Mine and their winter home
on the Fish Creek Flats into the town of Carey and into
their farm home on the Little Wood River Canal.
Mother's youngest brother, Elwin, was born when she was ten
and the roles within the family were by then quite clearly worked out.
Mother was her mother's helper and perfected her art of mothering
as she did much to care for her baby brother and she and he
bonded almost as mother and child as the first and last children.
Mid and Bob helped their father even as ten and twelve year
old children trailing sheep from Carey and Picaboo and the
railroad shipping station built by the Union Pacific for sheep.
So mother bonded in a dyadic relation with her mother
that never became monadic and self-centered because it was
quadratic when the new baby sister came and then the first
brother and six years later the second brother whom she babied.
Mother in the activity of her complex and passionate relations
was never the least bit bored for everyday was filled with
all kinds of tasks and it was difficult to find time for reading.
At the age of eleven the first signs of puberty started to show
and mother was reflecting on the many voices speaking
within her and to her and she was beginning to decide just how
she wanted to be as her exemplars picked her and she them.
The triadic and quadratic relations helped her through weanings.
And mother had identified with her mother's terrible weaning.
And Johannes de Silentio wrote: "When the child has grown big
and is to be weaned, the mother virginally conceals her breast,
and then the child no longer has a mother. How fortunate
the child who has not lost his mother in some other way."
And mother was fortunate as her own dear mother had not been.
With affectionate support mother was weaned through puberty.

I.2.3 In the Logic of Quadratic Weaning

Mother identified with the unlimited voices of her mother as
they chorused in her preconscious attitudes, moods, and feelings.
She identified with the unlimited voices of her father as
she knew them in his thoughts, words, and deeds, and as she
saw him in relation to his extended family in all their fun.
Mother was thus a very complicated mix of expanding relations.
She began to reflect on herself and to imitate certain teachers
and not to relate and identify with many around her who were
not in keeping with her taste, but even her taste was expanding.
In March her father brought her a black sheep bum-lamb.
She nursed it with the bottle and cared for it in the spirit of
the Good Shepherd story and picture in her Bible Story Book.
She played with it through the spring and summer and then
one day on about her twelfth birthday she went with her dad
to the barn yard and he took a sheep by the scruff of the neck
and cut its throat and hung it in the barn by its hind feet.
Then he grabbed a black lamb like hers and did the same.
She felt sick and thought that that lamb could have been her own.
Then he asked her to go to her mother and get a platter.
She brought it to him and he put the head of the first sheep
on the chopping block and split it open with the axe and then
he put the brain on the platter and he did the same with the lamb.
He told her that tomorrow they could have scrambled eggs
and brains for breakfast and he said it with obvious delight.
She talked to her mother about her feelings and her mother
told her what a good sheep-man her father was and how
lucky they were to have such a good life during the depression.
At breakfast next morning the twelve year old Joneva could not
identify with the hearty appetite of her parents and siblings.
And she was being weaned again and through her life.
Traumas can either break us or make us stronger teacher-healers.

I.2.4 In the First Deceptive Weaning

Although Grandpa Coates' family pioneered with the Mormons
they were not practicing Latter Day Saints and as "Jack Mormons"
with a completely secular attitude they loved drinking and good times
and would not enter the church except for the occasional funeral.
The parents agreed that the two girls would be raised Episcopalian
and the boys raised Mormon but mother was the only one with
any religious inclinations and she often went to the Mormon church
and primary school with her school friends and she liked to pray.
She greatly admired the healthy family life of her Mormon friends.
For Christmas Aunt Sadie gave the thirteen-year-old Joneva
a golden necklace chain with a beautiful golden cross and
she loved it so much she could hardly wait to wear it to school.
But one of the Mormon boys whom she admired asked her
"What kind of charm is that?" And she felt embarrassed.
And though the cross of the Good Shepherd was dear to her she
wore it to school no more and though she loved and admired
her Mormon friends she would not let them know that she
wore it at home and she prayed for them when she took it off.
And she began to hide many of her thoughts and to reflect on deceit.
Her mother got along well with the Mormons and they
admired her for she had winning and weaning ways
as she taught mother to be open to all and offensive to none.
And de Silentio wrote: "When the child is to be weaned, the
mother blackens her breast. It would be hard to have the breast
look inviting when the child must not have it. So the child
believes that the breast has changed, but the mother—she is still
the same, her gaze is tender and loving as ever. How fortunate
the one who did not need more terrible means to wean the child."
Her father thought it was only a black sheep and she should not fret.
The boy thought it was some evil, magical charm and she
became weaned by loving them with acting beyond deceit.

I.2.5 In the Third Weaning of Mutual Mourning

Mother loved her four years at Carey High School from the time
she was fourteen until eighteen and the Mormon atmosphere
suited her well as it fostered a sense of vocation-mission-destiny.
Some of her friends were already talking about going to college and
going on a mission to teach others that our Heavenly Father loves us.
Mother was especially impressed with the good Mormons in that
they did not drink or smoke or swear and in fact they did not
even drink coffee or tea and she could easily appreciate that.
When she visited her cousins Nelson, Burl and Frieda over
at her Uncle Chuck's and Aunt Omas' she loved them dearly.
Uncle Chuck was very funny, loveable and always joking
but sometimes he did drink a bottle of beer and go across the street
to the pool hall where some of his friends were just a bit rowdy.
Her father would also drink with his friends and even though
he was a very hard working and productive man mother asked
her mother about such activity and they both saw dark horizons.
They went into the Great Depression that swept the country and
even though farmers were fairly self-sufficient and they now
had their farm the banking system was failing and the sheep business
shut down and mother and her mother felt that an idle mind
is the devil's workshop and alcoholism began to make them anxious.
And de Silentio wrote: "When the child is weaned the mother, too,
is not without sorrow because she and the child are more and more
to be separated, because the child who first lay under her heart
and later rested upon her breast will never again be so close.
So they grieve together the brief sorrow. How fortunate the one
who kept the child so close and did not need to grieve anymore."
The weaning process is a kind of mourning process and the loss
of his mother when he was only five left Levaur Coates
with a lack of inner security that needed the boost
of alcohol and the warm camaraderie that it deceitfully fostered.

I.2.6 In the Fourth Weaning of Providing Sustenance

In the last of the four scenarios Johannes de Silentio wrote:

> When the child is to be weaned the mother has stronger
> sustenance at hand so that the child does not perish.
> How fortunate the one who has this stronger sustenance at hand.

This fourth weaning story helps us to understand the failures
of the other three for in none of them was better food provided.
Mother, like Abraham, grew in her faith by its often being tested.
How else could she have come to a loving, forgiving heart toward
her father when he was callous with black sheep bum-lambs like hers?
How else could she forgive the boy who ridiculed her cross?
How could she grow in love toward drinking, rowdy relatives?
Her mother helped her to understand and discover the better food
of loving forgiveness and thus mother was not enclosed in
the failed mourning process of merely aesthetically blackening
the breast or ethically of hiding the breast or in the resignation
of a mutual mourning since better sustenance was provided.
But the four Isaac-Abraham binding stories that parallel
the four weaning stories show us the inadequacies of even
the fourth weaning story for Abraham is not graceful in
his infinite resignation which indicates that he lacks faith
and that he will still retain Isaac and thus Isaac loses faith.
Gramma Coates as an only child must have been well weaned
by her mother and when her great test of being abandoned came
she must have been graced through her father and Aunt Sadie
so that like Abraham she could be graceful in her resignation.
Even though Gramma Coates provided mother with understanding
there was much more than only that food for conscious thought.
Gramma Coates' attitude, mood and feeling had a buoyant faith.
After all she had been through and successfully mourned
she could be an exemplar for mother so that when her father
or friends or relatives looked offensive she did not take offence.

I.2.7 Pauline Universalism—Johannine Exclusivism

What mother experienced even though it was not articulated was
the difference between her mother's Episcopalian universalism and
her father's and the Mormon's Beloved Community's exclusivism.
When the boy showed no tolerance for the cross she experienced
a thought, word and deed that was deeply rooted in an attitude
that was very surprising to her because it was not her mother's
universalistic attitude with which she had come to identify.
Her father, even though he was not a practicing Mormon, had
an attitude that may have been influenced by the English class system.
Later he would wonder why one of his children would marry a Basque,
another an Italian, another a Mexican and the other a poor girl.
Why didn't they just marry some nice white Anglo-Saxon types?
In John's Gospel the Word became flesh for the salvation of all
but the world of darkness that did not receive him remains
unsaved just as did Judas and the Jews upon whom John is hard.
Paul and John give different accounts of the Kingdom and the Cross.
Paul has his atonement view of the Cross that Christ died
in order to redeem all the fallen children of Adam and thus
the Kingdom was to come for all humans for there are
no longer Jews or Gentiles, Greeks or Barbarians but
with Christ's death and resurrection we are all members of
his body and can be members of the family of God and man.
John has a prophetic view of the cross that because Christ
was a prophet he made enemies of the authorities as did
so many of the prophets and thus they put him to death.
John and his people think that the second coming has
already happened at the resurrection and that Christ is
here now judging us and all those who fully believe
and keep his commandments are in his community or
his Kingdom now and mother could see these two views
in her mother's universalism and in the Mormon's exclusivism.

I.2.8 Dyadic Johannine Glory

Mother greatly loved her father and knew that he greatly loved her.
He seemed harsh and callous at times but she knew him better.
Gramma and Aunt Mid were helping mother get ready for her
junior prom and they came downstairs and Grandpa was reading
his paper and Gramma asked him: "Well Levaur, how does she look?"
And Grandpa stood up and came over to her and looking
at her from head to foot he said: "Sissy, you are so beautiful."
And he was so proud of his daughter and a lump welled up
in his throat and he nearly started to cry and mother had seen
him that way before and she began to wonder why he would cry.
Slowly over the years it began to dawn on her that he had the gift
of tears and that it was not sorrow or pain that would make him cry.
It had to do with the pride and glory of a beautiful love relation.
Just as Paul was touched by glory of the angelic face of Stephen
and just as the Roman Soldier said: "Truly this man is the son of God."
so Grandpa was touched by a moment of glory that made him tremble
and perhaps all his feeling for his lost mother was in his sobbing.
And in John's Gospel the Son glorifies and thus reveals the Father.
And the Father's love helps to glorify the Beloved Son's wonder.
And in John there are several dyadic one-on-one loving moments
such as when Magdalene did not recognize him after the Resurrection.
But in the way he said her name "Mary" as no one else could
ever say it she recognized her Lord and Master in a glory moment.
Did the beloved Mormon community somehow foster that kind of
sentiment that could feel the holy aura around a love of noble beauty?
Did it even go back into the Franciscan roots of English poetry and
had it to do with that shamanic presence that could heal and vitalize?
Mother thoroughly loved her father and even though he would become
a black-sheep bum-lamb wandering about as an alcoholic who
spent his last days at Pocatello in the Insane Asylum she knew
that in spite of it all our Heavenly Father loved him as did she.

I.2.9 Pauline Triadic Glory

In 1936, when mother was eighteen, Franklin Delano Roosevelt
was elected president of the United States and at once big things
began to happen even in the little town of Carey where the Mormons
were totally Republican and cared for as land owners by bankers.
Mrs. York, a Democrat, took over as head of the Carey Post Office
because jobs like that go to people of the party that makes it in.
They continued working on the big dams up Fish Creek and up
Little Wood River and Aunt Omas' boarding house was filled
with migrant workers and many town's people got new jobs.
Louie Arrian, a Basque, owned and ran the Carey pool hall and
he hired a young Basque poker player, Joe Goicoechea, to run
his games at the tables and Joe had been in jail for delivering
whiskey during the prohibition and in jail he learned card playing.
And Gramma Coates knew he was back in town for she had
known him as a youth up at the head of Fish Creek where
he often stayed with his uncle Pete Cennarrusa and Joe's
father had died when he was only five and he and Leona talked
together in the shamanic presence and she liked him very much.
And she told mother what a nice, intelligent young man he was.
And then one day Joe and Joneva met and started talking together.
And she told her father she was talking with him and her father
couldn't believe that his lovely young daughter would waste
her time on a vagrant, drinking, poker playing man with no
property or good job and he had to be fairly quiet because he saw
that Leona was their cupid and thus he could not speak his mind.
And when Joneva spoke with Joseph she sensed in him a
reverence she had never known before and it was as if he reverenced
her with the reverence his mother had when she said her rosary.
And in the triadic relation between Joseph, Leona and Joneva
there was a kind of triadic glory that gave glory to God in all things.
With coffee and cigarettes each morning he devoutly said his prayers.

I.3 With Her Catholic husband

I.3.1 The Holy Ideal and the Justice of Peace

In her last year of high school mother read *Just David*,
a novel by Eleanor Porter that revealed to her her destiny
so concretely that it inspired her with the directing dream
of a vision so vivid she felt it would guide her through life.
It was about a boy named David who was raised high
up in the mountains by his father alone in their little
mountain home with their books and violins and mother nature.
Daily David's father taught him in the pleasure of a shared joy
reading, writing, arithmetic, Latin, French and jujitsu.
Their home reminded her of her home high up Iron Mine.
And it connected in association with Joseph Manuel Goicoechea.
As a youth he spent his summers up Fish Creek with Pete,
the husband of his sister, Claudia, who was like a father to him.
Often by the sheep corrals where the Iron Mine Stream flowed
into Fish Creek mother's mother, Leona, and Joe's sister, Claudia,
would meet in friendly, laughing conversation and one day
young Joe with his dancing brown eyes gave Leona some trout.
As he cleaned them for her there in the clear, icy stream
he told her how he liked school and especially sports.
He ran in the hills each day to get in good shape for Fall.
Claudia named her first daughter after Leona because
she liked her so much and because she liked the name.
Now with her mother's blessing Joe and Joneva were ready
to be married, but mother knew that her father would not
like to give her away to this man of whom he disapproved.
So without any wedding dress or any wedding party
they eloped to Nevada to meet one of Joe's sisters and
there they were married, but only by a justice of the peace.
With the holiest of ideals she somehow felt in a deep down
and unspoken way that she married in a less than holy way.
They did plan to marry soon in the church to make it right.

I.3.2 Holy Child

On May 18,1938, at 1:30 a.m. in the same Hailey Hospital where
she had been born mother was delivered of her first child.
He was named David Levaur Goicoechea and his last name was
her husband's last name, and his middle name was her father's
name and David was the name she associated with the holy.
She now had nursing at her breast her own beautiful, healthy
well formed baby and she gave him the name for which she
wanted a son for she named him after *Just David* and now
she could teach him the holy arts as David's father taught him.
Her baby's name was also associated for her with David,
the shepherd boy who took care of lambs the way she did,
who was the conqueror of Goliath and the friend of Jonathan.
And she was so happy in the joy of her husband who was
the only one left with the name Goicoechea from his family.
For his father died when little Joe was five and his mother
raised him and his five sisters and now he was so proud
of this new Goicoechea that he had to quickly get out
the good news to all of her family and to his that mother
and baby were doing ever so excellently well and he brought
his wife and baby congratulations from those whom he called.
And also the baby's name was David Levaur and her own
dear father now had a little grandson named after him
and she knew that with him there would be those tears of glory.
She and her husband and her father loved her new little baby
with such great affection that it went beyond all contention
and in her baby all were united in the harmony of reconciliation.
Her mother and her sister and her brothers and all her friends
and relations were so happy and this was an image for her
of what the holy must be like and it was not so much
a *mysterium tremendum* of some mystery that makes you
tremble in fear, but it had the peace and joy of Baby Jesus.

I.3.3 Sacred Priest—Sacred Baptism—Sacred Matrimony

Baby David was born on May 18, and baptized on June 30. Even though mother was not catholic she was eager to have her child baptized and did not want the least procrastination. She and Joe had been married in a private mass by Father Dougherty once they got back from their Nevada elopement. Mother was completely taken by the priest and right away there was a master-disciple relation and she even asked him what was so different about a Catholic priest that she had never sensed in a Mormon priest or an Episcopalian Bishop. He told her that the Latin word of priest is *sacerdos* and that the priest in his celibacy lives apart from the profane so that through the sacraments he can help people be holy. He said that the *fanum* is the temple so that everything profane is outside the temple or even against the temple and that the temple is the place of the sacred sacrament of the real presence of the Body and the Blood of Jesus in the sacred Host and that that is why the red light burns in the Church and everyone genuflects. She sensed the sacred in the celibate *sacerdos* and wondered and pondered for years what he told her about the difference between the holy and the sacred and yet their significant relation. Joe's sister Claudia and her husband Pete were witnesses to the marriage and the Godparents for their nephew, David. There was nothing mother wanted more than the love that brings the reconciliation of joy and peace and she knew that with her baby and the priest and his sacraments there were intimations of a new hope that fit her *Just David* dream. And Mrs. Billingsley, one of her high school teachers, gave her a little pink baby book and mother wrote down the gifts and from whom they came and each of the gifts was a sign of love's power to turn any problem into a gift and they became memories of everyone's love.

I.3.4 The Holy, the Sacred, and the Profane

Father made his living by running poker games at the pool hall.
Deep down he was pleased that mother did not approve for he
loved her most of all because she was a holy woman like his
mother and he knew that she would be a very ideal wife and mother.
Even though he was involved in the most profane life
with his smoking, drinking and gambling she knew from
the way he loved her that he had a great reverence for the Holy.
She lived playfully with him in his play and he loved to
play with their little baby and with her in her playful delight.
In the baby book she wrote: "David looked like his daddy at birth."
Under *Recognition of Mother* she wrote: "He recognized his mother
before he was three months old." Under *Recognition of Father* she
wrote: "David thinks his dad is a play-fellow."
David identified with the moods and feelings of their play and it
was written: "When he was 11 weeks old we took him to Gooding
to the Rodeo. He behaved perfectly and slept in the dresser drawer."
Even that makeshift crib had something of their play about it.
And you can bet that many of dad's high school football,
basketball, boxing, and track and field friends would have
been there in his home town to meet his wife and baby boy
and to welcome them into the friendship of their play together.
To end the depression President Roosevelt initiated work programs
and mother was ever so happy that her husband Joe was hired
to work on building a road up Warm Springs near Ketchum.
But then with winter approaching they moved down to Ketchum
and dad got a job dealing poker at the Alpine Club for Lew Hill.
And so a pattern began for mother as she tried to influence
her husband away from gambling and toward wholesome work.
He was a strong hard worker who loved exercise and good health
but as an excellent poker player he could make much more by
dealing at casinos and he could get jobs there very easily.

I.3.5 Holy War—Holy Pregnancy—Holy Daughter

By 1942, the Second World War was already beginning to rage
in both the European and Asian theatres and uncle Bob would
soon be drafted into the navy and there was mounting anxiety.
There are so many kinds of war: within a person, between
the sexes, within different groups, between political parties.
The opposition of differences is an obvious fact and is
the source of the problem of evil which is the challenge for
all peace makers and those inclined to ways of reconciliation.
In many ways the war of the sexes is the paradigm case for
it is the source of bellicose and rebellious trouble makers and
if solutions could be found for it solutions could be found for all.
The first classical model for building up reconciliation has
always and paradoxically been the moral equivalent to war.
During a war the people on one side ban together strongly and
work with much more zeal than usual to survive and prevail.
The apocalyptic religious view sees the conquering of evil
as the way toward reconciliation and the attainment of peace.
"Peace without justice" or "Peace at any price" are criticized.
A second model is the moral equivalent to pregnancy and
while mother constantly saw various kinds of war around her
she had to keep herself in just the right attitude and to
perform all the right exercises for the sake of a healthy baby.
And she was highly motivated by the thought that whatever she
preferred, desired, thought, said or did was done to her baby.
And her new baby girl, Bette Jo, was born and again
the child was loved by all so that all loved each other.
And the quadratic logic of the little family had new blessings.
David was so happy with his new little sister and mother
loved the new happiness of father for his new daughter.
And each was as happy as a child and the way to reconciliation
also was seen as the moral equivalent to the joyful child.

I.3.6 The Holy and the Sacred

Daddy quickly made the money dealing cards at the saloon
so that their new house could be built down under the hill.
Then before they knew it daddy was called to do war duty
in a ship plant at Bremerton near Seattle, Washington.
They sold their home to Whitey Hirshman, a gambler friend
of daddy's and he drove their car to Port Orchard, a little town
on the Puget Sound where he found a house that they could rent.
Mother with myself and Bette Jo who was of course, only a baby
took the train day and night and day to Seattle where
daddy met us and he took us to our new home in a strange place.
Daddy left early each morning to take the Ferry to the Port to work.
Meanwhile Uncle Tony, Aunt Mid's husband, and Uncle Bob
were drafted into the army and navy respectively and Gramma
and Grandpa Coates went to Portland, Oregon, for defense work.
Gramma was constantly worrying about her son and son-in-law
and all the other young men whom she knew and was
hearing about on the radio week by week and some were killed.
Very difficult times were going on all around mother and her
little family, but in most ways with her work, prayers
and spiritual reading she still lived in the enchanted world
that she had read about in *Just David* and that Father Dougherty
helped her think about with his distinction between holy and sacred.
When he baptized Bette Jo he referred to her as Elizabeth Josephine
and daddy said to mother: "Now see what you have done!"
But to mother it was only funny and with her two children
she was learning to be child-like and she read those words:
"Unless you are like little children you cannot enter the Kingdom."
And she had named Bette Jo after a youth named Joe in
Just David and his sister Bette for they were friends of David.
Her children's very names reminded her of the realm of the Holy
and she kept pondering the sacred priest and his sacred sacraments.

I.3.7 Paul and John Becoming Mark

Mother and all around her were going through much upheaval by living through the war years and those trials were bringing her to a new religious outlook and fundamental attitude as she began to raise her family with her husband and in his world. His mother and five sisters and especially Father Dougherty all helped her to understand him as a new profile of Jesus. She had learned the missionary way of St. Paul from her mother and of a universal love for the goodness of all who are redeemed by Christ who suffered and died to pay the penalty for sin. She had learned the way of John's beloved community from the Mormon community of Carey in which she grew up. The cross of suffering which builds up the Beloved Kingdom here on earth as in Carey had to do with prophetic suffering which would come to those who live contrary to the world. But as mother and everyone coped with the anxieties and inconveniences of war and as she lived in a child-like attitude for, with and from her children the speech that Peter gave at Pentecost and that became the skeleton of Mark's Gospel and of the Synoptic Tradition began to form her heart. Jesus (1) whom the prophets foretold (2) went about doing good (3) but he was made to suffer and put to death. (4) However, he arose from the dead and ascended into heaven. (5) Now his Holy Spirit has descended upon us to protect us and guide us. Mother began to imitate Jesus in caring for others as did the Good Samaritan and in offering up her own and all suffering with the Suffering Servant who bore the Cross to teach us all how to suffer and she saw that reacting negatively creates more poison within us than do bad eating habits. She welcomed her husband, children and neighbors with joy and she prayed especially for any who annoyed or persecuted her. She pondered how the sacred sacraments might cultivate the Holy.

I.3.8 Communicating in Sacred Silence

Those years of '45, '46 and '47 were a turmoil of activity and
yet for mother, Bette Jo, and myself they were a time of harmony.
Mother loved a life centered on home and family and of good, clean
productive farm work that made each person happy, healthy, and holy.
Daddy was driving a milk truck for the dairy and mother was
pleased with his honest work for she always felt that gambling
was a wrongful taking of someone else's money and not honest.
We all lived at Gramma and Grandpa's farmhouse and everything
seemed to go along in an exciting and smooth way without friction.
Mother would wash the dishes and I got to help Aunt Mid dry them.
And I marveled at how much silverware she could hold in
her left hand and I would try to imitate her as we laughed together.
Uncle El taught me how to play monopoly and told me stories
at night before we went to sleep in our bedroom upstairs.
Gramma listened often to the radio and talked a lot about
the war but still had lots of fun in the extended family.
Mother had many voices within her and she lived partly
in her mother's world, partly in her father's world, partly
in her husband's world, and, of course, always in her own world.
And she knew that the writing was on the wall and that her
husband would never be content being a farmer in Carey
even though that idea seemed so ideal for her and the children.
And she was an acting person who made constant
decisions that built up the loving attitude within herself
and within others and she performed good actions knowing
that they contributed to good habits of heart, mind and soul.
But, she was also an acting person in another sense of the word
for from her mother who was quite dramatic she had a sense
of the drama of life and she had to get each voice just right.
She had to keep still voices that would lead to strife and friction
and to strengthen the sweet tone of her voice of reconciliation.

I.3.9 Third Holy Child and Sacred Community

And big changes took place a mile a minute as we moved
to a farm we rented and my dad milked eighteen Holsteins
and grew hay and hunted and fished and visited Ketchum.
Uncle El lived with us and we took the school bus together
as I was in the first grade and he was a sophomore in high school.
And our new little baby brother, Bobby Brian, was born
and named after uncle Bob and my dad's friend Brian
who was a gambler up in Ketchum and found us a house
right across the street from his. And the war ended and
I washed baby diapers in the irrigation ditch with mother
just as she had with her mother up Iron Mine. And we
did move to Ketchum and Whitey Hirshman and my dad
bought a little nightclub together called *The Rumba Club*
and their gambling was very successful and we paid $3,500
for our little old house and I started second grade in Ketchum.
We had Catechism school once a week and mother and I learned
the answers together as we had the book propped up on
the window-sill over the kitchen sink as we did dishes together.
She had watched as my dad taught me the *Angel of God* and
Hail Mary in Carey and now she learned them too and she
decided to become a Catholic when I received first communion.
What William James said about getting down on your knees
and praying if you want to receive faith describes good acting.
We can cultivate the whole network of right attitude, right
mood, right sensing, right feeling, right thoughts, words
and deeds if we are good actors and keep acting out the way
we want to be in sacred reflection that cultivates holy living.
Mother was strongly motivated to live the most excellent way
she could imagine because her children would follow that way too.
Father Dougherty in the reflective standing back of his sacred
celibacy inspired her to focus on sacred communion and love.

II. Søren Kierkegaard

II.1 Reconciling the God-Man and Socrates

II.1.1 The Paradoxical Logic of Erotic Inspiration

On May 19, 1838, at 10:30 a.m., the Existential Movement was born when Kierkegaard wrote in his journal:

> There is such a thing as an indescribable joy
> which grows through us as unaccountably
> as the Apostles' outburst is unexpected:
> "Rejoice, and again I say, Rejoice!:
> Not a joy over this or that, but full jubilation,
> "with hearts, and souls, and voices."
> I rejoice over my joy,
> of, in, by, at, on, through, with my joy,
> a heavenly refrain, which cuts short,
> as it were, our ordinary song;
> a joy which cools and refreshes like a breeze,
> a gust of the trade wind which blows from
> the Grove of mamre to the eternal mansions.[1]

Kierkegaard as a young student in his mid-twenties
suffered from a sort of genetic depression.
He moved out of his beloved father's home
and became estranged from the melancholic old man.
He thought of himself as no longer religious.
He experimented with alcohol and prostitution.
He could not write his Master's thesis.
He found that he had a secret thorn in the flesh.
But then he fell in love with Regina Olsen,
a beautiful young girl of fourteen.
With the above outburst of existential joy he
realized what had happened as he became reconciled
with his father, with his God and with himself.
His erotic love made of him a celibate religious genius
and his celibacy increased the passion of his *eros*.
Kierkegaard discovered the paradox of Socratic reconciliation.

II.1.2 The Logic of Socratic Irony

Kierkegaard's father was a lonely, wretched shepherd boy
on Denmark's Jutland heath where one day he cursed God.
Then as a teenage orphan he went to Copenhagen to live with
his uncle who employed him in his fine clothing store.
His father married, but his wife died and soon thereafter
his first child was born of the servant girl whom he married.
After a few years his father inherited the store and became wealthy.
Several other children were born and then came Søren who,
as a hunch-back cripple, became his father's favorite.
The father and the little boy were always together and
Søren sat in on his father's theology discussion group.
Then the father's children began to die one after the other
and the father began to think he was cursed by God because
he had cursed God and committed adultery and he was
consumed in a guilt complex with which Søren identified.
At university Kierkegaard was caught up in boredom
and felt he was an ugly little critter who was unlovable.
But then when Regina really loved him he was astounded.
All of a sudden he realized that the reconciliation process
that Socrates describes in the *Phaedrus* was happening to him.
Socrates said that our body is like a chariot that is
pulled by a vulgar black horse and a noble white horse
and driven by the charioteer of our rational intellect.
When the black horse beholds a beautiful boy he wants sex.
He is so strong that the white horse and the charioteer are dragged
along into sexual activity and since exercise builds strength
the addiction increases and vulgar lust is all powerful.
But it can happen that the soul can fall in love with
the right beloved soul and then the white horse and
the charioteer will sublimate the energy of the black horse
in a reconciling, life changing enthusiasm of Divine Madness.

II.1.3 The Logic of Skeptical Irony

When Kierkegaard and Regina fell in love the indescribable joy
of his erotic inspiration took him totally beyond boredom
and awakened the genius of his creative illness with the energy
of that ancient Platonic love of the *Symposium* and the *Phaedrus*.
Kierkegaard now knew Socrates from within and with the energy
of the black horse he could now write his brilliant Master's Thesis
on *The Concept of Irony with Constant Reference to Socrates*.
Socrates was the master of irony because he became the wisest
man in Athens by knowing that he could know nothing.
He clearly saw that the Pre-Socratic philosophical physicists
only had theories when they claimed that all things came from
the one, or the two, or the few, or the many or the infinite.
He knew that they could never know the truth about the becoming
of all things and that allowed him to ironically move from
their proud, pretending, pompously ponderous prejudice
to a new humble, honest, hilariously humorous health.
Kierkegaard saw how true philosophical irony is more than
a literary trope which says one thing and means its opposite.
When the skeptic moves from knowing nothing to being wise
he is working with the logic of mixed opposites that became
for Kierkegaard the very logic of Christian agapeic reconciliation.
Søren saw that the aesthete's inclusive opposites reconcile
in a common poverty that is always bored but never boring.
The ethical exclusivistic opposites do not reconcile in
a common mediocrity that is never bored but always boring.
Socrates went beyond either inclusive or exclusive opposites
to parallel opposites of the neither/nor of infinite resignation.
In his skeptical irony he was resigned to never knowing
but his wisdom was open to his Daimon for direction.
Socrates had discovered the religion of the second immediacy
but Søren saw that it was not the God man's reconciliation.

II.1.4 The Logic of Agapeic Reconciliation

The Socratic reconciliation with which Søren was so gifted
when he fell in love with his beautiful and adorable Regina
did harmonize him in three dimensions of his personhood.
But it did not reconcile him to marrying with her.
He was reconciled within himself, with the world and with God.
But after his engagement with Regina he called it off
because he saw that if he married her he would lose
his erotic inspiration and all its religious creative energy.
His thorn in the flesh which troubled him even more than
being a hunchbacked, little cripple probably had to do
with homosexual inclinations and so he felt so
unbelievably blessed to be able to really love his Regina.
Socrates, like so many Greeks, saw Platonic love as
the homosexual love of a man for a beautiful youth.
When Socrates and Plato discovered Platonic love in which
erotic passion made possible celibacy and celibacy's greater passion
they were astounded at the reconciliation of the black and
white horse with its love of wisdom and even of holiness.
Søren saw at once the difference between Platonic erotic love
and agapeic erotic love and he knew his was not agapeic.
He thought that if he had Christian faith he would be able
to marry her and still have his erotic inspiration.
Agapeic reconciliation in its logic moves from either the aesthetic
or the ethical to neither the aesthetic nor the ethical to the both-and.
Søren beheld Socrates, the Shaman, discover presence in absence.
Socratic wisdom had to do with the three great secret things.
As the sexiest man in Athens Socrates refrained from sex.
As about to die he thought he might live on forever.
As an atheist his familiar Divine Sign protected him.
But Søren's good Lutheran Christ as incarnate God-man
should be able both to sublimate black horse energy and marry.

II.1.5 The Logic of Personal Growth

As Søren pondered the differences between Socrates and Jesus
he saw that they were not irreconcilable and he defined
the four loves and the stages of personal growth precisely.
For Socrates there was the first immediacy of black horse *eros*.
Then, there was the noetic reflective realm of friendship.
Finally, there was the second immediacy of Platonic *eros*.
For Søren there is either the first immediacy of the aesthetic erotic
or the ethical reflection of decisive married affection or
the infinite resignation of the neither/nor that opens religiousness A.
Thus Søren in *Sickness unto Death* defines the person
"as a relation (aesthetic) that relates to itself (the ethical)
and relating to itself relates to the others (as the absolute and
then as the relative)." So it is our personal task to grow
through the stages on life's way not only with the great
burst of growth that the Platonic lover experiences with Socrates
but also in such a way that what Socrates leaves behind
with the celibate love of his enthusiasm and Divine Madness
Søren as a good Lutheran thinks he can recover in marriage.
Søren was hoping that even after he broke the engagement
his faith would blossom and he could happily marry Regina.
He did not want to be a burden to her with his melancholy
which he thought might return if he lived in marriage.
He was afraid he would hurt her by breaking the engagement.
But to his surprise she quickly married another and while
she was happily married he kept on loving his inspiration.
In 1848, at Easter time, he did think he could have faith
and become a Lutheran pastor; but even that failed him and
he lived on as a philosophical genius of erotic inspiration.

II.1.6 The Logic of the Both-And

Søren's logic of the both-and seeks to reconcile opposites
and in this case the opposites are Socrates and Jesus.
He had identified with his father's quest to be religiously ethical.
But, his father deeply felt his failure and so did Søren
As a university student he tried to escape his father's ideals,
and in following the black horse of wine, women and song,
even though he was brilliant, he could not follow the white horse
and write his Master's Thesis in a satisfactory manner.
Then through Regina he found the way of Socrates and with
all the energy of the black and white horses he wrote his thesis.
The gift of Socratic, erotic inspiration had truly saved him
and he knew it could forever if he but loved his muse.
His thorn in the flesh could have been masturbation as well
as homosexuality and he was miraculously delivered from both.
If he was sexually tempted he need but focus on her who
was always powerfully present in his soul's adoration and
his temptation would flee away and he could continue
to ponder his new philosophy of love and his writing project.
The Socratic way in its paradoxical irony let him follow Jesus.
But what about Regina and the ethical way of Christian marriage?
With Socrates he had been gifted with the reconciliation
of me, myself andI. for the black horse me-id and the
white horse myself-super-ego were harmonized with the charioteer ego.
Socrates reconciled him with Jesus, but would Jesus let him
be reconciled with Socrates and homosexual celibacy
and no real concern with Regina's quest for marriage?
He began to see that to be an integrated person he had
to move from aesthetic happiness, to ethical health,
to the religious holy and then to have the wisdom that
after leaving the aesthetic and ethical he could so transform
the holy that he could return and renew the aesthetic and ethical.

II.1.7 Loving Socrates as More Important

Can Socrates and Jesus be fully reconciled in Søren's thinking
if Jesus is like the prodigal son and Socrates like the elder brother?
While Socrates lived and died as a philosopher Jesus lived
and died as a God and such a claim could offend Socrates.
Jesus could look like a prodigal with his claim to be the one
and only Son of the one and only Creator, Father God.
According to Søren if Jesus is to win over the elder brother
he would begin by loving Socrates as more important and
then Socrates might begin to love him as more important.
Søren believed that Jesus did love Socrates more than himself.
In his incarnation Jesus stepped down in self-emptying.
His life was one of self denial for all his brothers and sisters.
He offered his passion and death for the redemption of all.
Jesus loves everyone as more important than himself.
With his love of Jesus Søren really loved Socrates too.
Søren had tried his best to live with purity of heart.
He had tried to will one thing in knowing, loving and serving God.
He had tried to be the best student and philosopher possible.
He had tried to follow his vocation and make it his profession.
But all his effort failed and he felt he was going mad.
Then he fell in love with Regina and Socrates became
his teacher and his guide and helped him understand himself.
His love for Regina let him understand Socrates
and Socrates let him understand his love for Regina.
His writing began going better than he could ever imagine
as he began writing about his beloved Socrates
and that sexual love that ironically took him beyond sex.
In Søren the love of Jesus loved the love of Socrates even
more than himself for the love of Socrates let him
attain the purity of heart that Jesus demanded of him.
Socrates' praise of love taught Søren how to praise love.

II.1.8 The Noble Socratic Return

Søren greatly admired Socrates and thought that if he had
known of Jesus he would have believed in him and loved him.
That is so because of Socrates' conversion which revealed how
he would follow his conscience with humility and honesty.
At the heart of Søren's philosophy of love is the "like for like."
Before Jesus revealed his *agape* the "like for like" was that
of "an eye for an eye and a tooth for a tooth" and that
"like for like" wanted justice without a primacy of forgiveness.
But the "like for like" of the judging Christ is mercifully just.
Whatever goes out from my heart will return with exactly
its same quantity and quality in upbuilding my heart's habit.
As Søren saw more clearly and loved more dearly each day
as he prayed for his lovely Regina, the queen of his heart,
and as he daily wrote about Socrates, the teacher of his soul,
he knew that the Christ in his heart loved Socrates as more
important so that Socrates could love Jesus as more important.
That is the way the "like for like" always has to work.
It is the law of agapeic love that accomplishes reconciliation.
Christ in justice can truly love Socrates as more important
for Socrates' love makes up for what is lacking in Christ's love.
That is so because the heart cannot say to the head: "I have
no need of you." For in the Mystical Body of Christ
each member is lacking what only the other members can do.
Socrates was not afraid of dying and ironically he comforted
those who were trying to comfort him by telling them that
perhaps after he drank the hemlock he would be with Homer.
And Jesus after he was put to death descended to the dead
and there he no doubt gathered up Socrates and all the others
and let them arise from the dead with him and let them ascend
with him into the realm of God who is universal love.
How could the noble Socrates not love Jesus as more important?

II.1.9 Loving the God-Man as More Important

Søren knew in his mind and his heart that the prodigal Jesus
could win over the elder brother, Socrates, and reconcile with him.
Søren had tried to be reconciled within himself and with others
and with God, but he only sank deeper and deeper into despair.
Then one day he met Regina and she inspired him into integrity
and the reconciliation of Platonic love as his crippled chariot
began to fly with the black and white horse teaming and the charioteer
driving them with poetic, philosophic and holy religious harmony.
Socrates and his wondrous Platonic love reconciled Søren with Jesus.
His aesthetic me, his ethical myself, and his religious I could
harmonize in the happy, healthy, holy wisdom that could
yield great grades, a terrific job and a great life as he became
a relation that relates to itself and in relating to itself relates to God.
The elder brother, Socrates, had a love that won Søren over to Jesus.
But how about the Thou and the you? Could the prophetic Jesus
be reconciled with the mystic Socrates so that Søren could
love Regina for herself and let his muse become his wife?
How could the prodigal Jesus win over the elder brother, Socrates?
Søren's strategy for winning over the grudging elder brother
has the three parts of: (1) loving him as more important so that
with the like for like he will love the prodigal as more important,
(2) praising love so that he too will come to praise love, and
(3) recollecting the dead so that he will do likewise.
Praising the God who is Love praises all love that truly loves
and praises all of Love's lovely beings so that the elder brother
knows that he is always being loved and praised by the prodigal.
If they both pray for the dead and trust the dead to pray for them
then in the community of Saints which is Jesus' Mystical Body
no matter what happens they can trust in eventual reconciliation.
In his heart and authorship Søren understood Socrates by
reconciling him with Jesus and Christ with Socrates.

II.2 Reconciling the God-Man and Abraham

II.2.1 The Absurd Contingency of the Single Individual

S.K. writes his pseudonymical literature as indirect communication to let himself and his reader be deceived out of self-deceit into truth. Thus, Johannes de Silentio or John of Silence, is writing about many secret affairs with this story about Abraham's sacrifice of Isaac. It is a story about Kierkegaard and his estranged father and it is a story about Søren sacrificing Regina with the broken engagement. It is a story about Abraham, the father of faith, who believed in God's promise of land, nation and name which could be fulfilled through Isaac, but, if Isaac is to be sacrificed then God and his promise are absurd for the promise depends totally on Isaac. So the story is about how faith reconciles Abraham and God. All the stories in the Abraham cycle are about threats to either land, or nation or name, but Abraham endures and the threats and challenges become opportunities that show that Abraham is truly called by God to be the father of his people. But this threat is the worst of all because it is not a threat from other people against the promise, but from God himself. If God is making the promise and then breaking it he is absurd. But, by virtue of the absurd Abraham believes and gets Isaac back. However, Kierkegaard does not get Regina back even though he thinks that he might be given faith that will let him marry. This lets Kierkegaard see that for Jesus things are much worse than for Abraham, for in this case the Father does sacrifice his Son. What kind of reconciliation can there be when child sacrifice which ended for the Jews with Abraham is reinitiated with Jesus? What counted for Abraham was his family and the promise. But now Søren begins to see that love is a matter for each single individual's conscience and things are much more absurd. He is absurdly called to be a sacrifice as a witness for his generation. He is not even a part of the whole so that his witnessing can be logically understood by his generation for he is an exception.

II.2.2 The Absurd Contingency of Postmodern Doubting

Johannes de Silentio's *Fear and Trembling* builds up through
eight parts beginning with a Preface about modern doubting.
Descartes, the father of modern philosophy, begins by doubting
and in his very doubting gets his Archimedean point which is
certainty that ends the doubting and lets him get his system.
St. Augustine actually began this modern move when he
hit upon the notion: "*Si fallor, sum.*" "*If I fail, I am.*"
Descartes who copies St. Augustine at several key points
argued that the "Cogito ergo sum," "I think therefore I am"
is logically sound and that to contradict it is self-contradictory.
Kierkegaard began as a good modernist with Augustine and Luther.
When he fell in love with Regina he was certain that he should marry.
But in being called to break the engagement he discovered Socrates
and his ongoing skepticism and he was in doubt and his
life and writing became a constant experimenting in doubt.
After writing his thesis about the irony of Socratic doubting
he then wrote *Either/Or* which is about either various forms
of aesthetic non-married immediacy or ethical reflective
married commitment and as a good Lutheran he felt he should marry.
But, just as he began to write *Fear and Trembling* he learned that
Regina was engaged to another and that shook him with doubt.
For Abraham and Luther there was no doubt about the universal
value of marriage for Luther had tried an Augustinian monastery
and he found that celibacy was not for him and he married.
Good Lutherans are certain that if they want direction
in their marriage and family life they should go to a pastor
who knows about marital problems from his own real experience.
How could an old celibate be a good pastor for the married?
And Kierkegaard saw that he was an individual exception
to the general rule and so were Jesus, Paul, and Augustine
and he doubted that they would be foolish about married life.

II.2.3 The Absurd Contingency of Unlimited Voices

Søren was a troubled young man with many relation problems.
He fell in love with Regina, the love of his life, and they got engaged
and that was a serious promise for him, but he broke the engagement.
Søren was in fear and trembling about breaking his commitment.
How much would it hurt her? What consequences would it have for him?
Fear and anxiety are two distinct passions for fear is a being
threatened by something definite such as a bear growling at me
as we come face to face unexpectedly out in the woods unarmed.
Anxiety is being threatened by the indefinite or something that
may or may not be which is the meaning of contingency.
Formal logicians work with abstract ideas such as "the necessary,"
"the possible" and "impossible;" but once you think about
the actual with all its concrete possibilities you are outside of
the realm of formal logic and fear becomes anxiety as the definite
becomes indefinite in the blurring boundaries of relating contingency.
As Søren thought about making his promise then breaking it he
saw many actual possibilities or contingencies for himself and Regina.
In *The Exordium*, or the out of order, of *Fear and Trembling* he
experimented with some of the real concrete existential contingencies.
Johannes de Silentio saw that Isaac could be devastated as he
saw that he was to be the sacrificial victim and he could have
taken offence at God, so to prevent that, Abraham could tell
him that it was not God's command but his own demonic will.
That way Isaac could have kept faith in the God of Abraham.
In contingency two Abraham could have become dejected
and abject by wondering how God could be so monstrous to do this.
In contingency three Abraham could have concluded that even
to believe in God's command was the sin of child murder.
In contingency four Isaac could have lost his faith.
Søren had these and many more unlimited voices speaking
within himself and such complexity made logic absurd.

II.2.4 *The Absurd Contingency of Abraham's Faith in the Promise*

In part three of *Fear and Trembling*, *Eulogy on Abraham*, Silentio laments that life's unlimited absurd contingencies could bring us poor humans to the defiant defeat of doubt, dread and despair. Søren was so tempted when he felt called upon to break his promise as was Abraham when God seemed to be breaking His promise. But the challenges of complexities' contingencies can become opportunities for heroes, poets and orators to become great. "One became great by expecting the possible, another by expecting the eternal; but he who experienced the impossible became the greatest of all" and, of course, that is exactly what Abraham did. God looked like an impossible contradiction of opposites as Abraham went forth in faith to do His will because Isaac was the means by which God could keep His promise and by demanding Isaac as a sacrificial victim God would be taking away the means by which the promise could be kept with honor. The promise was for this finite, temporal life in that it had to do with a very large family and a very prosperous land and somehow becoming a blessing for all of humankind. So Abraham believed that God was only tempting him and that if he went forth in good faith to do God's will in sacrificing Isaac God would somehow give him back Isaac a second time. In his faith Abraham so believed and trusted in God that he reconciled the absurd opposites of God: God who promises good and wonderful things with God, the monster, who demands the sacrifice of Isaac and thus the end of the promise. But Kierkegaard had just as much to reconcile for he did identify with his father's melancholia and he did feel like a hunched back, little creep whom all of a sudden Regina redeemed. But he felt called to leave her and never get her back in this life a second time, but that had to do with the new complexity of Christian faith in the sacrifice of God's Son.

II.2.5 The Absurd Contingency of Double Movement Leaping

In his *Eulogy* Silentio writes that Abraham was the greatest of all

> "great by that power whose strength is powerlessness,
> great by that wisdom whose secret is foolishness
> great by that hope whose form is madness
> great by that love that is hatred to oneself."
> This is the language or the logos of the Cross as Paul sees it.

It is as if Silentio is quoting Paul here and this is the core of Søren's philosophy of love and reconciliation which he now spells out for the first time in this *Preliminary Expectoration*. Søren first spits out his philosophy of double movement leaping by comparing the Knights of Infinite Resignation and of Faith. With all of his energy and passion Abraham renounced Isaac and was willing to give him up as a Knight of Infinite Resignation. But by faith which is God's gift Abraham gets Isaac a second time. As Silentio puts it in thinking of Regina:

> By my own strength I can give up the princess
> and I will not sulk about it
> but find joy and peace and rest in my pain
> but by my own strength I cannot get her back again
> for I use all my strength in resigning.
> On the other hand, by faith,
> says that marvelous knight,
> by faith you will get her by virtue of the absurd.

With Infinite Resignation Buddhists renounce all desire and Platonists renounce the shadows and images of the cave and Hegelians renounce each thesis with an antithesis. But Søren, while renouncing the aesthetic basement and the ethical first floor of his house with the logic of the neither/nor and relating absolutely to the absolute, then in faith comes back and is free to live on all floors of his house at once by relatively loving the basement, first floor and the second floor.

II.2.6 The Absurdity of Ethically Suspending the Teleological

Silentio focuses on three major problems for Father Abraham.
He is called upon to murder, hate and lie in the worst way possible.
But, does not this make his faith absurd and totally unethical?
The ethical is the universal natural law and every individual,
as Hegel argues, should obey that law with a good conscience.
Socrates saw that we should care for our soul with good conscience.
While there is no mention of good conscience in the Hebrew Bible
it runs through Paul's writings as an element of his Stoic heritage.
Kierkegaard in *Works of Love* highlights the practice of cultivating
a sensitive conscience as the single individual's loving guide.
But here in *Problemata I* Silentio argues that faith is the paradox
that the single individual is higher than the universal and
that to respond to God's call Abraham should suspend the ethical
for the sake of his absolute duty to the *Horror Religiosus*.
There is not only a teleological suspension of the ethical here
but also an absurd suspension of the teleological for Abraham
faces the loss of all meaning as God becomes self-contradictory.
In his duty to the Mysterium Tremendum of the Holy, Abraham
is willing to be tried and tested by God believing all the while that
God will suspend his own command or He will no longer be God.
Silentio further eulogizes Abraham by comparing him to Mary.

> *She needs worldly admiration as little as Abraham needs tears*
> *for she is no heroine and he was no hero,*
> *but both of them became greater than these,*
> *not by being exempted in any way*
> *from the distress and the agony and the paradox,*
> *but became greater by means of these.* (65)

When you read Silentio's treatment of Abraham you see no
difference between Abraham and the God-man and that is why
Kierkegaard does not sign his name to this deceptive writing
which makes no distinction between the elder and younger brother.

II.2.7 Loving Abraham as More Important

In *Works of Love* after showing how love is a matter of conscience Kierkegaard writes a chapter on "The Duty to Love the People We See." This takes us right to the heart of our duty to so love Love that in praising Love we will be able to love each and every person. To cultivate the conscience that sees why I should love every person is the main point of *Problemata II* in which Silentio in order to comprehend Abraham goes to Luke's hard saying:

> If anyone comes to me and does not hate
> his father and mother and wife and children
> and brothers and sisters, yes, and even his own life,
> he cannot be my disciple. (Luke 14:26; see *Problemata II*, 72)

Abraham is pictured here as living out this highest command. Kierkegaard through Silentio seems to love Abraham as even more important than Jesus because Abraham seems to have been the first to practice this strange love that hates in order to follow. So what is this hard saying about hating each person we meet in order to love them all about in its absurd paradoxical way? Kierkegaard explains his usage of it in *Works of Love* by showing why the Christian is called to love the enemy and to hate the beloved and by explaining how the first depends on the second. When I love *my* child, *my* friend, *my* beloved with the emphasis on the *my*, I love with a preferential self love that I need to suspend with infinite resignation if I am truly to love every other person as they are in themselves and not as I see them. So this hard saying is part of the cultivation process in which I can come to love all persons in the very value of their personhood. In accord with Kierkegaard's existential dialectic after I stop loving *my* beloved absolutely and I come to love Love absolutely the I can love all persons as persons and then love my beloved relatively in all of his or her unique differences. According to Silentio Abraham is already called upon to do this.

II.2.8 The Abrahamic Blessing for All Peoples

Kierkegaard's understanding of the strategy of the highest love
that is the gift and task to reconcile all peoples should let
the prodigal son, Jesus, go out to the elder brother, Socrates, the Greek,
and Abraham, the Jew, and begin by loving them as more important.
Just as Socrates in Søren 's mind would nobly come to love Jesus
as more important in return so could Abraham also do that.
Abraham believes that the promise of being a blessing for all peoples
can be fulfilled through Isaac and his offspring and Jesus
could be the key person in that family line for blessing all peoples.
Silentio treats Abraham and Jesus as the same for the reader
could think that Abraham's double movement leap is the same
as that of the God-man who as eternal came into the finite flesh.
They do both have universalist intentions even though in Jesus'
case the Son is sacrificed for every single individual person,
whereas in Abraham's Isaac is not sacrificed for all peoples.
In *Problemata III* it is asked if it was ethically defensible
for Abraham to conceal his understanding from his family.
The main point is that Abraham did not have any certain understanding.
He acted as if he would sacrifice Isaac and believed as if he would not.
Abraham is trapped in a double bind that calls for the double
movement leap of faith and that makes him higher than other
heroes such as Agamemnon, Brutus, and Jephte who
did sacrifice their children for very clear teleological reasons.
They were Knights of Infinite Resignation, not Knights of Faith.
Silentio's Abraham is already being loved as a blessing for the peoples
by helping us to love the girl and the young swain, Ephigenia in Aulis,
Aristotle's bride and bridegroom, Axel and Valborg, Queen Elizabeth,
Agnes and Merman, Sara and Tobias, and Gretchen and Faust.
We must love Abraham as more important for he is greater than these.

II.2.9 Loving the God-Man as More Important

This pseudonym, Johannes de Silentio, is being used by Kierkegaard to deceive us out of our self-deceit into the truth and he tells us in the Epilogue at the end of *Fear and Trembling* the truth is that the highest passion in a person is faith and faith is:

> an honest earnestness that fearlessly
> and incorruptibly points to the tasks
> an honest earnestness
> that lovingly maintains the tasks
> that does not disquiet people into wanting
> to attain the highest too hastily
> but keep the tasks young'
> and beautiful and lovely to look at
> inviting to all and yet also difficult
> and inspiring to the noble mind. (121)

Our highest passion is faith in the gift and task of reconciliation. We can spend our life on this or we can become weary of it. *Fear and Trembling* is Kierkegaard's way of fulfilling his task. He wants to make the task young and beautiful as was Regina. She awakened him from his unmotivated lethargy and sleep walking. By showing us Abraham and his task we can come to love Jesus and the task He has given us of spending our lives for others. The actual is higher than the possible and the highest of all is to live out the highest possible actual which is the gift and the task which Paul and Kierkegaard were given and which we can all be given if we notice it and become earnest about it. *Fear and Trembling* is a motivational book that wants to move us to do nothing less than the best we can dream of for others. The promise and the task of faith in that promise so motivated Abraham that he lived out his belief that by giving up Isaac he would get him back a billion fold as a blessing for all peoples. Jesus as the grain of wheat died that all Abraham's might live.

II.3 Reconciling the God-Man and Job

II.3.1 Repetition's Reconciliation Is the Only Happy Love

In *Repetition*, the companion volume to *Fear and Trembling*, Søren also discusses his love for Regina and the engagement breaking. When he fell in love with her he became a poet who was religious but he believed that if he had faith he would be able to marry her. But the engagement breaking was complex and he wrote in his journal:

> *If I had not honored her higher than myself as my future wife,*
> *if I had not been prouder of her honor than my own,*
> *then I would have remained silent and fulfilled her wish and mine—*
> *I would have married her—*
> *there are so many marriages that conceal little stories.*

Such as being gay. Perhaps he worried that if he married her the whole network of his melancholy would return and she would have to live day in and day out with a depressed husband. But he believed that if he really had faith he would be able to remain in the enthusiasm of his Divine Madness and be married at the same time in the reconciliation of what he calls "repetition." When we think of repetition in English we think of a mechanical repetition in which the same thing happens over and over again in exactly the same way so that it is boring and completely non-eventful. The concept of Kierkegaard has to do with experiencing through life a reconciled mix of the old and the new at the same time. The young man falls in love poetically and mystically in a Platonic recollective love that is captivating for the young girl. She loves being adored by the melancholic poet as his muse. But this poetic love is an unhappy love for it expects the new and the interesting and would be bored with the repetition of the same. If a love relation is only aesthetically interesting it becomes unhappy. If it is an ethical mechanical repetition of the same it is unhappy. But "the dialectic of repetition is easy, for that which is repeated has been, otherwise it could not be repeated, but the very fact that it has been makes the repetition into something new."[2]

II.3.2 Beyond Platonic Recollection to a New Future

Kierkegaard argues that "repetition is the interest of metaphysics and also the interest upon which metaphysics comes to grief."[3] He demonstrates that by contrasting faith's repetition with Plato's metaphysics of recollection and Hegel's mediation. Kierkegaard clarifies his concept of repetition with several kinds of definition, nominal or etymological, essential, causal, and descriptive and for each of these he uses the method of free imaginative variation or the experimentation of comparisons. Kierkegaard is proud that Danish has such a good metaphysical word as *Gjentagelse* which contains all the religious, ethical and faith based metaphysical meanings that he will bring out. Repetition means to bring out or to fetch for *Gjen* means "again," and *tag* means "day" and *else* means "getting" so the word means re-getting it again in a new way each day so that even the English word *re-petition* is suggestive for petition as the first form of prayer is renewed with repentance, thanksgiving and praise. Petition means to earnestly ask for something from the other. Repetition for Kierkegaard is the renewal of Platonic Recollection. "Recollection" is also etymologically a very rich word for the root "lect" is connected with *legein* which means "to gather" and so to collect is to gather together into a logos or one. So Plato reconciled the being of Parmenides and the Becoming of Heraclitus with the concept of recollection which shows the identity of the logos with the ontos which connect the many. But repetition is much more humble and other-oriented for according to its basic attitude it constantly re-petitions the other because one is aware of one's lack and the need. For Plato one recollects by climbing up out of the cave and recovering the past truth that the soul knew before it fell. For Kierkegaard repletion is a forward recollection that renews all things because of the surprises of the unknown future.

II.3.3 Beyond Hegelian Mediation to a New Past

So recollection is a process that collects the many into the past in order to re-fetch their meaning and significance so that Plato would see the fallen soul rising through the remembrance of things past until he collected them in their originating form. Thus there is no genuine future or freedom in the realm of Platonic recollection because the moment of truth only recovers what has been and has been previously lost and lost sight of. Hegel's metaphysics of mediation goes in the opposite direction to a future and a *telos* or goal or purpose that makes the past only a quantitative, instrumental, utilitarian step on the way. Mediation has to do with the medium or middle premise by which a conclusion comes out of previous premises such that we can say that if an acorn is properly nourished and cultivated it will become an oak tree, but this acorn has been duly nourished and cultivated, therefore, it has reached its goal and is now this oak tree. Plato explains things by relating them through recollection to their archeological formal causes and Hegel explains them by relating them through mediation to their teleological or final cause. The moment of truth for Hegel is that moment of mediation when the thesis is negated by the mediating anti-thesis so that the new synthesis or new whole comes forth into a new future. Just as Plato does not have a true freedom or a true future because his recollection reduces things to the past so Hegel does not have a true and living past because his mediation negates the past in not keeping the actual acorn as it only becomes the oak. Plato's formal recollection and Hegel's Aristotelian final or teleological mediation are both mechanical or natural and quantitative whereas Kierkegaard's qualitative leap of repetition provides a metaphysics that preserves the freedom of a new future and the freedom of a renewing past so that in the present there is a reconciliation that keeps the past and allows the future.

II.3.4 Repetition as the Ethical Task of Freedom

The book, *Repetition*, has its small, powerful, metaphysical section at the beginning and then it is the story of the young man who falls in love and his mentor, Constantine Constantius, who helps him to think about his love affair and to explore repetitions' meanings. What the young man discovers is that the repetition can reconcile four different attitudes that make up the four stages on life's way. The young man learns that a lover can be a poet, a husband, a mystic and a person of faith who can repeat all four at once. Ordinarily and for the most part good husbands love their wives ethically and with reflective decisions that promote their welfare. Job was a good ethical man and husband and father and according to the Deuteronomic morality and religious vision he should have been blessed, but instead he was cursed for he lost his flocks, and his land and his children which proved that ethics can fail. And this often does happen to good people for ethical love need not be rewarded since the good can suffer more than the wicked. The relation between the Kierkegaard-Regina story and the Job and his children story and the Abraham Isaac story is that they each want to get back again what they have had taken away. That would be repetition and a happy beginning reconciliation. If Job lived happily with his family and they were taken away life would be renewed in repetition if they were united again. In the epilogue Job does get his children back but that seems like a fairy tale for no one has experienced such a thing. However, eternity is the true repetition and when it begins in faith in the incarnation, the death and the resurrection the followers of Jesus believe that each individual lives in eternity. Kierkegaard writes this book under the pseudonym of the Constant Constant one and by remaining in love's debt to Regina he knows that he will always love her come what may and he believes that in some ways she will always love him too.

II.3.5 Metaphysic's Interest on Which Metaphysics Founders

Both Plato and Hegel base their ethics on their metaphysics but
Kierkegaard makes clear that neither of them can account for
the genuine new and thus neither can account for freedom and
without the qualitative leap of freedom decisions are impossible.
Metaphysics seeks to account for becoming but if becoming is
a process of necessity which can be logically accounted for
then it lacks the really new and the contingency and possibility
that are the opposite of necessity and which make freedom possible.
The interest of metaphysics is to give a logical account of freedom
but since metaphysics must be truly logical and based on
necessity it falls into self-contradiction in accounting for freedom.
If there is to be a truly free decision then one must make a
qualitative leap into that decision that is not based upon
a merely quantitative build up of necessary antecedents.
If freedom is a lifting up of oneself by one's boot straps then
the potency for such a leap must be a real potency in oneself
like the potency in the acorn out of which the oak comes forth
but again that potency only works with a quantitative
build up and this model cannot be one of freedom's qualitative leap.
So what Kierkegaard shows by contrasting repetition's
qualitative leap of freedom with the quantitative build ups
of Plato and Hegel is that if we really value freedom then
we have to affirm faith in the God-man whose leap from
being God to becoming man alone is a model for freedom.
Kierkegaard is arguing that if we value freedom and all
that it implies in our Western culture then we cannot deny
faith in *agape* and personhood without which our secular society
has no real metaphysical basis but only hidden assumptions.
Kierkegaard and Job with their faith could have for themselves
the ethical task of always loving their beloved no matter what
and of remaining in debt to those who are present in their absence.

II.3.6 The Single Individual and the Posthorn

Constantius tells the story of a stagecoach driver who arrives in a town with the mail and blows a posthorn to let the people know that he and the mail are there and this horn is unpredictable. It never sounds the same twice and thus symbolizes no repetition. However, the dialectic of true repetition is to be found with it. The repetition that renews is a transition from one state (such as religiousness A) to another (such as religiousness B) and the states are as different from one another as the creatures of the ocean are from those of land and air for repetition takes place not through an immanent continuity with the former existence which is a contradiction, but through a transcendence. Any person as a single individual is as unpredictable as the posthorn. Kierkegaard came to see that clearly as he grieved over Regina's grieving at his breaking of the engagement and then discovered that she was not grieving at all but was about to marry another. He was totally surprised and the idea crossed his mind that she must not have cared so much for him if she could so quickly seemingly forget him and become engaged to another. This news of her new engagement brought him to identify with Job at the moment of the Storm when God asked him how he could question God when God and his creation were so great and Job did not know all that God was up to with his universe. However, he came to see that she gave him to himself a second time. First she inspired him to a full life of witnessing faith and now she relieved him that he was not hurting her. That is true repetition for what has been can be again. However, the second time is like and yet unlike the first. What has been does not determine what will be and in his surprise that she went with an other so quickly he could see how his second experience of erotic inspiration was different from the first for she loved him and then freed him.

II.3.7 Loving Job as More Important

Satan made a bet with God that if Job should experience
the problem of evil and suffer he would lose his faith in God.
Job lost the prosperity of his flocks and he continued to pray:
"The Lord had given. The Lord has taken. Blessed be the Lord."
Then Satan upped the ante and God took away Job's children.
Just as Kierkegaard's father began to lose his children so Job
lost his and there was the dramatic story of Job's friends
who claimed that Job must have done evil to be so punished.
That is the Deuteronomic vision that those who are good will be
blessed and those who are evil will be cursed and destroyed.
But that logic did not hold and the unpredictable happened.
At first Job did begin to doubt and despair and to think that
it would have been better if he would had never have been born.
He even thought in the back of his mind that he would like
to take God to a court of law and show God's injustice.
But then when it looked like Satan was winning the wager
there was the storm and God spoke to Job out of the thunder
and asked him where he was when God created the stars and
the seas and the Leviathan of the deep and Job recognized
his pride and he repented in sack cloth and ashes for doubting.
So with the posthorn we see that doubt about the next note
at first seems to make repetition impossible but then it can
help one to see the non-mechanical true repetition and its doubt.
In *Works of Love* Kierkegaard explains the role of doubt in the
life of a loving and trusting faith when he writes:

> *If someone can demonstrate on the basis of the possibility*
> *of deception that one should not believe anything at all,*
> *I can demonstrate that one should believe in everything*
> *on the basis of the possibility of deception.* (228)

In his own experience Søren knew that the younger brother, Jesus,
could truly love the elder brother, Job, especially in his ambivalence.

II.3.8 Job's Faithful Love That Justifies the Exception

At the end of the book in a Concluding Letter by Constantine Constantius the logic of repetition is explained in terms of a battle between the universal order and the exception such as Abraham, Job, or Søren Constantine mentions that the 1, 2, 3 of the ordinary syllogisms that draw conclusions from the universal and particular do not work in the case of the individual exception and:

> *It is asking too much of an ordinary reviewer*
> *to be interested in the dialectical battle in which*
> *the exception arises in the midst of the universal,*
> *the protracted and very complicated procedure*
> *in which the exception battles his way through*
> *and affirms himself as justified,*
> *for the unjustified exception is recognized precisely*
> *by his wanting to bypass the universal.* (226)

Job began like Abraham with a vision of land, nation and name and he was promised he would attain his aesthetic dream if he would be ethically good and follow the laws of God and he did that and he did gain prosperity, posterity and rich blessings for all. Then at step three of the dialectic he was challenged by the universal and losing prosperity, posterity and blessing he stood face to face with the problem of evil and wondered how a good God could be so unjust as to punish him so when he was good. Then in step four the universal order of God appeared in the great storm and Job repented in infinite resignation and absolutely loved the absolute so that he now in step five saw God anew. In step six according to the epilogue of the miracle he got his children back a second time and in step seven he was prosperous once again having recovered the aesthetic. This battle is the same one that the prodigal must go through when he wants to win over the elder brother in reconciliation for the elder brother represents the universal order of the law.

II.3.9 Loving the God-Man as More Important

So Job like Abraham is a type of the God-man who gives up all
for the other in a spirit of praising love that recollects the dead.
When Job first lost everything he still prayed: "The Lord has
given; the Lord has taken away, blessed be the name of the Lord."
But, as he was taunted by his friends he began to give in
to temptation and sigh and lament the very day he was born.
Finally he wished he could take God before a court of law.
At first Job saw all the world as a gift from God and then he came
to see it only as the problem of evil that looked worse and worse.
So it was with Kierkegaard. He came to see himself as a problem.
He could no longer stand his depressed father and moved out.
He was a small, hunch-back, gay, little guy who could not
even write his thesis. He not only had problems; he was a problem.
He was a physical, social, sexual, intellectual mess of problems.
But then Regina loved him and he loved her and all his problems
turned into gifts for now he was reconciled with his father.
He wrote a brilliant Master's Thesis on the *Irony of Socrates*.
Regina gave him the gift of himself and he felt like a gift for others.
He experienced the magic of love that transforms problems into gifts.
Still he had his secret thorn in the flesh and he decided not
to inflict himself upon Regina and he broke the engagement
and he was pining away about her pining away in rejection.
All his gifts were taken away for he believed that if he
only could get genuine faith he would be able to marry her.
But then he read in the newspaper she was to marry another.
That was like Job's thunder storm and she gave him to himself
a second time and he could praise Love as did Job.
He discovered the love of the God-man who could be a sacrifice
for others and like St. Paul he could now make up for what was
lacking in the suffering of Christ and teach others that if they
like his father lost their children they could get them back in heaven.

III. St. Paul

III.1 Conversion to Reconciliation

III.1.1 The New Agape

Paul's conversion was the mother of all conversions.
Converts like Augustine and Kierkegaard have his story
as a story within their own confessional conversion stories.
Saul became Paul in about AD 33, precisely
at the moment when Ananias came to him and said:

> "Brother Saul, I have been sent by the Lord Jesus
> who appeared to you on your way here
> so that you may recover your sight
> and be filled with the Holy Spirit."
> Immediately it was as though scales fell away
> from Saul's eyes and he could see again.
> So he was baptized there and then, and after
> taking some food he regained his strength. (Acts 9:17–19)

As Kierkegaard's conversion began with the love in Regina's face
so Paul's began with the love of Jesus in Stephen's face.
The young Stephen, a freshly ordained Deacon, was
arrested by the Jews for preaching the Good News of Jesus.

> The members of the Sanhedrin
> all looked intently at Stephen
> and his face appeared to them
> like the face of an angel. (Acts 6:15)

As the Roman soldier saw Jesus on the cross and said:
"Truly this man is the Son of God" (Mark 15:39), so Stephen touched Saul.

> The witnesses put down their clothes
> at the feet of a young man called Saul.
> As they were stoning him, Stephen said
> "Lord Jesus, receive my spirit."
> Then he knelt down and said out loud,
> "Lord do not hold this sin against them."
> And with these words he fell asleep.
> And Saul entirely approved of the killing. (Acts 7:58b—8:1a)

III.1.2 The New Personal Agape

Saul as a Pharisee believed in life after death but
all this started becoming real for him in a new way
as he experienced the death and dying of Stephen
for Stephen loved and forgave him while being stoned.
All of this was very vivid in Saul's mind.
Many jeering Jews gathered round just as they had for Jesus.
Saul was right up front very close to Stephen.
To free their throwing arms the witnesses took off their cloaks
and tossed them to the young Saul who was in training
to become a full-fledged witness and killer of Christians.
The witnesses each had their bag of well chosen stones.
They were each about a quarter pound and round like baseballs.
There stood Stephen relaxed and radiant with eyes of compassion.
The stones started pounding into him and he fell to his knees.
Saul watched a witness get right up close and throw his stone.
It hit Stephen right in the forehead and crushed his skull.
Stephen crumpled and fell like a dropped sack of potatoes.
The stoners picked up their stones and wiping them off
put them back in their leather stone-bag for next time.
Saul did not forget the glory on the face of Stephen
that made present the love of Jesus even in his absence.
Saul got on his horse and started riding back to Damascus.
The loving, beautiful, glorious face of Stephen haunted him.
That look became for him the agapeic event that converted
the negative, hateful heart of Saul into the loving heart of Paul.
He heard the words: "Saul, Saul, why do you persecute me?" (Acts 9:4)
And at once he was able to ask: "Who are you, Lord?" (9:5)
And that was it. Paul knew the resurrected Jesus and his Spirit
in the agapeic face of Stephen and he knew that through
the person Jesus in the person Stephen he was called to be Paul.
Paul was given reconciliation and now he must give it to others.

III.1.3 The New Universal Agape

Paul had always believed in the Jewish double command of love:

> Love the Lord, your God,
> with your whole heart, mind and soul
> and your neighbor as yourself. (Deut 6:5 and Lev 19:18)

What happened when he experienced Jesus' love in Stephen
is that Paul's understanding of "neighbor" began to change.
The Jew thought that his neighbor was his fellow Jew.
But Stephen loved each and every person as his neighbor
and he especially loved his enemies and his persecutors.
What Paul experienced in Stephen was a universal love
for all persons and especially for the most unlovable
such as Saul who was bent on slaughtering Christians.
Paul was a passionate man who believed in excellence
and as soon as he beheld the love of Jesus working in Stephen
he knew that if he really believed in excellence he would have to
undergo a change of attitude from restricted to universal love.
Of course, there was complexity in the Jewish tradition and
there was the long tradition of loving widows, orphans and aliens.
Those aliens could be Gentiles and in Second Isaiah there was
the Suffering Servant who prays for and forgives his persecutors.
Gamaliel in *The Acts of the Apostles* right before the Stephen story
advises the Jews not to persecute the followers of Jesus because
if they are not of God they will soon fizzle out and if they
are of God who should have or do anything against them?
Paul very much belonged to the apocalyptic tradition which
was a meaningful way of thinking for those who are persecuted.
It started with Ezekiel on the banks of the Euphrates when
the deported Jewish people wept when they remembered Jerusalem.
It had a universal outlook in its cosmological and ethical dualism.
There was a great battle between the forces of good and evil and
very soon according to Paul the final showdown would come.

III.1.4 A New Apocalyptic Universalism

So in Paul's mind there was a great urgency to decide to be
either with the forces of evil or with the forces of good.
A long history of apocalyptic thinking had prepared him
for this exclusivistic logic of the either/or and thus he
was always a very passionate man and never lukewarm.
From Ezekiel to Daniel to the Maccabees, apocalyptic writing,
which was unveiled in symbols to console a persecuted people
was concerned with death, judgment and either heaven or hell.
Apocalyptic thinking assumed a resurrection of the dead
and the persecuted were waiting for "the day of Yahweh"
or the end of the world when the judge of the nations would
come to reward the good and punish the evil.
The Jewish religion of the covenant and the law up until
the apocalyptic movement was exclusively for Jews
and not for Gentiles who were not people of the covenant.
But in apocalyptic thinking there was a universal dualism
that was cosmic, psychological, and ethical so that all
of humankind was engaged in a battle of chaos against cosmos.
When Paul converted to the Lord Jesus Christ he saw him as
the Apocalyptic Christ who would provide salvation for all
if they would but convert from evil to good as he did.
Paul saw himself as called to be the apostle to the Gentiles.
Many Greco-Roman Hellenists already knew of the apocalyptic battle
because of the Stoic idea about the coming of the end of the world.
Paul experienced first hand the love of the resurrected Christ
in the loving face of Stephen and he heard the voice of the Spirit
of the resurrected Christ calling him on the road to Damascus.
He felt that Christ had placed him at the centre of the human drama
and that now Christ's universal love could come to replace
the power of the forces of evil in the apocalyptic battle.
Now instead of universal war a universal love was possible.

III.1.5 The New Agapeic Logic of Suffering

Paul's mission to save the world was the moral equivalent to war.
He was not living as people did ordinarily and for the most part.
The enemy was out there ready to devour each precious person
for whom Christ had suffered and died in atonement on the cross.
Paul's love for Christ who saved him from his wicked ways
put Paul under a compulsion to go out and save others.
His life was a living prayer of love, repentance, thanksgiving
and petition to Christ his savior and with the most
passionate inwardness he preached the Good News to the world.
Before Paul was converted he did not know that he needed saving.
He thought of himself as a devout Jew doing God's will.
But then he experienced the power of the suffering Stephen
and he began to understand the power of the suffering Christ.
He began to see how the problem of suffering could be understood
for the cross and all the suffering it represented was the
weakness of Christ and of God which could redeem all weakness
and bring about the kingdom of love, justice, joy, peace, etc.
Paul first experienced the solution and then he began to
understand the problem in a way he never saw it before.
Paul came from Tarsus and was a Roman citizen and
a Stoic as well as a Jew and an apocalyptic Pharisee.
He knew the great Stoic answer to the problem of suffering
which went back to Alexander the Great and his General, Pyrrho,
who brought to Greece the Buddhist idea of universal suffering
and the answer to it is apathy or detachment from passion.
Paul's conversion took him to a new solution to the problem
of suffering which he saw in Stephen and in Jesus who
showed that a passionate and graceful suffering for others
was a way of loving that could reveal the worth of all suffering.
Just as Stephen had lovingly suffered for Paul so now
Paul spent his life suffering for others to teach them its worth.

III.1.6 Paul's Logic of Mixed Opposites

Paul was a man of mixed opposites; enormously self-confident
yet full of fear and trembling; very successful and yet always
on the brink of failure; threatened by both Jews and Gentiles.
But in this way he was a true follower and apostle of Christ.
What set Christ apart from philosophers and other
religious leaders was that he redeemed weakness by weakness.
God has always been thought of as omnipotent and impassible
or as all powerful and beyond the imperfection of suffering, but
now the weakness and suffering of Jesus who is the Son of God
revealed the weakness and suffering of God and so Paul too
could be confident in his anxiety and successful through failures.
Love suffers for others and reveals the value of all suffering
because Jesus died and yet rose again and it was the resurrected
Jesus who lived on and appeared to Paul and saved him.
In the Incarnation, in the Crucifixion and in the Resurrection
there was the logic of mixed opposites that guided the unique
personality of Paul that was so different from the character of Saul.
In the joy, sorrow and glory of those three mysteries Paul was
born again through the death of Saul as a member of Christ's body.
What Paul's conversion meant was that he came to love the church.
First he persecuted her and then he spent his life building her up.
Paul came to love the church because he came to believe that she was
the people of God, the family of God, the body of Christ, the temple
of God and the Bride of Christ and thus he was on a mission as
the most passionate missionary ever to bring all persons to her.
As a Jew Paul was a devoted member of the people of God and
of the family of God but it was clear that all belong to God's family.
All the multitude of the earth were not only his neighbors
whom he should love but they were members of his family
and members of the Body of Christ for whom Christ died.
At his conversion the problem of evil became the mystery of suffering.

III.1.7 The New Logic of the Body of Christ

What amazed Paul in his conversion experience was the presence
of the loving body of Christ first in Stephen's suffering love
and then in the loving words that spoke to him in his blindness.
Paul knew that Jesus was dead and yet he spoke to him with
such love that Paul wanted only to love him in return.
This mystery of the Incarnate, Crucified and Resurrected body is
the core of Paul's preaching and writing for the rest of his life.
He will have to go beyond Greek and Hebrew ideas of the body
and work out a new theology of the body that has to do with
love and personal growth, the Kingdom and the Cross and
the very nature of our common and individual personhood.
When Paul moved from the Jewish people to the human people
and from the Jewish family of Abraham to the family of the new Adam
he had to start working out a new logic of mixed opposites.
Before his conversion he had always thought in terms of a logic
of exclusive opposites in that the Gentiles were excluded from
the Jewish family and Greeks excluded Barbarians.
When he thought about all persons being members of Christ's body
if they were baptized into his body he saw that that could not
work according to a logic of inclusivity as with Platonists.
For individuals cannot be mere appearances who participate
in a common soul as things participate in a common form,
as drops of water would be swallowed up in a great common ocean.
The members of the body each have to be really distinct
even though each is dependent on the other members.
The great human family has Christ as its head and Stephen
and Peter and Paul are all members of his Body even though
as single individuals Peter and Paul do not always see eye to eye.
So Peter and Paul are not even a pair of parallel opposites.
When single individuals are members of one Body logics of
exclusive, inclusive and parallel opposites do not work.

III.1.8 The Logic of the Communal Person

Throughout his seven authentic letters Paul will work away
at clarifying his concept of the body and the body of Christ.
The plan of salvation history according to Paul is that God
created Adam and because Adam sinned his children are fallen.
Other origination beliefs besides the Biblical assume that evil
is equiprimordial with good and thus there can be no notion
of personhood or of moral creatures who are responsible for evil.
But the plan of salvation history according to Paul is that
God's son was sent to redeem us by being crucified,
resurrected and taken into heaven to take us there too.
The mystery of salvation has to do with the body in three ways:
as the Incarnate Body, the Crucified Body and the Resurrected Body.
God has redeemed his people and the fallen family of man
by the body of Christ and now we are all members of his body.
The Jewish people believed that God was personal but the body
of Christ has complicated the understanding of the personal God.
Is the Son of God who has become man a person distinct
from the Father and is the Holy Spirit another third person?
Paul has enough to do without working out these problems.
But they are there in the background of his own set of problems.
Christ appeared to him in his Resurrected Body which
according to Paul is a Spiritual Body he heard but did
not see; but is not a spiritual body a contradiction?
The Greeks would have thought so because body and soul
or matter and form are exclusively opposite kinds of being.
It is not as if the person is an immortal soul that
at death will depart from the body into an eternal life.
Paul believed in the resurrected body and that we will be
taken up as members of the Resurrected and Ascended Body
of the Lord to be also with the Father and the Holy Spirit
who though not embodied will be present to us as to Christ.

III.1.9 The Logic of Individual Persons

Philosophers following Boethius defined the person as
"an individual substance of a rational nature" and
the relationality of persons was seen as accidental
because they worked with a metaphysics of substance
and thus thought of each thing as individuated by matter.
So when Kierkegaard redefines the person as "a relation
that can relate to itself and to the Other both Divine and human"
he is trying to recover a Biblical view of personhood.
In Paul's thinking even though we are each members of
Christ's body and not independent entities we are still
individuated and different as each member is differentiated.
The eye cannot say to the hand I have no need of you.
This may sound as if we are individuated by our functions.
But we are also individuated by our special gifts and tasks.
The Holy Spirit gives us each different gifts and we can use
them and act with them or not for the good of the whole body.
Paul found that by his conversion he was freed and he could
use his freedom to serve others or for his own self-indulgence.
Paul had a notion of the moral individual or the acting person.
We are what we do, individuated by every thought, word and deed,
and we will be unique forever not only in the gifts we receive
but in our attitudes, moods, and feelings which give rise to
our thoughts, words and deeds all of which we can cultivate.
As members of Christ's body we are not self-made persons.
God creates each person as unique and we are further
individuated by heredity and environment and our heredity
has to do with the interpersonal relations of our parents.
Our environment has to do with all the complexity that
impinges upon us, but when Paul was freed by meeting
Christ in his conversion he became also a maker of himself
and others with Christ beyond any heredity and environment.

III.2 Paul's Love Letter to the Thessalonians

III.2.1 Motivating Thessalonians to Universal Love

Saul turned away from his old ways of negativity to his new life and mission of love when he beheld the loving face of the persecuted Stephen, when he was called by the Resurrected Christ and when he was served with love by Ananias and the little Christian community. Now the new Paul after years of urgent missionary work to bring the Good News of *agape* and personhood to all others is writing his first letter to his beloved Thessalonians. Paul's letter to them is written in the form of a prayer for them: "May the Lord be generous in increasing your love and make you love one another and the whole human race as much as we love you" (1 Thess 3:12). This is the new Christian Gospel for which Paul is constantly on a mission and for which he is constantly working and praying with great energy and most passionate urgency. This prayer is his mission statement and it must be a prayer for Paul knows that by himself he would not even have known of this universal love let alone dream that it could become reality. Paul loves his Thessalonian community and he wants them to love each other just as he loves them and he wants their love to increase constantly not only for each other but for the whole human race. The notion of constantly increasing love is central to true love. Loves that are not fulfilled in *agape* often tend to whither away and with *agape* there must always be love and personal growth. Constant growth is the nature of true love and it is the nature of personhood both for communities and for individuals as they see it as their sacred task to bring that love to every single other. As a Jew and as a Greek with both of those languages as his mother tongue Saul would never have dreamed of loving all other persons as his neighbor and as his own, but this new love is the fulfillment of those old loves which always distinguished Jew and Gentile, and Greek and Barbarian and now for Paul the Roman and Stoic idea of universal love can really happen.

III.2.2 Bonds Them in Familial Affection

When we consider Paul's *agape* in terms of affection, friendship and *eros* it is clear that while Plato put the emphasis on *eros* and Aristotle on friendship, Paul following the Hebrew tradition puts the emphasis on affection. Paul loves the Thessalonians like a mother, like a father and like a brother. He writes: "Like a mother feeding and looking after her own children, we felt so protective and devoted to you, and had come to love you so much, that we were eager to hand over to you not only the Good News but our whole lives as well" (1:7b–8). Paul sees in maternal affection a feeling so great that the mother will sacrifice herself for her offspring. He finds that he has this kind of maternal affection for his own and the whole human race. But also he loves them like a father for he writes: "You can remember how we treated every one of you as a father treats his children, teaching you what was right, encouraging you and appealing to you to live a life worthy of God, who is calling you to share the glory of his Kingdom" (1:11–12). So Paul distinguishes maternal and paternal affection as self-sacrificing in its nourishment and protection as distinct from guiding, teaching, encouraging and appealing. The criterion for Paul's paternal ethics is being worthy of God. It is not that we will be virtuous that we might be happy or that we seek the greatest good for the greatest number by subordinating utilitarian to intrinsic value, but rather the ultimate motivational goal that Paul as a fatherly figure aims at for his children is to be worthy of God and the glory of his Kingdom. In that Kingdom there will be the affection of brotherly love. "As for loving our brothers, there is no need for anyone to write to you about that, since you have learned from God yourselves to love one another" (4:9). He ends by saying: "Greet all the brothers with a Holy Kiss" (5:26). And he gives orders that this letter be read to all the brothers.

III.2.3 So That He Constantly Loves Them in Prayer

Paul's love letter to the Thessalonians is also a prayer for them.
He begins his letter with thanksgiving and congratulation for them
and to them by writing: "We always mention you in our prayers
and thank God for you all, and constantly remember before God
our Father how you have shown your faith in action, worked
for love and preserved through hope, in our Lord Jesus Christ" (1:2–3).
Prayer for others is a way of cultivating love for them, for Paul
does not think we have to love people but not like them.
For him love as affection is a joy and pleasure in the other.
Some might wonder how we can love unpleasant others on demand.
But prayer can cultivate that special atmosphere of love:
by praising, adoring, worshiping and loving, by begging for
forgiveness, healing, deliverance and salvation; by abiding
in a spirit of thanksgiving and gratitude and by asking God
to mother, father, brother, sister all of ours and especially enemies.
Prayer is always positive and it cultivates positivity in the heart
of the one who intones and envisions the other in the heart of God.
Paul believes that his prayer will help the Thessalonians to grow
in their love of love for one another and the whole human race.
His prayer will bring the Lord to bless their hearts with love.
By his prayer and his example Paul seeks to further love
his Thessalonians by giving them the best gift possible,
namely, a constant increase and growth of their loving hearts.
Paul also ends his letter with prayer: "May the God of peace make
you perfect and holy; and may you all be kept safe and
blameless in spirit, soul and body, for the coming of our Lord" (5:23)
To really love others is to be a peace maker and the loved one
can have peace and joy if she or he is blameless and holy.
Prayer is a loving communication with God who is love
and his Thessalonians will cultivate love if they constantly
pray even as Jesus and Paul prayed especially for those in need.

III.2.4 To the Father, Son, and Holy Spirit

As a Jew Paul had developed the habit of prayer to the Father
and here he prays for the Thessalonians to the Father.
But he also prays to God the Son who has revealed the Father
in a new way and is now the mediator to the Father.
"May God our Father himself, and our Lord Jesus Christ,
make it easy for us to come to you" (3:11). But Paul also prays
to the Holy Spirit who likewise is at the center of his love life.
"We have been called by God to be holy, not to be immoral;
in other words, any one who objects is not objecting to
a human authority, but to God, who gives you his Holy Spirit" (4:7–8).
So God the Father gave us his Son to redeems us and to call
us to help him to let all humans know they have been saved.
But he also gives his Holy Spirit who sanctifies and inspires us
with his gifts to be holy and to serve others in the freedom of love.
Even though all have been redeemed by the Son there still are
many negative and un-loving thoughts, words and deeds, which
arise spontaneously out of our negative moods and feelings.
Jesus and his love converted Paul and his Thessalonians by
the love of Stephen and then of Paul but ongoing conversion of self
and of others is still imperative for we are saved but not sanctified.
As soon as we go out to others in love the Holy Spirit of the Risen
Lord Jesus can continue to give us the gifts of the spirit which
can continue to sanctify and free us from our negative habits.
It is important to pray the Trinitarian prayer as does Paul
because we are Trinitarian in our make-up as spirit, soul and body.
Jesus became embodied that all flesh might see the Lord's salvation
and he continuously sends Spirit to us that we might grow
in sensitivity for the loveliness of each member of the human race.
In Father we father, in Son we brother and in Spirit we sister,
and, even though Paul did not know Mary, in each we mother.
In Paul's spirit we pray to Holy Mother, Father, Sister, Brother.

III.2.5 But There Is the Problem of Death

So Paul greatly loves his Thessalonians and he wants the best for them, namely, that they have an attitude of complacent love for the whole human race, but he also takes their concern to heart. He has interpreted the coming of the Kingdom to mean not only that Christ has merited justification for all humans, but that he will come a second time and establish his Kingdom of peace on earth. Christ will come in our lifetime and we will all be taken into his Kingdom. However, some of the Thessalonians have already died before the coming of the Kingdom, so what is going to happen to them? Paul says: "We want you to be quite certain, brothers, about those who have died, to make sure that you do not grieve about them. We believe that Jesus died and rose again, and that it will be the same for those who have died in Jesus: God will bring them with him" (4:13–14). So Paul is led into theological thinking by the practical problems of his dear ones. His theologizing is also directed by his love for them because he has to think out the most loving solution possible. He wants to be fair to everyone and to comfort those whose loved ones have died. To comfort them he writes that those who have died in Christ will be the first to rise. Each of them will be with the Lord forever. This question of the coming of the Kingdom is a major problem for each of the New Testament writers and just as there will be nine different models of the Kingdom and the Cross, so there will be different models concerning the Parousia or the fullness of time. Once more we will see that there are many different and opposing voices within the New Testament. Others have taught different views of the coming Kingdom and Paul is doing his best to articulate his faith and even he and his school will try different articulations as to whether it will come very soon or maybe a bit later as it is not clear. One of the great problems of reconciliation is to work out a model for reconciling the very different voices within the New Testament.

III.2.6 Set in the Context of Christ's Resurrection

As Paul considers individual immortality in the light of Christ's Resurrection and ponders what kind of body will be resurrected he receives many questions and objections that will lead him step by step into his theology of the nature and place of the body. Will each of us have an ordinary or spiritual body after death? Paul is led into a discussion of the body and of the Holy Spirit. Right at the beginning of his letter Paul reminds the Thessalonians that the Good News came to them: "not only as words, but as power and as the Holy Spirit and as utter conviction" (1:5). This is also a description of how his own conversion took place. So what is the Holy Spirit of the Risen Lord Jesus and how are our resurrected bodies to be related to the Holy Spirit? "It was with the joy of the Holy Spirit that you took the Gospel" (1:6b). As Christians we will live in accord with the gifts of the Holy Spirit: faith, hope and love and by the fruits of the Holy Spirit: love, joy, peace, patience, kindness, etc., which will keep us healthy. As we live in the Body of Christ and in the Holy Spirit so we will die with them and be with them throughout eternity and our bodies will be spiritual bodies when we are resurrected. As Paul begins to think about life after death he has to raise the issue of the resurrection of our bodies and the coming of a new kingdom in which there will be no more death. Paul teaches that the Lord will soon come to establish a Kingdom of love, justice, joy and peace so that the Christians with him are thinking about the immediate future when this will happen. It will come at an unexpected time like a thief in the night. Christ's Resurrection becomes evident to others through the gifts of the Holy Spirit so we should live in accord with these gifts so that we might manifest Christ to others through these gifts. The questions that will give rise to Paul's theology of love and of the universal and eternal worth of individuals here appear.

III.2.7 And His Second Coming in Our Lifetime

So what is Paul thinking about The Day of the Lord which is going to come like a thief in the night in relation to the whole human race which we should love as much as he loves the Thessalonians? Are only those who have converted to the Lord Jesus as did Paul and the Thessalonians going to be saved when the day comes and they are taken up in the clouds to meet the Lord in the air? He does speak of the Christians as being sons of light and sons of day. He says that we do not belong to darkness. But we are supposed to love the whole human race and it would seem that God does too. So when he says "You are all sons of light" (5:5) is he referring to the whole human race? Are only a few counted as brothers now, but will all be saved and counted as brothers when Christ returns on the Day of the Lord? Paul does write about a battle between the forces of good and the forces of evil. We are all supposed to partake in the battle and "Put on faith and love for a breastplate, and the hope of salvation for a helmet" (5:8b). So there is a cosmic battle between the forces of light and the forces of darkness and the battle is also ethical. If we really live in the Kingdom of Love which is about to come should we be loving the whole human race and hoping for the salvation of the human race and having faith that the whole human race will be saved when the Lord comes? If this is the case then it is not as if the Lord is going to judge the nations and we are going to be saved and they are all going to be condemned. Is that the view that Saul held before he became Paul? Is Paul distinguishing between all persons who are to be loved and those impersonal forces that might still have control over non-Christians as they had over Saul before conversion? Does Paul think that all the souls of the world are going to be converted as was he on the Day of the Lord? Did the Thessalonians have a pre-taste of the Day of the Lord when they converted?

III.2.8 Which Gives Urgency to Our Ethical Task

The battle in Paul's thinking is not only cosmic and psychological but also ethical for he is "encouraging you and appealing to you to live a life worthy of God, who is calling you to share the glory of his Kingdom" (2:12). He writes: "We have been called by God to be holy, not to be immoral" (4:7). He says that God always punishes sins of that sort. So Paul and the Thessalonians have been freed from their old, narrow unloving attitude. But they can still sin and be punished. So once we come to the postmodern insight of unlimited complex voices in everything including scripture, reading scripture becomes a challenge like that of loving. As we grow in loving the challenges of complexity keep increasing but they can become if we have the right attitude greater opportunities for growing in love. Paul is being challenged and he is searching for understanding and greater faith as new questions come his way. If the whole human race is loveable how can they be excluded from God even if they sin? What is the role of morality in promoting the Kingdom of Love? On the one hand Paul has a great urgency about personal virtue. The Day of the Lord will come any day and we should be ready for it. But will we be punished to the extent of being excluded from the Kingdom if we are immoral? The answer seems to be no. We will be punished for any immorality but that may just be a natural law for everybody. The Lord did come to save sinners like Saul and Saul was a pretty bad sinner until after he was converted. So Paul urges his loved ones not to be immoral and get punished now because they are supposed to be happy and joyful. He does not want them to suffer the natural punishment that will be the consequence of any sin. However, it could be that no one will be excluded from the Kingdom that is to come. There is no time for all to be converted but we must love them.

III.2.9 As We Abide in the Grace, Peace, and Joy of Jesus

There is a peculiar paradox in Paul's thinking about morality and the coming of the Day of the Lord. On the one hand there is a great urgency about being just and avoiding punishment, but on the other hand Paul is complacent concerning social justice. He believes that in Christ Jesus there is no longer master or slave for we are all brothers and neighbors but he will urge the slave to go back and submit to his master even though he does admonish the master to treat the slave like a brother. The point is that it is not Paul's concern to bring about a social revolution. Christ Jesus will do that very soon when the Day of the Lord comes. In Christ Jesus there is no longer the whole set of customs governing the traditional rituals of male and female. But Paul is not interested in changing the social customs of his day, for the Lord will do that when he comes very soon. Paul is urgent about personal justice and virtue but he is complacent about social justice and virtue because the Lord will take care of that. Paul urges the Thessalonians to mind their own business and to let the Lord take care of his. They should have faith and patience in the face of any persecution and temptation. Paul does speak of the Jews as enemies. "They have been persecuting us, and acting in a way that cannot please God and makes them the enemy of the whole human race" (2:15). But in Christ there is neither Greek nor Jew. There is only the whole human race and they belong to it. So surely they too are loveable and they are not the real enemy any more than the Romans are. Paul tried to visit the Thessalonians, "but Satan prevented us" (2:18) and he has been afraid that "the temptation might have tried you too hard, and all our work might have been wasted" (3:5).
So the battle seems to be between Christ and the tempter. They are at war in the hearts, souls and bodies of all persons but all persons are loveable and should be constantly prayed for.

III.3 Paul's Love Letter to the Corinthians

III.3.1 No Gift of Worth but Love

Once Paul converted he began to see and wonder about many problems in his own way of life and once his communities began to form many problems arose in each of them.
In his first letter to the Corinthians he agonizes over problems that to his eyes of faith or conscience could seem insurmountable because there was alienation, bickering and infighting within each person, within many families, within the little community between different Christian communities, between the Jews and the Romans, between the forces of good and evil and between God and the forces of evil that still raged in spite of redemption. Paul and his people were experiencing war on all seven fronts. This letter to the Corinthians is another love letter in which Paul is constantly praying for his community with love.
In chapter one he gives a succinct summary of the logic of love as Jesus revealed the folly and weakness of God's love. Then he addresses many of the problems and gives his advice. In chapter thirteen he writes his famous ode to love and in chapter fifteen he relates love to the resurrection of the body. The main point about the solution to all the problems is that we have received the gift of love and it alone will let the other gifts of faith, hope, understanding, teaching prophecy, etc., be efficacious and really heal the root cause of all our problems which torment each and every person. Paul knew that the love that forgives is a gift because he had received it already from the loving, forgiving face of Stephen. If we truly love others because each one of them is a lovely and beautiful child of God then any problems we might suffer with them or because of them can be offered up for them and the very suffering of our problem can be an act of love for them. The gift of forgiving love if we are worthy of it by our loving gives worth not only to faith and hope but to all of our problems.

III.3.2 Which Gives Worth to Suffering

When Paul describes *agape* in First Corinthians chapter thirteen its first attribute that he lists is patience and that makes sense. A real problem is a passion that we suffer and with *agape* we can suffer it patiently, but without the joy of love we will be impatient and the pain, paranoia and anger of that impatience can give rise to a network of negative passions that parallel the positive passions such as unkindness, jealousy and rudeness. The first problem over which Paul agonizes is factionalism. Different factions within the Christian Corinthian community argue and unkindly proclaim: "I am for Paul," "I am for Apollos," "I am for Cephas," "I am for Christ" (1 Cor 1:12). So right from the start there were sects in conflict and rather than loving each other and giving a good example they were against *agape*. The political root of the problem was the occupation of Jerusalem by the Romans for orthodox Jews thought that if they would really be good and holy Jews then God would liberate Jerusalem. They saw the occupation as punishment for their sins and thus if the males would be circumcised and if they would follow all the laws and commandments then as in the past God would relent his jealous and punishing anger and save them. Some of the Christians such as Cephas could still be seen as good Jews because they saw Christianity as a fulfillment of the Law and the Prophets and still argued for circumcision. Paul was looked upon as a bad and renegade Jew by the orthodox Zealots and so there were these political factions. Of course, the political problems were rooted in religious factions for there were Pharisees, Sadducees, Essenes, and Zealots and they covered the theological-political spectrum from the arch conservative to the two in the middle to the liberal. Paul had assumed that in a community of *agape* these scandalous divisions would not exist so he learns to suffer in patience.

III.3.3 And to God's Foolishness and Ours.

The second attribute of love in Paul's list is kindness and
that too makes sense for both his Hebrew and Stoic background.
In the prophetic tradition Hosea, for example, showed a God
who was rich in mercy and instead of being jealous and angry
practiced forgiveness as Hosea did toward his wife Gomer.
In the Stoic tradition there is a network of positive
passions which Paul grounds in *agape* and a network of
negative emotions and if there is love and joy there will be kindness.
But God's new logic which is never jealous and wrathful
as it is revealed in the Incarnation and suffering of the Christ
is neither Greek nor Jew for the logic of the Cross is folly.
In no other religion is God thought of as foolish but for Paul
his loving kindness is so great that in comparison to other Gods
the Cross of Jesus reveals that God the Father is not wisdom itself.
Agape as Christ practiced and taught it does not look after its own.
It looks after the needs and suffering of others, of all others
including one's enemies and persecutors for even Paul was loved.
The logic of God's foolish love was right at the heart
of Paul's conversion experience as he saw Stephen, Christ
and God himself giving up well being in sacrifice for others.
All other theologies would set up a series of perfectly positive
attributes with which to think of God and they would exclude
negative attributes such as suffering, folly and weakness from God.
But the notion of God's suffering, weak and foolish love
that Paul experienced in his conversion becomes the key
to Paul's concept of how to live with our sufferings.
By Christ's and Stephen's and now Paul's example we
are given the gift of a love that makes all suffering
worth while including the suffering of factions and quarrels.
If we bear our cross in patience and kindness then we
will make up in our suffering what was lacking in Christ's.

III.3.4 And to God's Weakness and Ours

How foolish can you get to talk about making up in your
own suffering what is lacking in Christ's; for was not
his, as the Son of God, the perfect and all redeeming sacrifice?
But what Paul brings out as the new logic of the Cross
is the weakness of Christ and the weakness of God as the essence
of true patient and kind suffering that is never jealous.
Deep down in the logic of the Cross is the end of God as a
jealous God who would be angry if others shared his weakness
or if his weakness was lacking so that others had to make up for it.
Before the new event of the Cross God was always thought of
as omnipotent or all powerful with no weakness in Him.
So what does Paul mean when he believes in God's weakness?
The traditional creed says, "I believe in God, the Father
Almighty, the creator of heaven and earth." Mixed in with
God's almighty power is there now some weakness that
Paul knew of and is now becoming evident in our times?
Already in the words "creator of heaven and earth" is there
something that tells us about God's love that makes Him weak?
So God created each and everything that is out of the formless
void and out of the watery depths. These two images had
to do with a chaos out of which God made a cosmos.
Of course, those are Greek terms but still they can
somewhat gropingly but accurately get the meaning
of the Biblical notion of creation of things out of contingency.
God's created world is not simply a cosmos of necessity.
He did not create things out of nothing as if untouched
by contingency. He created them as untouched by necessity
and thus free to evolve and free to be free with choice.
When God out of love brings forth His creatures as free
he has become weak before the freedom he has given them.
God is weak and we are each weak before the other's freedom.

III.3.5 In a Logic of the Cross

So as Paul thinks about his Corinthians and their agonizing problems in this war that is being fought on all seven fronts at once he is well aware of all the problems of each individual person such as himself and he is aware of all the kinds of problems that come because we are complicated interpersonal relational persons. His faith helps him to be aware of these problems and the conditions that give rise to them. That is why at the beginning of his letter he already ponders with them the logic of the Cross which reveals God as weak and foolish out of love and shows us how to suffer too. In chapter thirteen in his ode to love he says that love does not take offense and that love is not resentful. Love as not taking offense has become the key to Kierkegaard's philosophy of love, while love as not being resentful has become the key to Nietzsche's philosophy. They both explicate and work out philosophies of freedom that have to do with ways of creative love that see in the contingent complexities of our mysterious suffering ways of letting all our suffering become meaningful for others and thus they solve the great problem of evil. The ordinary logic of everyday philosophers across the globe had to do with collecting parts into a whole by connecting the dots of apparent chaos into an ordered and cosmic whole. But Paul is beginning to see a new logic that can never connect the dots. Socrates already saw that the human mind can never connect the dots so he had a new logic of skepticism that ironically made ethics possible. But, Paul sees that even God in his weakness cannot connect the dots because his creatures are out of His control and to love them anyway is Paul's new logic of the Cross.

III.3.6 That Can Reconcile Factions

So in Paul's mind there are these seven major battles going on
at once and they will continue until Christ comes a second time
and as the victorious apocalyptic judge conquers the forces of evil.
Of course, in the meanwhile we should receive God's grace
and the great gift of love that will free us to suffer in service
for others that they might become members of the body of Christ
in love's joy, peace, patience, kindness in not taking offense
and in having no resentment that blocks healing in our hearts.
This solution of forgiving love will not really put an end
to the factions but for each Christian there can be the
reconciliation of the forgiving and suffering heart just
as there was for Jesus and for Stephen. Jesus was weak,
and God is weak and we are weak and being aware of
our weakness is already the beginning of a new power.
If we meet Jesus in all of his foolishness and weakness then
we will become aware of the new logic that forgives and
thus, though Paul was at odds with Cephas and Apollos
he truly believed that they were both members of the
suffering factionalized body of Christ and Paul truly
loved Peter and Apollos and the Judaizing Apostles
even though he was called to be an apostle to the Gentiles.
So his very calling factionalized him but there was a deeper
reconciliation that let them all know that they were
united in a love deeper than their factionalizing functions.
To reconcile is to be aware that all flesh will see
the salvation of the Lord. It is to constantly pray with
Jesus. "Father forgive them for they know not what they do."
The logic of love operates at a level of awareness
that is different from the logic of knowledge and in
that loving trust and hope that surpasses understanding
there is the peace of a reconciliation that Paul is teaching.

III.3.7 As Well as Marital Alienation

In his first letter to the Thessalonians Paul meditated
on the mystery of death and tried to bring the community
to an attitude of faith, hope and love about life after death.
Now in this letter to the Corinthians the root of the problem
is the mystery of sex for which it seems the circumcision
is the point of the debate and the cause of the faction scandal.
But the problem goes deeper than that for the Jewish culture
had at its core a deep cultivated bond between monotheism
and monogamy whereas the culture of Corinth had a deep
cultivated bond between polytheism and polygamy and polyandry.
The fourth commandment right after the three concerning God
ordered the Jews to honor their father and mother and that was
connected with centering on family life in Judaism.
So the question of circumcision was only the tip of an entire
cultural clash between Paul's understanding of religion
and that of the Corinthians for whom conversion to Christianity
was a leap of major cultural proportions and even though
Paul argued that Gentiles did not have to become Jewish
in becoming Christian they really did have to leave behind
sexual promiscuity and move from a culture of *eros*
to one of affection as they converted into the world of *agape*.
Paul was aware of a secret thorn in his own flesh that
seems to have had to do with sexuality and kept him humble.
But what he recommended to the Corinthians went beyond
even what the Jewish religion asked of her people for Paul
recommended celibacy and argued that his would free
the followers of Christ who wanted to evangelize others to
be totally committed to serving others with their own sacrifice.
Paul seemed to sense that his could appeal to Corinthians
who knew of Plato's move away from polytheism to
a monotheism and that Platonic love of celibate enthusiasm.

III.3.8 In the Lord's Supper

The new culture of *agape* into which Paul is channeling
the Jewish culture of familial affection and the Greek culture of *eros*
has at its centre the new covenant meal which sometimes
would begin with a sort of pot luck supper called the agapete
or love feast and Paul was disturbed over this because the
more wealthy would not share adequately with the poor.
And then there was the Lord's supper which should have been
the centering source for reconciliation of all differences.
There was the offering of the bread and the wine and then
there was the consecration in which the bread became the
real presence of the body of the Lord and the wine became
the real presence of the blood of the Lord. This real presence
in which the bread is believed to be the body of Christ and
the wine his blood was the mystery or the sacrament
in which believers took their stand and gave new meaning
to their life both as individual persons and as community.
The Lord's supper took them into *agape*'s new logic of opposites
for just as God became body so now the bread became
the body of Christ and so also the crucified body of Christ
would be resurrected into a new spiritual body which
Paul thought would return and transform our whole earth.
This sacrament of the Lord's supper is an event that renews
what has already been most deeply human, namely, the
shamanic presence of the invisible in the visible and
the then in the now and the sacred in the profane so that
for the believer who takes his or her stand in this mystery is
already in possession of the reconciliation of all differences.
At the consecration of the bread and wine there was also
the separation of Christ's body and blood so that his
death was reenacted and then there was communion
which was the real sacramental renewal of reconciliation.

III.3.9 Of Christ's Resurrected Body

Death is truly the ultimate destroyer and when life goes out
in our body the final alienation takes place when our body
disintegrates and we are consumed by little flesh eaters.
When Christ's spirit appeared to Paul in the love of Stephen
and when the spiritual body of Christ asked Paul why he was
persecuting him that for Paul was the ultimate reconciliation.
Jesus met the great mystery of death and gave a response
to it that became Paul's answer to all of our problems.
We might be at war on all seven fronts but we do not
need to be afraid for Jesus conquered death with his
resurrection from the dead and we too can be resurrected.
That is Paul's apocalyptic and militant way of understanding
his faith that he has in the resurrected Christ who
in death moved from an ensouled body to an enspirited body.
When we repeat his death and resurrection in the Lord's Supper
we bring the mystery of the Lord's reconciliation into
our individual lives and into the lives of the loving community.
There is a direct relation between our loving and forgiving
heart and the health of our bodies for when Paul writes
of the Lord's supper he explains how the right heart
when receiving communion makes us healthy and then
he writes: "In fact that is why many of you are weak
and ill and some of you have died. If only we recollected
ourselves, we should not be punished like that. But when
the Lord does punish us like that, it is to correct us and
stop us from being condemned with the world" (11:30–31). So Paul
as he came into the shamanic world of Jesus was aware
of the health and well being of his community and he
warned them that an unforgiving heart destroys the
immune system. So God's weakness in His suffering teaches
us to suffer with grace and that will bring reconciliation.

The Place of the Seven Shamanic Powers

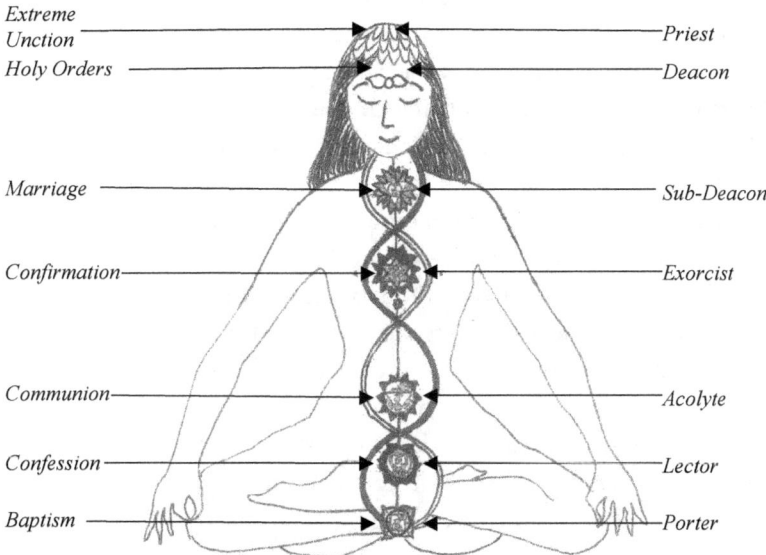

The Seven Chakras

IV. Personhood

IV.1 From Shamanic Humans in Relation

IV.1.1 Shamanic Humans

To think about the concept of personhood which is
the kind of subjectivity connected with the agapeic event
and its universality, it is helpful to compare and contrast
it with other theories and practices of the human subject.
Humans as the homo sapiens sapiens who have survived
have been forever shamanic in their fundamental attitude.
Shamanism has to do most of all with a sense of presence.
Shamans get in touch with the higher and lower worlds
of which ordinary members of the community are not aware.
Shamans heal and help through the awareness of this presence.
In hunter-gatherer societies the altered state of consciousness
called "vision trance" activates the awareness of this presence.
In agricultural societies the "ecstatic trance" of fertility cults
is the source of awareness of this presence of various spirits.
In a tribe, kingdom or empire there is a division of
shamanic labor and thus several different shamanic techniques.
The seven shamanic powers relate to the seven functions
of the body which in India are called the seven chakras:
(1) colon, (2) reproductive organs. (3) digestive organs, (4) heart,
(5) throat, (6) third eye, and (7) brain. These ground
the seven shamanic roles of (1) healer, (2) erotic artist,
(3) exorcist, (4) sorcerer, (5) medium, (6) diviner, and (7) shaman.
Shamanic society is highly traditional and thus disciples
learn their techniques of awareness and presence from masters.
Elemental forces, animistic spirits either good or evil,
gods, goddesses and demonic powers are discovered
in trance and ecstasy and remembered in the creeds
of oral then written traditions. Codes of customs, laws,
rules and regulations which shamans have formulated
are memorized and abided by. Mythologized cults,
creeds and codes are collected and preserved in sacred canons.

IV.1.2 Pelvis Healers and Porter Physicians

The health of a people is always of primary importance
and thus tribes had their herbalists and medicine men.
Colon cancer is often an early killer and preventative medicine
for that first chakra relies upon a healthy immune system
rooted in a positive attitude and nourished by healthy foods
and a habit of right exercise, right sociality and right sleep.
Young girls are especially adept at learning to diagnose ills.
Those who begin on the pathway toward shamanhood have
often had the traumatic experience of losing a parent when young.
In coping with absence they develop sensitivity for presence.
Many existential artists and philosophers such as Nietzsche,
Tolstoy, Sartre and Marcel lost a parent when they were young.
Marcel says that his mother, who died when he was two, was
always more present to him than his aunt who cared for him.
Rasputin lived alone with his father and spent much time with
horses in the barn communicating with and learning from them.
One night his father and several men were talking about a robbery
while little Rasputin was lying in his bed and listening.
The next morning he told his father which one was the thief.
He could detect him in the tone of his voice and thus it was
no wonder that he went on to become a savant in high places.
Hunter-gatherers who live in proximity with animals learn
from them, for each herd has an alpha female and lead male.
A shaman is like the alpha mare and a horse whisperer today
is a sort of shaman who learns from horses their kind
of awareness and how to guide them gently into cooperation.
In the Catholic Church, which was criticized by reformers
for retaining pagan cults, the first of the seven holy orders is
that of the porter who welcomes participants into the sacred place.
With his or her joyful, smiling welcome the healing gets started
as they leave the profane outside to enter the sacred presence.

IV.1.3 Erotic Artists and Lector Teachers

The second chakra of the reproductive organs is significant
because shamanic discipline aims at channeling sexual energy.
Sublimating that energy produces the building up of culture.
The nature, place and role of the female within shamanic societies
provides key clues to the history of our own human unfolding.
In hunter gatherer societies the males were hunter-warriors
and the females were gatherer-nurturers concerned with health.
As hunter-gatherers became herders and then farmers
humans slowly moved from mere survival habits to
subsistence farming and then to societies of leisure and culture.
In the agricultural lands of the great river valleys of
the Yellow River, the Ganges, the Nile and the Tigris-Euphrates
the movement of tantrism developed within shamanic culture.
There was the left-handed cultivation of sexual energy
and the right-handed cultivation into erotic awe and reverence.
The leisure made possible by agricultural economies that
banked and stored wealth gave rise to the priestly caste who
sublimated sexual energy in the Taoist harmony in China
of the Yin and the Yang and of Shiva and Shakti in India.
The primary voice in Southern India's Tamil Literature
was that of the loving female who could guide the male
to develop his feminine anima through shamanic discipline.
The gross sexual orgies which sought to stimulate
the sexual energy of the divinities activated military force
for the maintenance and expansion of the great empires.
Buddhist tantrism produced a monasticism in which
the art of reverence came forth from the celibate practice.
Plato, the Jews and the protestants to protect their culture
from erotic excess developed monotheistic patriarchies
that could promote capitalistic and imperial expansion.
In Catholicism the second Holy Order of the Lector
sublimates sexual energy into the awesome power of the Word.

IV.1.4 Liver Cleansers and Exorcist Deliverers

The third chakra of the stomach calls forth the discipline of the
exorcists who cast out the whole network of demonic powers.
As the shamanic movement evolved from "vision trance" to
"ecstatic trance" the dangers and addictions of possessiveness
became a major problem for possessions can possess us.
Humans were not recognized as persons within shamanism,
but as role playing functionaries within the system.
Thus farm workers could become party animals or
be used as part of the war machine by possessed tyrants.
As shamans were cultivated they controlled the anal sphincter
first with potty training and then the herbalist's right diet.
Then there was need for control of the sex urge or all energy
could be dissipated by the ever growing monster of lust.
Finally, there was cultivation of the stomach and the urge
for food supply which could become the deadly sin of gluttony.
Obedience, chastity and poverty became antidotes to
the territorial imperative of self-will at territorial boundaries,
of lust at its display point and greed at its center.
There were malevolent and benevolent spirits that
personified the passion of the vegetative soul and
exorcism was cultivated as a key shamanic power so that
evil spirits could be driven out making room for good ones.
Exorcism became a major spiritual exercise in mysticism.
Bernard of Clairvaux gave his sermons on the *Song of Songs*
and climbing the ladder of love through the four kisses.
The kiss of the feet could exorcise the nine evil demons.
The kiss of the hands could welcome the nine choirs of angels.
The kiss of the mouth could enable Mary within us to say
"yes" to the holy Spirit and let the baby Jesus be born within us.
The kiss of the breasts could release the flow of milk that
could nourish God's children which shamanic milk and honey.
Cleansing the liver can deliver us from belly aching negativities.

IV.1.5 From Sorcerer Heart to Acolyte Heart

Animals are territorial. At the centre of their territory they follow
the nesting instinct to protect themselves with familial affections.
At the display point they go through their erotic mating rituals.
The boarder around the periphery is protected by bonded friends.
It is here that brave heart warriors play out their roles.
Be it among hunters, herders or farmers, strong hearted
braves develop the fourth chakra of the brave courageous heart.
They must cultivate brave courage because there is always war.
Enemies are always threatening each of us as is bad luck.
The special helper of the heroic warrior brave is the sorcerer.
In his sorcerer war paint he improves his odds against enemies.
In his sorcerer camouflage with his sorcerer cave paintings
he is a crafty warrior-hunter always seeking to improve his odds.
The sorcerer and the witch hex and curse the enemy that
he might be the loser and the brave heart might be the winner.
There are the shamanic arts of bringing down the evil spirits
of bad luck upon the competition and good spirits on the self.
The tribes of Israel hexed Jericho by blowing their trumpets
as they rode around the city three times discouraging the enemy.
Acolytes balance exorcists who cast out evil spirits by
bearing the heroic light that drives out all the darkness.
It is at this point that the agapeic revolution transforms
the shamanic network of functions for when we love our enemy
because our neighbor is now everyone there is no longer room
in the kingdom of light for sorcerers, witches and their hexing.
Shamanic healers, celibates and pure spirits are fine,
but once we get to the realm of defending the territory
all bewitching of the enemy is counterproductive for those
who live by the sword will die by the sword and if it is
to pierce our enemy it must go through our own body first.
Exorcising the negative demons invites in the affirmative angels.

IV.1.6 From Prophetic Mediums to Sub-Deacons

The fifth chakra is located in the throat, the place of
the glottal sphincter and the voice box, and the shamanic
meditation and practice aim at dissolving the lump
in the throat, getting the digestive process started right
and letting the voice be one of liberating shamanic song.
In the shamanic world it used to be the medium who was expert
with the voice and in the *Phaedrus* when Plato discusses four
kinds of divine madness he connects the medium with the prophetic.
He says that prophetic mediums give military and political advice.
The early prophets of the Hebrew Bible were ecstatic prophets
and prophetic holy places were so potent it was said that
whenever Saul approached Samuel's prophesying hut at Ramah
he would begin to break out in a mad ecstatic prophecy.
Prophets would often live at certain key spots along the borders
gaining an awareness of enemy ways and in a trance they
could be spoken through with an efficacy that was marvelous.
Pagan peoples of the great agricultural lands would often keep
many prophets as did Queen Jezebel and when she married Ahab
she brought with her nearly 2000 prophets, a thousand of whom
were ecstatic prophets of sacred song and sacred dance.
Elijah, the Jewish prophet, entered into a prophesizing contest
with them and did them in just as the agapeic revolution
would later do in mediums and all of their militarism.
As the agapeic revolution unfolded mediums became deacons'
helpers or sub-deacons who helped the deacons to serve
the needs of the poor and helpless of the community.
The agapeic institutions of the Christian assembly or church
had a threefold responsibility of bringing people together and
telling them the stories of the good news and feeding them the
sacrament of the real presence and finally finding all the needy
and letting them be served and cared for by deacons and helpers.

IV.1.7 Sixth Sense Diviner Leaders

The diviner is a genius of the sixth chakra located in the
mystical third eye of the forehead above and between the eyes.
The essence of shamanism is the divinization made possible
by the heightened extrasensory awareness of paranormal presence.
Diviners have encounters with totems, spirits, ancestors
and the inner essence of natural persons, places and things.
This special awareness makes them adept at locating
fish and game, knowing the movements of the enemy, finding
curative herbs, getting rid of evil spirits, welcoming good
spirits and caring for the community in countless ways.
They become leaders through their activities of accessing
secrets, directing spiritual activities, employing special
powers and influencing and guiding others as their exemplars.
With the special focus of the ecstatic, be it in vision trance
or possession ecstasy, the diviner loses visual focus
in attending to felt perceptions and with this sixth sense
he or she attains an uncommon grasp of details in the big picture.
He or she is the sage who intuits common structures
within diversity and thus better appreciates concrete singularities.
In the dreams and visions of his of her trances the diviner
receives the special symbols out of which rituals are formed.
Out of these rituals arise mythological stories and traditions.
Out of possession trances arise the dance rhythms that are
the basis for art, for highland, lowland and island rhythms
break forth from the muses of music and then wordless song.
Then lyrics, rhapsodies and epic songs arise and out of them
proceed the plastic arts of painting, sculpture and architecture.
Thus shamanic divinization has been the source of culture.
Beyond the self-control of the vegetative soul and the courage
of the animal soul there is the special genius of the human soul.
The sixth of the Holy Orders ordains the deacon for such leadership.

IV.1.8 The Head Shaman as Integrator

The seventh chakra of the brain receives all information from the sensory nervous system and sends directions to all parts of the body through the motor nervous system and thus the shaman as the trance expert integrates the six lower powers. As Krippner puts it the shamanic powers were mastered by: "humanities' original specialists; healers, storytellers, weather forecasters, performing artists, ritualists, and magicians. A chief or chieftainess directed the tribe's political, civic and military life, but occasionally these two roles converged in a single remarkable individual."[4] In hunter-gatherer societies the several charismatic powers were employed equally by men and women for these societies were egalitarian, not hierarchical. These seven powers are common in shamanic peoples all across the face of the earth and thus ground a unifying universalism. The shamanic is integrative within an individual, within a tribe and between all peoples. Shamanic integration provides a multidimensional awareness of more than the present-at-hand. For shamans there was the "upper world" and the "lower world" besides this world we see and thus monasticism in Tibet while negotiating with the left handed power of the lower developed strong and vibrant right handed powers of the higher. With each stage of human history shamanism has been altered. Our point has been to clarify the network of shamanic powers and to hint that it has endured in Roman Catholic Holy Orders. In our modern world Spinoza demythologized the spirit world. Instead of warring upper world angels and lower demon worlds he understood liberation as being freed from reactive negative passions and freed for proactive affirmative passions.

To see how this logic of the passions was used by postmodernists but set in the world of *agape* and personhood is now our task. Anti-Shamanic individualism was the very basis for modernity.

IV.1. 9 From Shamanic Bishops and Abbots to Modernity

The multidimensional awareness, the sense of presence, and
the variety of charismatic powers that the shamans cultivated
have always been of utmost importance for the human family.
Now we are prepared to explore the history of personhood in terms
of the transformation of the shamanic bonds of affection,
friendship and *eros* into the new bonding of shamanic *agape*.
We must now explore how the Greeks moved to a psychology
of the human as besouled through their productive abstract thinking.
We must explore how the Hebrews in reaction to the fertility cult
possession culture of their powerful neighbors developed
their belief in and practice of spirit for the history of both
Hellenic psyche and Hebrew spirit will prepare us to see how
the belief in personhood came forth with the *agape* of Jesus.
How much of a shaman was he? Was Stephen a shamanic person
captivated by the charismatic powers of the tantric Jesus?
Was Paul taken into a trance-like state of real presence by
the spirit of the resurrected Christ who was present in Stephen?
Is John's Jesus a tantric shaman whose first apostles were women?
Do the women in Luke find in Jesus even more of a right-
handed tantric, shamanic power than is revealed in John?
In terms of the shamanic what is the significance of the
orthodox interpretation that Augustine gives to *caritas*
and do Francis and other new-millennial mystics get in touch
with a heterodox return of renewed charismatic shamanism?
Do the Lutheran and Calvinist modernists by dropping
monastic shamanism and getting rid of pagan cults
lay the ground in the West for the tycoons and captains of industry?
What is the great value of Protestantism and the rise of capitalism?
What are its dangers that call for a postmodern shamanic renewal?
Can our shamanic beginnings help us better understand
Stephen, Paul, mother, and Kierkegaard's postmodern beginnings?

IV.2 To Classical Soul and Spirit

IV.2.1 From Shamans to Pre-Socratics

In their quest to know the truth about the becoming of all things
Pre-Socratic philosophers move from mythical stories to logical theories
as they sought to connect all the dots or explain how the many arise
form one source, or from two, or a few, or many or an infinite.
Thales began Greek philosophy in the Eastern provinces of Ionia
by theorizing that all things arise from one material source of water.
Parmenides moved from Ionia to the Western provinces of Italy
and argued that all things arise from the immaterial source of the One.
Anaximander, a student of Thales, argued that limited things cannot
come forth from the limited but must come from the unlimited.
His student, Anaximenes, thought that positing an unlimited infinite
was unjustified and argued that all things could come out of the material
cause of air through the efficient cause of condensation and rarefaction.
Heraclitus also argued that the two causes of war and peace could
account for the beginning and ending of all things in accord with
the logos which is the logic of meaning and the meaning of logic.
Empedocles, an other Italian, made a synthesis of a few basic
principles and came up with the first philosophy of love by arguing
that water, air, fire and earth account for the beginning and ending
of things as love and strife move them circularly between
cosmic orderly states and chaotic disorderly collapsing.
Democritus and Leucippus did not want to suppose mythical
forces such as love and strife so as consistent materialists
they posited several kinds of atoms falling through the void and thus
accounted for physics or natural becoming of all the manifold things.
When Anaxagoras brought philosophy to Athens and taught Socrates
he argued that all things came forth out of seeds in an evolutionary
process that brings forth a series of different species.
The Greek word for becoming, *physis* is translated into
Latin as *natura* or the birthing of things and in knowing
the law of nature these wise men guided and healed like shamans.

IV.2.2 From Pre-Socratics to Sophists

The Sophists sought to get truth by getting rid of mythologizing and shamanizing by claiming that man is the measure of all things. By stressing culture instead of nature they argued that our behavior is guided not by any law of nature or logos but rather by the heredity and environment of various peoples and their geography. The political decisions of peoples arise from their own special needs. If we were to imagine a Christian who believed in reconciliation according to Kierkegaard we could think of the younger brother as approaching Shamans, Pre-Socratics and Sophists and in learning much from each of them he could treat each as more important than himself by loving them in the praise of love. From the Pre-Socratics he would learn that there are five theories about the beginning and the ending of the many things of becoming. This notion of the five different voices in a discussion on anything could be very helpful to him for if he learned from the Sophists about his own Jewish culture he would see that there would be five different factions making Judaism vibrant by arguing against each other and in need of reconciliation, namely, the Sadducees, the Pharisees, the Essenes, the Zealots, and the secular Cynics. When Jesus loved the five different kinds of Jews and prayed for their forgiveness because they knew not what they were doing when they persecuted him and put him to death he was only being a very good cynic against any isolated, fixated voice, and as zealous as a Zealot about the coming of love's kingdom, and a firm believer in the monastic wisdom of the Essenes, and one who completely believed in the Resurrection, and one who trusted the traditional Law and Prophets with the Sadducees. Without the ideal of loving reconciliation it is only natural for the Pre-Socratics to go to war with the Shamans and the Sophists to go to war with both in the spirit of the Greek contest which would put dramatists, athletes and philosophers all against each other.

IV.2.3 From Sophists to Socrates

Greek Philosophers moved from polytheism to pantheism
to gain a better moral and religious understanding of our world.
Socrates played the key pivotal role in Greek philosophy with
his paradigm shift from theorizing to caring for the soul by
questioning all theories and pathways with a positive skepticism.
With his emphasis upon holy, honest, humble, humorous health
he may have looked like a Sophist and have been put on trial
for atheism and for leading the youth astray as a mere relativist.
But he stood between the early Greek polytheists and the pantheism
to which his questioning pushed the post Socratic philosophers.
The familiar divine sign of Socrates steered him clear of
either outright polytheism or outright pantheism and while
he was put to death as an atheist he could be reconciled with
Sophists, Platonists, Aristotelians, Stoics, Skeptics, and Cynics.
Only Epicurean materialists were irreconcilable with Socrates
and yet their ruthless questioning of others was truly Socratic.
Besides his familiar divine sign who warned him what not
to do there was the oracle at Delphi who through his friend
told him he was the wisest man in Athens and thus
set him questioning to find that he alone really knew nothing.
It has been said that Socrates and Sophists are but two
different sides of the same leaf and they are the same in their
questioning of nature; but they are different in that Socrates
even more is always questioning one's own religious culture.
By focusing upon and caring for the soul Socrates brought
Greek philosophers to their fundamental conception of the human.
The Greek word *prosopon* became translated into Latin as *persona*.
It means *face* and the *prosopon* was the mask that actors
wore in the Greek dramas and thus in Latin the *persona*
was that through which there sounded the character's voice.
Thus the term *persona* did not yet have its new Christian meaning.

IV.2.4 From Socrates to Plato

Plato developed a complete psychology to ground our ethical and religious aspirations and the self for him was not personal. The Ladder of Love in the *Symposium* explains the nature of the soul as with it we arise out of the Cave in the story of his *Republic*. The soul or the life force has powers of knowing and of loving. We have fallen into the bottom of the cave as he says in the *Phaedrus* because of a double burden of forgetfulness and wrong doing and thus as all knowing Gnostics argue evil was there in the beginning. In our everyday knowledge at the bottom of the cave we believe that the shadows we see on the walls are the real things of our life. But then by reading great literature as in Homer and the Dramatists we can rise up to another level of opinion and see images in a pool of water that let us realize that our former knowledge deceived. Then with science such as physics and mathematics we can get a true knowledge that is not only opinion and it reveals the things themselves that cast their shadows and their images. Finally with philosophy we can get true wisdom in a dialectical process that leads us to a knowledge of the sun which is the light that lets the things be shadowed and imaged down below. Thus through higher and higher gnosis we get back to where we started as part of the world-soul contemplating the one Good. While Plato is ultimately a Gnostic who thinks that knowledge saves us by letting us get beyond our individuality which is only a false impression for really we are part of the world soul, he does emphasize erotic love which at the bottom of the cave lets us love one beautiful body and then several in that that shadowy world where we believe in bodies as really beautiful. But then we can fall in love with a beautiful soul as the life force. But then we can fall in love with the intellectual part of the soul and then come to love science and then laws and institutions and finally we can love Absolute Beauty itself which is the Good.

IV.2.5 From Plato to Aristotle

For twenty years Aristotle thought deeply about his teacher's philosophy and most of all he felt the need to reform Plato's theory of the soul which did not adequately account for individuals. All souls were immaterial forms and thus in the end would only be parts of the same world-soul just as they were before falling. Aristotle developed his hylemorphic theory to account for individuality such as we find in this horse and not in that one. For Plato humans are spiritual forms that know and are in a body only accidentally, but for Aristotle each living being is individuated by its *hyle* or material, essential principle. Aristotle used the principle of "action follows being" in order to study the soul and thus he was a biologist and psychologist. If you examine the activities of a human you will see that we have vegetative, animal and human souls since our powers of nutrition, growth and reproduction indicate a vegetative soul while powers of sensation both external and internal and powers of local motion indicate an animal soul. We have a human soul because we can think abstractly and arrive at universal, immaterial ideas and make judgments about them and use them in reasoning process which brute animals cannot do, so we are rational, vegetative animals. We are individuated by our vegetative animal bodies, but when Aristotle proves the existence of the immortal soul he does it in terms of the formal, immaterial, spiritual and universal soul. Material things are extended and made up of parts and thus can break into parts and be destroyed , but an immaterial thing cannot break into parts and thus it is immortally indestructible. Aristotle did have a theory about love as *philia* or friendship but the chief aspect of the soul is its universal knowledge for that alone lets it be immortal and thus as a Gnostic Aristotle is ultimately like Plato with no individual soul.

IV.2.6 Stoic Recta Ratio

The noble Stoics stressed above all a universal love for all the living and to do that philosophically they built up their own tradition and held that philosophy is like an egg the yoke of which is physics, the white ethics and the shell logic. For them the common element of all things is the Divine Fire or Pneuma which is the material life breath of things that is governed by the logos or a logic of harmonic process. It is the task of the Stoic to live in accord with nature and thus they have a natural law ethics which has a definite criterion for each decision and that is: "Human nature adequately viewed in all its essential relations." We should consider the consequences of our actions for ourselves, those around us and all others including God. So the yoke at the centre is physical nature out of which living beings come forth as thoughts, words and deeds come out of attitudes, moods and feelings or the oak out of the acorn. The shell is the logos that collects all the parts in a whole and protects the yoke with definite fated laws. The white or the ethics nourishes the living beings proceeding from the yoke and helps it bring forth healthy life. Because they think and act by taking into account their destiny within the totality of reality their basic prayer came to be not only the prayer of St. Francis but the Guiding Wisdom from St. Paul to Spinoza to Nietzsche. "God grant me the SERENITY to accept the things I cannot change, the COURAGE to change the things I can, and the WISDOM to know the difference." As the Greco-Roman tradition of the five philosophical schools developed the Stoics by seeing logos as right reason stressed a universal brotherhood of all humans and thus differed from Platonists with *eros* and Aristotelians with friendship.

IV.2.7 Matter Matters in Epicurean Friendship

Epicureans aimed at a simple, scientific view of life that would make all happy without superstition or idolatry. They used the philosophical method of gardening (1) to acquire the sure and secure in a world of uncertainty, (2) to build a firm foundation that makes no concession either to skepticism or idealism, (3) to start with the incontestability of immediate experience for sense data are true, (4) to see that feelings of pleasure and pain that accompany sense experience are the ultimate good and evil, (5) to choose the physical theory of atoms falling through the void to avoid fear of afterlife and give peace to the soul. In their anthropology they argue (1) when we exist death is not yet present; when death is present we do not exist. (2) The human soul is, like the gods, composed of finer kinds of atoms. (3) The soul has a rational and an irrational part. (4) Desires can be controlled. (5) We are not necessitated but because of chance can be free. In their ethics they argue that (1) it is in pleasure alone that happiness consists. (2) There are short term pleasures that imply pain and there are long term pleasures that imply no pain. (3) So true pleasure is not momentary but enduring. (4) Pleasure consists in absence of pain rather than in positive satisfaction. (5) Pleasure consists of serenity of soul and health of body. In their theology they argue: (1) God is an indestructible and blessed animal. (2) Complacent in his own happiness he is not concerned with human affairs. (3) He either wants to eliminate bad things and cannot, or can but does not want to, or neither wishes to nor can, or both wants to and can. (4) But given the fact of evil, if he cares he is then weak or spiteful or both. (5) So he must be without concern for us and will not judge us. Epicurus was known as a most friendly man and as a materialist his friendship was not elitist nor exclusivistic like Aristotle's.

IV.2.8 Non-Judgmental and Serene Skeptics

Pyrrho went to the East with Alexander the Great and discovered the Buddhists who were tranquil in their skeptical attitude. After Alexander the breakup of the Hellenic empire brought anxiety and Pyrrho combined the nonjudgmental tranquility of Buddhists with the skepticism of the Socratic examined life and started a school of thinking that eventually flowed into the nominalism of the Franciscans and the postmodern complexity theories of today. The Stoics and the Epicureans also quested for the tranquility of the Skeptics but they continued to develop their physics and logic and were thus seen as dogmatists together with Platonists and Aristotelians. Sextus Empiricus, who made a summa of skepticism, held that because the skeptic loves humanity he wishes to cure dogmatists of their opinions and rashness with reasoning so far as possible. So, just as doctors have remedies of different strengths for bodily ailments, and for those suffering excessively employ the strong ones and for those suffering mildly the mild ones, so the skeptic puts forth different arguments. The most general skeptical argument against the dogmatists is the argument of equipollence that to every argument an equal argument can be opposed which is rooted in opposites. This is expanded upon by Agrippa with his five modes: (1) constant disagreement shows that every question advanced by philosophers or by everyday life is a matter full of confusion. (2) The argument from the infinite regress shows that there is no ultimate cause that is a simple explanation of things. (3) The argument based on relativity shows that things are received relatively by our senses, our minds and our customs. (4) Assuming an hypothesis is not fundamental for the opposite can be assumed. (5) Upon close examination the circular argument shows that the premise of an argument is also a conclusion. So there is good reason with Socrates and the Buddhists to be serene skeptics.

IV.2.9 The Neo-Platonic Synthesis

As the Neo-Platonists gave an account of our human destiny
they did reconcile all five Hellenic Philosophies in a synthesis.
We do live in an Epicurean universe as many, changing
material humans, but if we practice Epicurean discipline it
will become a catharsis or purification which will focus us
on the pleasure of the soul and the inner life which will abide
and withstand all the many and changing difficulties which pain us.
Thus, the purification of the mystic way will take our attention
inward and upward and we will discover the realm of apathy
and the Stoic soul which is the Spirit of the whole universe.
But, as we go deeper into contemplation we will receive
the illumination which reveals to us the inner most essence
of soul which as Aristotle would say is the Agent Intellect.
This highest power of the soul which lets us be human is
the Nous or intellect which is a self-knowing knower or
which is the Divine to which Aristotle's argument for the
existence of God leads us as the self moving mover of all.
But, notice, at each stage along the way it is a skepticism
about the present stage that leads us higher in the process
of reconciliation through skeptical purification and illumination.
Finally, we see the limits of duality and know that that
cannot be ultimate perfection so that too is negated
as we go to the mystical experience of unification and
abide in the One which is the ultimate principle of Platonism.
Thus the mystical and rational process reveals through the skepticism
of negative theology that we can go up from bodies, to soul, to intellect
to the One and the way down is being thought of as parallel to
the way up so that through the emanation which is like
heat and light coming from the sun intellect emanates
out of the One and the soul out of intellect and then the
changing many out of the soul so that there is no real freedom.

IV.3 To the Chosen People's Nine Revelations against Gnosticism

IV.3.1 The Law and Creation Stories against Gnostic Origins

When the Priests put together the Torah or the Pentateuch or the first five books of the Bible, they put their own creation story right up front against the Gnosis of all the rest of humankind. Other stories of origination portrayed evil as there in the beginning. The Babylonian story (and Father Abraham was from that region) saw Marduk fighting a great dragon, Tiamat, and things came from the hacked up parts of her body, so that, as with Heraclitus, war was there in the beginning with peace in a primal struggle. Plato's story, like that of the Hindus, also sees an original forgetfulness and wrongdoing as there as the archeological source. We fall away from the world soul or Brahman because of some knowledge which is false or only appearance or *maya*. The Hebrew creation story sees the almighty Father God as bringing forth from the *tohu wabohu*, or formless void, on six progressive days, things which are emphasized as good. On the Shabat or seventh day the Good God rested and enjoyed all the good things which his sweet work had brought forth. In chapters two and three, immediately after the priestly story, the Priests edit in the Yahwists' story of the creation of Adam and then of Eve and their dwelling in the good Garden of Eden. Then we see how evil first came on the scene from humans and not from God, so that, with God's help, it can be rectified. In order to put Gnostic knowledge in its place, it is emphasized that the knowledge of good and evil comes only after the Fall, as Kierkegaard so brilliantly brings out against Augustine and Milton. The Gnostics, with their original evil, set up a context of cosmos and chaos in which the evil chaos cannot be overcome. The individual is ultimately tainted with matter, which is evil, and when God is blamed for evil, humans cannot overcome it. But when man is blamed, then, with God's help, it can be overcome and that is the special revelation of the Hebrew Bible.

IV.3.2 Mosaic Redemption Stories against Gnostic Determinism

According to the Gnostics, the Father was the Redeemer-God and Yahweh was the Creator-God, an inferior deity who allowed himself to get mixed up with matter, which was essentially evil. But for the Hebrew people, the point is not to distinguish them. When Moses was in the Arabian desert and saw the Burning Bush, he was told that God's name is Yahweh—I am who I am. This Yahweh delivered the people of Israel out of Egypt and was their Redeemer-God who saved them from slavery and eventually delivered them back into their promised land of milk and honey. At Mt. Sinai the Redeemer-God made a covenant with his people. He would be their God if they would keep his commandments. Gnostics can never be freed from determinism, for if evil is the wicked mother of all material things, then there is no possibility as long as they are material, of their being freed. Even the very Revelation of the Torah is a chorus of many voices and is worked out in a conflict of interpretations that permits there to be a constant freedom of new unpredictable possibilities. When the priests at the time of Ezra and Nehemiah put the Pentateuch together at around 450 BC, they edited together the four written traditions, without concern for conflicting views. At about 930 B.C., the Yahwist wrote her story from the viewpoint of the Davidic Promise Theology and then, in opposition, the Elohist in the Northern Kingdom at Samaria in about 850 BC, wrote his epic narrative in terms of the Mosaic Covenant Theology. In about 620 BC, as the Babylonians were threatening Jerusalem and one hundred years after the Northern Kingdom had been destroyed by the Assyrians, the Deuteronomist wrote his version of historical events, trying to bring back Mosaic Covenant Theology into the temple worship in Jerusalem and avert God's curse. Thus, against Gnostic determinism, the matter and form of Hebrew History have to do with a God-given freedom from slavery.

IV.3.3 Davidic Promise Stories against Gnostic Fatalism

If the very matter out of which we come to be is evil, then there can be no freedom from a deterministic past, nor freedom for a future filled with promises of unpredictably new and wonderful gifts. Gnosticism is not only a determinism from out of the past, but it is also a fatalism for the future, since evil must be there from beginning to end, and even through all eternity, for matter persists. In 2 Samuel 7, the Good-Shepherd God promises his beloved David that the Kingdom of *hesed* or of everlasting, merciful love will never be taken from the house of David, and that, although he will sin, he will only be punished with the rods of men, but not everlastingly. For Gnostics, life will always be a war of all against all, with no hope for a theodicy that can justify the ways of God to humankind. But this Davidic Promise is a theodicy of the best possible world. For the evil which man causes and the suffering that comes from it will be overcome by the loving God who created all things good. As J wrote her epic at the same time that the court Historian wrote his stories of David's triumphs and of his failures, there was a great realism in both of them that let humans take responsibility for their own evil without blaming God or others. Because the Lord is our Shepherd, we shall not want, for in spite of our sin and suffering, His kindness will pursue us.
The main point about the promise that takes it beyond Gnosticism is the new notion of *hesed* or everlasting, merciful love.
We are not only knowing beings for whom only knowing counts, but we are also, and most of all, loving beings with its promise. God is a good and loving Father and Redeemer who, out of love, made us good and forgives us when we sin and frees us when we get caught in slavery and thus we should love God and each other. J's story of Abraham shows him as receiving the promise of land, nation and name and all the stories about him concern threats to those promises and how he prevails through faith in God.

IV.3.4 The Prophets and Elijah against Gnostic Orgies

When the great agricultural empires emerged from out of primitive
hunter-gatherer shamanism, the shamanic trance was replaced
by the ecstatic orgy of the three great festivals after the harvest
of the winter wheat, the early summer planting and the fall harvest.
Gnosticism, which began to flourish with the great river civilizations,
always took pleasure in wine, women and song and found ways
of approaching union with divinities in sacred song and sacred dance.
Samuel, at his prophesying huts, up in the hill country of Ramah,
was first known as a seer and became known as a prophet
or one who is a spokesman for another, as was the prophet Moses.
When King Saul tried to capture David up at Ramah, he sent
his agents, but when they saw the company of prophets prophesying,
the spirit of God came upon them and they, too, fell into an ecstasy.
When Saul went up, he too stripped off his clothes and fell into
an ecstasy, and, falling down, lay there naked all day and all night.
So the Hebrews took their three great festival celebrations from
their neighbors and transformed them and also they took prophecy
and slowly transformed it in terms of the Mosaic Law and Davidic Love.
After the Northern Kingdom split away from Jerusalem and
when King Ahab married the foreign Queen Jezebel, she brought
with her to Samaria a very large number of her pagan prophets.
The prophet Elijah, that troubler of Israel, challenged four
hundred and fifty of them to a prophesying contest on Mt. Carmel.
They called upon their God Baal in their prophetic dancing and
ecstasy, but he brought no fire to the wood they assembled.
Then Elijah called upon Yahweh who lit the fire and the four
hundred and fifty were put to death and Elijah, without any
ecstatic transport, took the Hebrews beyond Gnostic titillation.
So the sacred song and sacred dance of left handed Tantrism
was transformed by the Gnostics into a sublimated spirituality
and then, by the Hebrews into their new prophecy of moral order.

IV.3.5 *The Minor Prophets against Gnostic Immorality*

The twelve minor prophets were called by the Lord God to speak for social justice, loving *hesed* and a humble walk with their God that his beloved people might grow in just holy love. The Chosen people went through nine periods of history with nine different empires: the Chaldeans, the Egyptians, the Canaanites, the Philistines, the Assyrians, the Babylonians, the Persians, the Greeks and the Romans and they had to be constantly warned by God and his prophets not to be like their Gnostic neighbors in their exploitation of their own people for the sake of power, wealth, pleasure and their false gods. Samuel spoke for the tribal confederacy, because, under a king, the people would have to pay heavy taxes, and men would be conscripted into the king's army, but the people would not listen. The people of Israel wanted to be like the other nations and thus Amos was called to speak to them, especially against injustice, because they sold virtuous men for silver and the poor man for a pair of sandals and they trampled on the heads of ordinary people and pushed the poor out of their path and father and son both resorted to the same girl and the weak were downtrodden. Hosea was called to speak against Ephraim and Judah, for their love was like a morning cloud, like the dew that quickly disappears. That is why God tore them to pieces by his prophets, and why he slaughtered them with the words of his mouth, for he wanted love, not sacrifice, and knowledge of God, not holocausts. Many nations would come and go and Israel would be destroyed and the tribes scattered and lost, but God would forgive his people, and if they would lie low and walk humbly with him, they would be saved, for as Zephaniah said: "In your midst I will leave a humble and lowly people" (Zeph 3:12). And in justice, love and humility, and not in the Gnostic way of sex and violence. God, through his prophets, would bring his people to love and the law.

IV.3.6 The Major Prophets against Gnostic Disaster

Toynbee wrote that there have been twenty-six great civilizations
in the past and nineteen of them collapsed through internal corruption.
During their two-thousand-year history before Christ, the Hebrews
saw many peoples come and go, and their four major prophets
were God's spokesmen to them about how not to succumb to disaster.
Isaiah saw the Northern Kingdom fall to the Assyrians and he saw
Jerusalem nearly fall, but then the Assyrians left them alone.
However, during the prophetic time of Jeremiah and Ezekiel,
Jerusalem did fall to the Babylonians and the temple was destroyed.
It seemed that God's promise of an everlasting Kingdom for the
House of David had been broken, as there were no more Davidic kings.
But whereas history repeated itself in a circular series of
ups and downs for all of their Gnostic neighbors, the Hebrew
history, as the prophets spoke of it in terms of the promised Messiah,
kept going in a progressive straight line with qualitative leaps
into the new and unexpected turning all bad tricks into good ones.
As the four main themes of covenant, promise, Messiah and
sacred signs went through their nine periods of progressive history,
it often seemed as if there were total disaster, but the great prophets
spoke for their God to the people, assuring them the promise was true.
As Ezekiel, in a vision, saw old, dead, dry bones get up and
start to form together, they began to believe in life after death,
and out of their terrible captivity in Babylon, Ezekiel helped them
to begin to see an apocalyptic vision of the future reconciliation.
Second Isaiah saw the rise to power to Cyrus, the Persian, and
the people of God started to return to their beloved Jerusalem
and he saw that, as God's suffering servant, they could be
a light to the nations and thus a blessing to all peoples.
During the time of Hellenic persecution and the Maccabean revolt,
Daniel delivered his prophecy to sustain the hope of the Jewish
people through faith in a Son of Man "who would reign forever."

IV.3.7 The Writings and Prayers Replacing Gnostic Non-Prayer

Throughout Hebrew history, revelation took place in a contesting of four institutions made up of prophets, priests, kings and sages. At Jeremiah 18:18, as the false prophets and people were planning to kill the prophet, it was written:

> Let us concoct a plot against Jeremiah.
> The priest will not run short of instruction without him,
> nor the sage of his advice
> nor the Prophets of the word.

The King administered with the Law and Jewish lawyers to help. The wisdom movement began with King Solomon and his proverbs and the book of 150 psalms was central to the seven books of wisdom. The Psalter became the prayer book of the Jewish people in their temple worship and in their own prayer life, as it taught them the spirit of praise, thanksgiving, repentance and petition. Whereas Gnostics do not pray in the Hebrew sense because they do not have faith in a personal God who revealed himself, prayer formed the heart, mind, body and soul of the Chosen People. The first words of the first psalm reveal prayer's significance:

> Happy the man
> who never follows the advice of the wicked,
> or loiters on the way that sinners take,
> or sits down with scoffers
> as he meditates on the Law of the Lord
> day and night
> and finds therein all of his delight. (Ps 1:1–2)

This very Psalm is a wisdom prayer and gives advice about from whom to get or not to get advice and it shows the spirit of prayer which meditates day and night on the Torah of Yahweh and that is a life of *hesed's* joy and peace, no matter what sorrow will come, for prayerfully dwelling in God's Glory can let sorrow become joy, though it remains sorrow.

IV.3.8 Lady Sophia's Joyful Wisdom against Gnostic Nihilism

In the books of Proverbs, *Wisdom*, and *Ecclesiasticus*,
we meet Lady Sophia, that created creatrix of playful delight,
that word-breath mediatrix and that mirror image radiatrix.
In Proverbs 8, she says of herself:

> Yahweh created me
> when his purpose first unfolded
> before the oldest of his works. . . .
> I was a master Craftsman,
> delighting him day after day,
> ever at play in his presence,
> at play everywhere in his world,
> delighting to be with the sons of men. (Prov 8:22, 30–31)

This is another creation story with Wisdom in joy and goodness
there in the beginning, exactly the opposite of Gnostic stories.
Gnostics look into the abyss of evil matter and fall into nihilism.
God's people look into the abyss of sorrow and are found by Wisdom.
The book of Job is another wisdom text that tells the story of
the chosen Job, with his beloved family and tremendous wealth.
But then, step by step, all is taken from him, and as he looks
down, down, down into the abyss, he is at first very patient.
God has given. God has taken away. Blessed be the Name of the Lord.
But slowly he begins to question God and take offence at him.
If I could get God into a Jewish Law Court, I could prove him wrong.
But the story does not end in that Gnostic vision of primeval evil.
After all the Gnostic drama and questioning with Job and his friends,
we receive another creation story as God challenges Job from
out of the tempest with a series of poetic questions that reveal
that God is the creator of all good and master of all the forces of evil.
Job becomes a wise man who repents in dust and in ashes.
And God rebukes the false sages and tells them that Job,
his servant, will offer prayers for them which God will hear.

IV.3.9 Apocalyptic Progression against Gnostic Regression

Once the Davidic line of Kings and the temple of Jerusalem were destroyed the model of *hesed* as everlasting, merciful love was no longer dominant and a new somewhat Gnostic dualism became prominent in the realm of priestly and apocalyptic vision. Ezekiel was a priest and he became an apocalyptic prophet as he and his people were deported from Jerusalem to Babylon and they sat and wept when they remembered Jerusalem. For the priests the concept of the holy was given a dualistic meaning, as the profane or that which is outside the temple was radically distinguished from the sacred of the sacraments of the *sacerdos*. Apoclyptic thinking, which flourished during times of persecution, had to do with the future and how a remnant would be saved. The Son of Man would come to save the people who followed the Law and lived holy lives while the profane would perish. According to the *hesed* model, no man is an island, for we are all part of the main and the sins of the fathers will be visited upon the heads of their children to the third and fourth generation. But according to the apocalyptic vision, individuals would be judged according to their own profane or sacred attitudes and Jewish shunning began to be practiced, as it was best to segregate a cancerous, profane individual from the sacred community, so that all would not be punished and destroyed as was the case with Jerusalem for all her illegal ways. The grapes of wrath would no longer pass on from father to children, for if there were three righteous men in a sinful city—Noah, Daniel, and Job—they would be spared. The general Gnosticism of the way of knowing tended to see a threefold cosmic, psychological and moral dualism between the forces of the good spiritual and the evil material and the Apocalyptic movement tended in that direction without *hesed*. But for the Apocalyptic prophets, there was still a line of time.

NOTES

1. Walter Lowrie, *A Short Life of Kierkegaard* (Princeton, NJ: Princeton University Press, 1942) 56.
2. Søren Kierkegaard, *Fear and Trembling*, trans. and ed. Howard V. Hong and Edna H. Hong (Princeton, NJ: Princeton University Press, 1983) 149.
3. Ibid.
4. Krippner, "Epistemology and Technologies," 97.

Gramma Coats at the time of her marriage   Mother with her Mother up Iron Mine

Mother's Anglican Mother

Mother's Morman Father   Uncle El with Gramma and Grampa Coates

Myself and Mother with Grandpa Coates and his Father

Mother with her Catholic husband and me

Myself and our sheepcamp up Dollarhyde Summit

Myself with Dixie and her puppy, Penny

Mother's five children

Myself and Aunt Sadie

Part Two

Sorrowful Proceedings

I. Mother

I.4 With Her Son, David, and Father Dougherty

I.4.1 Cultivating the Holy with the Sacred Heart of Jesus

When mother converted to Catholicism Aunt Claudia gave her
a beautiful picture of the Sacred Heart of Jesus and as mother knelt
in the little Ketchum church before Mass that picture became for her
a symbol of this new atmosphere unlike any she had known before.
Here the red light, as a sign of the real presence of Jesus, burned.
And while friends greeted each other outside there was silence
and total reverence within as they took their places and prayed.
Mother was a very eager student of Catholicism and Father Dougherty
was an excellent mentor in whom she had a total confidence.
She immediately began to go to confession on a weekly basis
and he introduced her into the practice of spiritual reading.
He let her borrow a book called *The Devout Life* by Francis de Sales.
She read a little section each day and thought about it frequently.
She began to see that as an Anglican and as a Mormon she was
like St. Augustine who said, "You have made us for Yourself,
Oh God, and our hearts are not at rest until they rest in You."
To be religious had meant primarily to be happy as an individual
and within a community, but now she began to see that
primarily doing God's will and primarily serving others was
more important than a religion of self-interest's self-realization.
She was struck by the words: "make frequent confession, and
choose thee a good confessor who shall faithfully teach thee
in the way of salvation." And she felt that Father Dougherty was
such a confessor and that this book was teaching her the truth.
She began to reflect upon and to pray the holy sacrifice of the Mass.
She tried to understand the offertory, consecration and communion.
Each Sunday when she and her family went to Mass she took
everything she would do and undergo during the week
and offer it with the bread and the wine on the altar to God.
She began the habit of letting her life be the living out of the Mass.
With the sacred *sacerdos* sacrifice she loved the Sacred Heart of Jesus.

I.4.2 Cultivating Holy Health with the Sacred Sacerdos

On October 15, 1947, Brian Coppinger, dad's friend after whom
Bobby Brian was named and who found our house for us
in Ketchum, looked up in the evening twilight to the top of
a hilly ridge and saw there a buck deer feeding with head down.
He aimed his rifle right at the neck, fired, and the deer
dropped. He hurried to his prize and there lay my dad.
He had blown the ankle bone right out of my father's
right foot and my dad could hardly stand to remove his shoe.
They had to put their handkerchiefs into both sides of
the messy, mangled hole in order to try to stop the bleeding.
Daddy had already been praying that God would let him live.
As he waited for Brian he said the *Angel of God*, the *Hail Mary*,
the *Our Father*, and the *Act of Contrition* as he prayed for his life.
Brian helped him to the car and got him to the Hailey Hospital.
Doctor Fox took out as much of the shattered bone as he could
and set the leg in a cast. On Sunday morning Brian
came to Carey to Gramma Coates' to tell us and get us.
We went to daddy's room and in the bed next to him was one
of the Smith boys who had broken his leg playing football.
Mother, myself, Bette Jo, and Bobby Brian were with him and he
hardly felt like talking and I admired him that he did not complain.
He was a tough guy who always believed in acting like a man.
On the next day Father Dougherty visited him and said to him:
"Be not afraid! Have faith!" He told my dad to offer up
his suffering with the suffering of the Lord and he told mother
what he had said to daddy and she began to do that also.
She was thirty years old with three young children and
a seriously wounded husband in the midst of great suffering.
She was very, very anxious and yet through her husband's
and her family's suffering the passion of her faith in
the Sacred Heart of Jesus did begin to grow in a brand new way.

I.4.3 Cultivating Holy Happiness with Sacred Sacrifice

Her husband's ankle did not quickly heal and Doctor Moritz
up at Sun Valley re-broke it to take out all the shattered bone.
He was on crutches for more than a year and he got about
with a cane until finally he walked with less and less of a limp.
He still received some money from his share in the Rumba Club
but in 1948 the gambling tables were all closed down by law
and, of course, mother and father worried about how they were
going to make a living. Mother sold Christmas cards and
watched every penny and daddy's friend, Art Winters, took him
to hidden and secret, illegal pinochle and poker games.
And Clifford Scott was born on January 24, 1949. They
named him after Clifford Toone, a football friend of dad's,
and he won first prize from a photo company's baby beauty contest.
Mother always called him "sunshine" and, even though they were
in what seemed to be desperate straits, mother felt
that God was becoming more and more present to her.
Francis wrote: "Begin all your prayers, be they mental or vocal,
with the presence of God, and make no exception to this rule,
and you will soon see how profitable it will be to you."
Mother from her Anglican days always liked the proverb:
"Early to bed, early to rise, makes a man healthy, wealthy and wise."
She always had her four children early to bed and as she fell
asleep she noted more and more that she went to sleep
saying the name of Jesus. She would envision her husband and
say: "My Jesus, mercy." She prayed always for him and
for them and early each morning before she arose she offered
her day and all of her joys and sorrows and everything she did
up with Christ on the altar and all her daily life permeated
into the Mass even though she could not go to weekday Mass.
As she took the newspaper and the kindling and started
the fire she was praising God and begging him to help them.

I.4.4 Cultivating Holy Wisdom with the Sacred Sacrament

Father Dougherty told her that he was going to be moved
and that a new priest, Father Heeren, would replace him.
He told Father Heeren about her and that she was truly devout
for the good person keeps the commandments of God but she was
devout because she did so willingly, promptly, and with good heart.
She was poor and she was troubled over many things not the least
of which was her husband's drinking and his quick temper
as he too was troubled with his condition both of pain and anxiety.
When Father Heeren arrived they became spiritual friends at once
and he let her use one of his books called *The Dark Night of the Soul*
by St. John of the Cross and she was amazed by its poetic beauty.
She slowly read and daily meditated on the first fifty or so pages
that explained what it meant for the soul's house to be at rest.
"On a Dark Night, enkindled in love with yearning oh happy chance,
my house being now at rest." And she was especially struck by
the line "leaving all my cares forgotten among the lilies."
Mother was expecting her fifth child. Their little house only had
two small bedrooms. Her mother asked mother why she did not
use birth control. There was hardly any income and if it were
a boy the four boys could sleep in the bedroom and Bette Jo
would not have a room but would sleep on the couch in the front room.
If it were a girl mother did not know what they would do.
But she offered it all up to God with the bread and the wine
and she was not afraid but had faith that it would be all
transformed into the body and blood of Jesus. And she was
happy to be pregnant for a fifth time and Father Heeren told her
that he prayed for her and her family each day and she
prayed for him too and she ached that such a lovely
man could never marry and have a wife and child, but in
wisdom his cares were forgotten among the lilies as were hers
and in this representative of Jesus she loved Jesus the more.

I.4.5 Cultivating Holy Work with the Sacred Consecration

Her fifth child was born on April 12, 1950 and she named him
Thomas Joseph after Father Thomas Heeren her dear confessor
and after her dearest husband, Joseph, who was so brave in his
affliction and who shared with her their tranquility in anxiety
and the great passion to raise their family in faith and in excellence.
And Tommy Joe's dark brown eyes sparkled like his father's and
she called him "Little Lamb" and instead of feeling like her
children were a problem she felt that each of them was a most
precious gift of God and they planned a college education for each.
Instead of being a problem each of her children was a gift of
reconciliation between her and her husband and between each
of the children and their parents and they all loved little Tom
and the three older children loved to take care of him and he
and Cliff became the best friends two brothers could ever be.
Father Heeren baptized Thomas who was named after him and
when he moved from his crib in his parents' room into the
other bedroom. Bette Jo gracefully learned to be without a room
even though she still had her space in the closet and chest of
drawers in the boy's room and at nine she never complained.
David was an alter boy and mother got him off early on Tuesdays
and Fridays to hitchhike to Sun Valley and to serve Mass
for Father Heeren and then ride back to school with Father Heeren.
From their mother's attitude and feeling each child learned that
all they did was holy for it was all consecrated at Mass.
Bette Jo was always a most excellent student and she was
her Father's special love even though he said that mother would
raise the girls and it was his job to raise the boys.
Mother began to pray the rosary each day and she felt that God
truly was their Father and that he would give them their daily bread.
And her husband did get a job at Sun Valley the year round.
And she sought to do God's will by consecrating all at Mass.

I.4.6 Cultivating Holy Forgiving with Q's Jesus

As mother continued to read Francis de Sales different types
of spirituality became clear to her especially the way of forgiving.
Her mother as a good Anglican had always been community
minded and as an Anglican mother belonged to the Rebecca Lodge.
She also greatly admired the Mormon Community and how they
were so focused on family values and in some ways she
preferred to continue living in the healthy farming community.
She also greatly admired Aunt Claudia who had fallen down the
basement stairs when pregnant with her fourth child, Donny.
He could never speak and walked with difficulty but Aunt Claudia
had him with her all the time and took such loving care of him
that she showed to mother the suffering servant Jesus of Mark.
But, now high up in the mountain valley of Ketchum, Sun Valley,
she lived in an atmosphere unlike that of the lowland farmers.
And *The Imitation of Christ* written by the lowlander Thomas a Kempis
was loved by mother in Anglican and Mormon ways, but
as Francis of Sales directed the soul of *Philothea* mother grew
especially with his help in the spirit of loving forgiveness.
The Jesus of Q and of St. Francis of Assisi appealed to her
as she read in *The Devout Life*:

> St. Francis, seeing a sheep alone amongst a herd of goats,
> said to his companion, "Look at the poor sheep, how
> gentle it is amongst the goats—even so our Blessed
> Lord was gentle and lowly amidst the Pharisees." And
> another time seeing a tender lamb devoured by a boar,
> "Oh, little lamb!" he exclaimed with tears, "thou
> settest forth to me the death of my Savior."[1]

And mother had her "Little Lamb." And from *The Devout Life*
she learned the lives of the saints and they taught her of her Jesus.
And Jesus, Father Heeren, and Frances of Assisi helped her
to imitate was the Jesus who was forgiving and positive to all.

I.4.7 Offering All in the Dark Night

In mid-summer of 1952 daddy and I dug the grave out at
the Ketchum cemetery for Mary Theresa, our little stillborn
daughter and sister. The earth was dry, hard, and rocky and
we were both perspiring profusely as we took turns in
the deepening hole. I saw my dad pick up my mother's
rosary and he kissed and held it reverently as we took it
to her up at the hospital. We dug the grave in that same
reverence and silence. And mother had a hysterectomy.
She came home and she was weak and for the first time ever
could not do her work. Donna Chaney whom I loved
came over and they hired her to help with all the cleaning
and washing and ironing. Mother would lie on the couch
with a washcloth on her forehead and pray her rosary
through the day. We all pitched in and made things work.
Tommy was still only a two year old so she had to get well
soon as there was no time to be sick and depressed.
Gramma Coates came to visit her but she could not stay
for there was no room for an extra person to sleep over.
No one said anything about it but mother did thank God for her
operation since now she would not have to have more children.
The notion and image of the Dark Night of the Soul became
a consolation and a guide for her, and that she could offer all
her suffering up with Jesus cheered her and healed her and
her virtuous life and loving attitude did strengthen her
immune system and very quickly she was back into her full routine.
Her husband now had work that he liked much better than
working on the ground crew up at Sun Valley and on the ski lift
up on Baldy during the winter. He cleaned the Sawtooth Club
for Louis Accaturri each morning and got the franchise for
the trash route in Ketchum and I helped him each day
and made money to go away to the seminary in the Fall.

I.4.8 Offering Her Son to the Seed Bed

On September 6, 1952, Father Heeren came over for my mother's
birthday dinner and the next day he picked up myself and
then David LePrise and drove me to Mt. Angel Seminary and
David to the Benedictine College in Olympia Washington.
Mother was so happy that Holy Mother Church was there to help
her raise and educate her children. In my grade school class there
were ten pupils and none of the others would go on to college.
Mom and Dad had always saved for a college education for each
of their children and even though they were in the lowest 20% of
Ketchum's economic spectrum and even though her dear husband
was an alcoholic garbage man they were so blessed to have first
Father Dougherty and then Father Heeren to be role models and
guides and advisors and mother felt totally secure with their help.
When I was at the seminary mother and I wrote letters to
each other once a month and I told her about our life in the
seminary and for Christmas she gave me *The Confessions* of
St. Augustine and as a fourteen year old I began to read them
and to take notes during spiritual reading and I liked them and
a couple of years later I asked her if I should give a copy
to dad for Christmas and she said that he would not read them
so I bought some fishing flies instead for my fishing friend.
Mother became the god-mother for Janice McDermott,
Bobby Junior, her nephew, and Michael McPheters, the boy
next door, and she loved them and encouraged them and
they talked with her and Michael went to Carol College and Fordham.
The people of the church and of the town all admired mother
for her sweet, loving way and her neat, clean children.
Bette Jo became a favorite babysitter and Bobby Brian
began serving Mass as had David for years and she prayed
for David each day that he might be like Father Dougherty
and Father Heeren and she prayed especially for his purity.

I.4.9 With the 'Jesus' of the Hail Mary

In that part of the *Devout Life* called *The Invocation of the Saints* mother read: "Honor, reverence and love the holy and glorious Virgin Mary, for she is the mother of our Lord, and therefore our mother also. Fly to her as her child, and cast yourself at her knees with a perfect confidence at all times and on all occasions. Call on this dear mother, appeal to her maternal love, and strive to imitate her virtues."[2] Mother was eager to do this and so her family had three mothers: Holy Mother Church, Mother Mary, and she herself who learned from both how to be the kind of mother she wanted to be to do God's will. She read the opening quotation at the beginning of her book: "But even as Josue and Caleb declared that the Land of Promise was good and fair, and that the possession of it would be easy and pleasant; so the Holy Spirit, speaking by all the Saints, and our blessed Lord Himself assure us that a devout life is a lovely, pleasant, and a happy life."[3] Mother truly believed this and her book opened for her this wonderful world of the Saints. Living with the community of Saints and with Mary, the Queen of the Angels and Saints, daily inspired mother. As she looked back it seemed that the first 27 years of her life were almost carefree and joyful and that now she was beginning to be united with her Lord in the sorrowful mysteries. She shared daily in her husband's affliction and she knew that he loved and revered her even as he might Mother Mary. She did go through the Dark Night of the loss of her daughter, Mary Theresa, whom she named after Mary and the Theresas. All of her sorrow and affliction was taken into the realm of the glorious mysteries and transformed into joy as she offered them all on the altar as gifts and as they were consecrated by the sacred *sacerdos* priests Fathers Dougherty and Heeren who were unlike any she had known.

I.5 With Her Daughter, Bette Jo, and Father Heeren

I.5.1 The Holy Communion Covenant with the Sacred Heart

In mother's heart Father Heeren truly was the representative of Jesus.
By his ordination he was set apart from the everyday world in order
to make holy all those who would but touch the hem of his garment.
As a woman she knew him well in the devotion of his celibacy.
He had taken his masculine desire and offered it on the altar with
the bread and the wine and it became the Lord's love which she
received from him in Holy communion as she attended his Mass.
He was for her a mirror image of the Sacred Heart of Jesus
so that she could know Jesus in him as she knew him in Jesus.
She was inspired by him as an exemplar not only to offer her
heart, mind and soul with the bread and the wine but to pray that
they too might be consecrated and transformed into a new desire.
She did have a conflict of desires within her so that she feared
that which threatened the covenant bond of her dear family.
Her husband was drinking more and more and while he provided
for his family with all of his hard work on the trash route
he still spent a lot of his time in illegal gambling and according to
the rules of his mind he would spend the winnings on drinking.
Francis of Sales wrote straight to her heart: "Dice, cards, and
similar games, in which success depends mainly on chance, are
not only dangerous amusements like dancing, but actually
and naturally bad and blamable. For this reason they are
forbidden both by civil and ecclesiastical law."[4] And that is
exactly what happened for in November of 1952 even slot machines
were outlawed and daddy's friends moved to Nevada
and he wanted to go to, but mother's friendly persuasion won out.
She even thought of breaking her covenant and divorcing him
and she did know that other men noticed and liked her.
But she took her troubled heart to the altar Sunday after Sunday
with her husband and her children and even though her husband
often did not receive communion he loved the sacred sacrament.

I.5.2 Dear Father's Affliction and Holy Communion Code

What Mother hated most she had to live with most closely for
she saw the addiction of her husband to gambling and drinking
becoming worse and worse and her own dear father was
drinking all the time and squandering everything that he
and Gramma Coates had worked so hard for, for so long.
Gramma felt she had to divorce him to save the ranch
that Uncle El daily worked so hard on and her own little house.
Grandpa Coates came to mother for help and she knew not what to do.
She could feed him some but there was no place for him to sleep.
So daddy let him sleep in the cab of his garbage truck and
mother even took him to Mass up at Sun Valley one time.
But he said that all that Latin was not for him.
They loved each other so much and he still always called her Sissy.
She remembered that poor little bum lamb, black sheep.
And now he was that very black sheep. At first he had
a pickup truck, but he wrecked that driving drunk.
At Mass and in her rosary mother prayed for him always.
At Holy Communion she pleaded with Jesus to save him and
at the beginning of each Mass when they said the Confiteor
she knew that he and all had to follow the covenant law code.
And in the Kyrie she prayed for mercy for him and
believed that God would love him as she did and save him.
They took her father and put him in the Insane Asylum over
in Blackfoot, Idaho, which also served as a kind of detox center.
She offered her father's suffering and all the suffering
he brought to others in the sacred liturgy of the Eucharist.
She knew all their suffering would be consecrated with
the body and blood of Jesus and in receiving his body
in Holy Communion she trusted that all their sorrow would
be joined with that of Jesus and in the long run throughout
eternity help save them in communion with God forever.

I.5.3 Loss of Father Heeren and Holy Communion Cult

Father Heeren told her he was being transferred and that Father O'Connor who went to the seminary in Ireland would replace him. Father O'Connor was of a more rugged body type than the more slight and gentle Father Heeren and mother was in need of his *Imitation of Christ* spirituality and the "Royal Road of the Cross." Father O'Connor had a great sense of Irish humor and daddy and Bette Jo seemed to like him even more than they did Father Heeren. Father Heeren was the closest soul mate mother would ever have. And his very spirit taught her that they could not be separated. In the Liturgy of the Word at the beginning of Mass she loved to pray the Gloria and that was for her the way to cultivate all sorrow so that it could become joy though remaining sorrow. The Liturgy of the Word in the first half of the Mass prepared her for the Liturgy of the Eucharist in the Mass's second half. Receiving Holy Communion for her was the apex of adoration. In the Anglican and Mormon worlds she did not know of this kind of adoration which the sacred *sacerdos* brought. Holy Communion for her was the very essence of Catholicism and of the New Covenant that Jesus made with his Church. It had within it all the power and mystery of sacred sexuality and of sacred death which were the moments of the life force. The priest's sacred celibacy so set him apart from anything in the world that Father O'Connor was like a combination of Father Dougherty and of Father Heeren and in the Mass she would always love Jesus through Father Heeren and he could never be gone for every time she said her son, Tommy's name he was there in the name like the little lamb. And the first part of the Mass had its code, cult, canon, and creed and it was all condensed in Holy Communion at the end of the Mass for the Gloria was there throughout letting God's glory shine especially in all suffering.

I.5.4 The Mary-Like Crusading and Holy Communion Canon

Mother kept reading not only Francis of Sales and St. John of the Cross and St. Theresa of Avila and the *Imitation of Christ*, but Father O'Connor advised her to be more practical and to also read the Catholic Register and she noticed several different Catholic publications and got on their mailing list and she started receiving a little journal called *Mary-like Crusaders*. And it came just at the right time for Bette Jo was entering her teenage years and they got a new television set and Elvis Presley and the spirit of the Rock and Rollers was starting to move across the land and Bette Jo wanted to go to dances with her friends and even to wear lipstick. Just as Francis of Sales warned against gambling and dancing so the *Mary-like Crusaders* warned against any skirt or dress that was not below the knees. And Bette Jo felt that her mother was overly strict and straight-laced and that she was becoming overly scrupulous towards herself. And Aunt Mid's husband, Uncle Tony, was killed in the war and she remarried Uncle Larry who was a divorcee and mother told us not to call him Uncle Larry but only Larry because they were not really married in the eyes of the Church. Mother meditated on the chapter in the *Devout Life* entitled "Balls and Recreations which are Lawful but Dangerous" and she felt that she had to become a law enforcer even concerning the dangerous because she knew from her own experience in Carey how most young people got caught in the dating game and never made it to college and she had her clear goals. In the Liturgy of the Word they read through the canon of both the old and the new covenant and mother knew of law and grace and she knew from experience that if the law code of the sacred were not followed a natural punishment was there for any immorality.

I.5.5 Dear Husband's Addictions and Holy Communion Creed

Even though mother knew that she could not directly help
her father and her husband she did believe in the power of prayer
and she prayed for them daily and she loved them more and more.
She believed strongly in the mystical Body of Jesus and that
she could serve the freedom and health of others by taking
responsibility for them by working on her own health and freedom.
By the grace of her conversion she had received gifts of freedom
to serve others and by not giving into any of her self-indulgent negativity
she firmly believed her positivity would also become their positivity.
She gave the reasons of Francis of Sales as to why she was
opposed to gambling and dancing. He said gambling was
forbidden because "the winner in such games does not win
on his deserts but according to chance, and the luck which
often falls to those who have exercised neither skill nor industry,
and this is contrary to reason."[5] None of her children really
believed this for they knew that there was skill in good
playing just as there was in Chinese checkers, which she played.
They looked upon their dad as a hero insofar as he was a
good gambler and they were ashamed of his being a garbage man.
Mother liked his honest work as he went out in his overalls,
which she washed with devotion each Monday, and cleaned up the town.
There were many points of friction that could have become
points of fraction that could have broken the family apart,
but because of a deep down adoration for the good which they
both had they became opportunities for reconciliation and love.
Mother taught her children how to love their father and
that was not hard because he was a very loveable person.
He taught them how to love and obey her and deep down
he was glad that she was naïve and innocent for he
did not want his children to smoke, drink, gamble,
and get angry and swear as did he out of strong habit.

I.5.6 Cultivating Petrine Authority with Matthew's Jesus

Mother's growth was analogous to the New Testament evolution. First, there was Paul, who like her Anglican mother, was community minded and with increasing love for all of humankind was open to communion with the rest of the world. Then, there was John, who like the beloved Mormon Community looked upon the world as being in darkness which tempts us to go astray from our heavenly Father's love and not to follow the Lord's way, the truth and the light. Then she discovered Mark through her husband's Catholic world which emphasized the right innerly direction in imitating Jesus. For first as the Good Samaritan he went about the hill country serving others and then going down to Jerusalem he was put to death. She learned the way of the suffering servant, that all must follow his direction in serving and suffering which is the synoptic direction for consecrating all serving and suffering as sacred. Fourthly, Fathers Dougherty and Heeren introduced her to the charismatic Jesus of Q, whose sayings are common to Matthew and to Luke, and who taught her the forgiving Sacred Heart of Jesus. Through *The Devout Life* and with St. Theresa of Avila and St. John of the Cross she learned to be forgiving and leave all her cares forgotten among the lilies as Jesus rested his weary head upon her flowery breasts kept wholly for him alone. And now fifthly with Father O'Connor she was learning about the institutional Church and the authority Jesus gave Peter. Her children were growing up in the world and the new technology of television and the new Rock and Roll spirit were terribly tempting and she needed above all a holy authority which they would obey so that they might live loving Catholic lives. And Fathers Dougherty, Heeren, and O'Connor lived in a vertical sacred relation with God through their poverty, chastity, and obedience and that let her see her poverty, chastity, and obedience as holy and she trusted it would be holy for her children too.

I.5.7 Obedience: Sacred Vertical and Holy Horizontal

St. Francis de Sales is especially good at directing lay persons into the depths, breadths, and heights of the inner spiritual world as they live their lives right in the world with all the worldly pressures. He helped mother to ponder poverty, chastity, and obedience. Father Heeren talked with mother about poverty during the time we were so poor and about his own practice of poverty as a sacred task that freed him to focus on God alone appealed to her. She came to see poverty not as a shameful disgrace but as a virtue. Mother had special concerns with sexuality since her own mother came from a broken home and she wondered if there were any connections between sexual addiction and the alcoholic addiction. But most of all she was beginning to see into the worth and the ways of obedience to authority. She was careful to always be obedient to her God, her conscience, her husband, and her parish priest. And though she began to have clashes with her children her constant prayer for and cultivation of obedience did enable her to command the children's obedience even though they disagreed. Bette Jo invited Ernest Hemmingway to come to Hailey High School and give a talk on his life and writing and he agreed to come but hearing of this mother asked Bette Jo not to attend her own meeting. She objected to Hemmingway's many wives and his worldly writing. Bette Jo felt that her mother's scruples were outrageously exaggerated and daddy tried to comfort her and persuade her to obey her mother. And out of obedience to her beloved father's wish she did come to graciously obey her mother's command. That September Bette Jo left on the train with David to Portland where she would go to Portland University with the Holy Cross Fathers. Daddy thought that was excellent because they were the same Fathers who ran Notre Dame and thus they had to be the best. Mother was relieved that now Bette Jo was the concern of Holy Mother Church who could train her in obedient active listening.

I.5.8 Chastity: Sacred Vertical and Holy Horizontal

Mother's second son, Robert, gave her no conflict and anxiety.
He was the middle child of the family and his character was kind,
mediating, empathetic, intelligent, balancing, obedient, and chaste.
Just as she could feel purity in the priests so she felt it in him.
But she did worry about her first son, David, because he was
impulsive and excitable and often got himself and others into trouble.
He had a hair-trigger habit of irascibility that would break out
in swearing and foul language even though it was gone as fast
as it came and he was also naturally given to the concupiscible.
His affection now became very interested in the female sex and she
had to censor lewd television shows or magazine pictures
because she knew that they were for him like honey for a bear.
She was so happy that the monks of Mount Angel Seminary and the
atmosphere there was building a whole other character within him
even though she knew that the irascibility-concupiscible complex
did not leave him in the least but was only becoming sublimated.
She knew that she herself had a quick temper like her husband's.
When he was four David was still wetting the bed and with an
angry energy she grabbed him and rubbed his nose in the wet sheets.
She so frightened him with the drenching that he stopped bed wetting.
With Bobby she did not have to use such drastic measures.
He without any violent desires either of the angry fighting type
or of the lusty pursuing type was deep down obedient with
an empathy like hers that was aware of the needs of others
no matter how slight and was at once attentive to other's wishes.
He had a quiet, playful laughter and a meditative artistic taste.
After a year of high school at home he announced that he too
would like to go to Mt. Angel Seminary and mother was overjoyed.
She lived out the consecration of the Mass by daily consecrating
her heart and she prayed that her sons might be consecrated priests.
As celibately sacred they could bring others to God's holy purity.

I.5.9 Poverty: Sacred Vertical and Holy Horizontal

Mother was quick to abandon herself to God's will and she was so happy
that her first two sons were studying to be priests and that her daughter
had transferred to Gonzaga University, the Jesuit University in Spokane.
Gramma Coates knew Gonzaga and confirmed for Bette Jo that
the Jesuits were the best and daddy liked them because even though
their football wasn't equal to Notre Dame their basketball was great.
Mother noticed that I was spending many evenings up at Sun Valley
and daddy's friends told him that I was spending a lot of time with a
particular girl and he was afraid that mother's heart would be broken
if after nine years I should leave the seminary and not be a priest.
In late August she asked me not to go out each and every evening.
So I went to the Church instead and wrote a good-bye love letter to Jane.
Daddy told me to tell him first if I were to leave the seminary
so that he could tell my mother in his own understanding way.
I went along with him even though I felt mother and I knew
each other in some spiritual way and I knew that she would not
really mind if it were God's will that I did not have a vocation.
When it seemed that I had a vocation mother was totally for it.
And as soon as I was told that I did not have a vocation to be a priest
she thought that I must have some other vocation right for me.
Mother was so totally obedient to the will of God that she could
accept a gigantic change in trusting faith without the bat of an eye.
Obedience or actively listening to and acting according to God's will
was quite easy for her because she trusted her obedient confessors.
They did what they were told by their Bishop who in turn was obedient
to the chair of Peter and her children united with her in obedience.
She knew I was not like the priests she loved in my need
to be affectionate with girls and women and their purity did not
quite seem to make me pure. But their practice of poverty did
help mother to have the spirit of poverty and we did seem to
seek first the Kingdom of God and trust the rest would come.

I.6 With Her Son, Bobby Brian, and Father O'Connor

I.6.1 How Sacred Communion Graced Her with Holy Love

What becoming a Catholic meant most of all for mother was being able to receive the body of Jesus in Holy Communion. Her favorite chapter in *An Introduction to The Devout Life* was the one on *How to Communicate* for it got right to the point: "Your chief aim in Holy Communion should be to advance, strengthen and comfort yourself in the love of God. There is nothing in which the love of Christ is set forth more tenderly or more touchingly than in this sacrament, by which He, so to say, annihilates Himself for us, and takes upon Him the form of bread, in order to feed us, and unite Himself closely to the body and souls of the faithful."[6] As soon as mother went to Mass she had not the slightest doubt that Jesus was present in the sacrament, present in the community of the faithful, present in her heart and present to all with whom she communicated. Her love really was strengthened and advanced each time she received Holy Communion because even though Jesus was not visible to her eyes his presence did become greater and greater for her as she prayed most fervently to him as she united her passion with all of his suffering and passion in the sacrifice of the Mass. In her prayer at the time of Holy Communion she brought all the suffering and passion of her husband into the passion of Jesus. She brought all of her dear father's deepest passion and suffering. She brought all of her mother's and all of her own which reached out to each of her loved ones and the presence of Jesus was as real for her as was all of her own love and suffering. Mother knew that Fathers Dougherty, Heeren, and O'Connor were totally dedicated to God in the verticality of their sacred celibacy. That brought holiness to her and others in a holy horizontality. Their seven sacraments, their subordination to authority and their contact with the community of saints and angels under the Queenship of Mary inspired mother's love of Holy Mother Church.

I.6.2 How Sacred Confession Graced Her with Holy Peace

St. Francis of Sales wrote: "If the most delicate and perishable
fruits, such as strawberries, cherries and apricots can
easily be preserved the whole year by means of sugar or honey,
surely it is no great marvel that our hearts, albeit frail
and weak, should be preserved from the corruption of sin
when they are immersed in the sweetness of the incorruptible
Body and Blood of the Son of God."[7] These words spoke to mother,
for each Fall she preserved about a hundred jars of fruit.
Confession for her was also a most important weekly sacrament.
She knew how well she cleaned all her fruit and took out
the core of the apples and pears and the pits from the apricots and
peaches and each little stem from the currents and choke-cherries.
The sacred *sacerdos* in sacred confession helped her to refine
the taste of her conscience more and more finely as she
prepared herself better and better for Jesus to come to her.
Confession was the preparation that helped her to come more
and more sweetly to Jesus as he came more sweetly to her.
The love of the Good Shepherd's Sacred Heart came right into
her heart at communion and it burst forth within her like
strong, sweet honey that she felt right up into her teeth.
Her heart too exploded so that his honey poured out into
each of her relationships and she knew her husband, and
her father, and all of her family, and all living things were saved
and preserved forever each in their dear and lovely uniqueness.
Mother watched her dear husband not receive communion Sunday
after Sunday until he went to confession at Easter and at Christmas.
She prayed for him that someday he might be freed from
his addiction and that he might be freed for the peace of
confession and preserved for Holy Communion love and joy.
She first learned the distinction between the sacred and the holy
from his Catholicism and his refraining from communion touched her.

I.6.3 How Sacred Matrimony Graced Her with Holy Joy

At forty-five as mother began to reach middle age she and father
began to taste the fruit of their parenting. She wrote:
"David transferred from St. Thomas Seminary in Kenmore, Wa.
to Loyola University in Jan. 1962. He received his Master's
Degree in Philosophy in 1963. 1963 was a big year of graduations
for our family. Bette Jo graduated from Gonzaga University
at Spokane with a sociology major. Bobby graduated from
Mt. Angel Seminary High School at St. Benedict, Oregon. Cliff
graduated from the 8th grade at Ketchum." By now mother's
prayer life was getting the order that she would keep and build on
for the rest of her life especially as she daily prayed her Rosary.
She had her order of intentions for herself, her family, and others.
She prayed by thinking about the words of the prayer and by
envisioning each person she prayed for in relation to the mystery
which she also envisioned. She prayed out loud to increase the vision.
She kept the same order of prayer so as not to forget anyone.
As she prayed with love she loved each person more and more.
In 1963, on August 5, on the Feast Day of our Lady of Snows,
who is the patroness of the parish at Ketchum, Sun Valley
her son, David, and Wilhelmina, a Dutch nurse from Holland
were married at the Cathedral of the Holy Name in Chicago, Illinois.
Right away mother loved Wilhelmina in a very special way
because she was also devout and loved Holy Mass and the Rosary.
She prayed always for the gifts of the Holy Spirit especially
that of healing for her patients and for all of her loved ones.
Mother felt that her own prayers were being answered and
it was now evident that all five of her children would go
through a university of Holy Mother Church for Father O'Connor
and then Fr. Waldman his replacement had inspired Bobby to go to
Mt. Angel. Cliff and Tom served Mass for Father Waldman and he and
his replacement Fr. DeNardis told them of Assumption College.

I.6.4 How Sacred Baptism Graced Her with Holy Hope

When Wilhelmina and I came to visit in Ketchum in July, 1964,
Mother asked me to drive her to Blackfoot and the Insane Asylum
so that we could visit Grampa Coates for perhaps the last time.
He came to the door to meet us and he was so happy and he
and my mother looked into each other's eyes and they took
each other in their arms and he said: "Sissy! Sissy!"
And she said: "Dad! Dad!" And he looked at me and we had
not seen each other for ten years. And I was David Levaur
and named after him. He looked into my face and took me
in his arms and said: "David! David!" And tears were
pouring down his cheeks and he was sobbing. We ate lunch
together and he asked about various people and kept saying how
he didn't like it here where they took such good care of him.
Looking around he said: "I just don't like the whole damn outfit."
He had become a black-sheep outcast no longer part of the herd.
Mother loved him with all the love they had always had
for each other and it was as if he were her bum lamb-black sheep.
It was as if he were the Prodigal Father and she was the child
who was helpless even to welcome her Prodigal Father home.
When she told Father DeNardis how she felt he told her that he
had been baptized and that God loved him even more than she did.
He died that Fall and she and dad drove to Carey for his funeral
service there in the little Carey cemetery on the side of the hill.
She knew how her mother loved him and her sister and two
brothers, and she loved him with all their love too in some
sort of secret faith, hope, and wisdom that he was very lovable
even though he was the town drunk and the lost black sheep.
She saw so many of her old friends and she began to pray for him
as the first of her blessed dead who could pray for her too.

I.6.5 How Sacred Extreme Unction Graced Her with Holy Promise

Mother continued to pray for her father especially at communion and with a special bead each day on her rosary and she continued to ponder the verse picked for his funeral card:

> Oh, deem not they are blest alone
> Whose lives a peaceful tenor keep;
> The Power who pities man, hath shown
>   A blessing for the eyes that weep.
>
> The light of smiles shall fill again
>   The lids that overflow with tears;
> And weary hours of woe and pain
>   Are promises of happier years. . . .
>
> For God has marked each sorrowing day
>   And numbered every secret tear,
> And heaven's long age of bliss shall pay
> For all his children suffer here.[8]

Mother did believe that each tear of her father dear was marked and loved by our heavenly Father who loves us. She wished that her father could have received the sacred sacrament of the sick and the dying and she began to ponder that definition of a sacrament which she taught each of her children. "An outward sign instituted by Christ to give grace." She thought of all the grace her father needed and missed out on. And yet she knew how he was so graced in the ups and even the downs of his life and she knew how his tears were tears of love. His tears poured forth from some kind of proud glorious joy. And as she prayed the "Our Father" sixteen times a day as she said her Rosary she began to think of the Heavenly Father who loves the Mormons and of how the Mormons loved her and the "Our Father" from now on had an Aura of her father about it.

I.6.6 Cultivating Freedom with the Jesus of Luke's Gospel

One morning at Mass in the Gospel reading she heard the words:

> The Spirit of the Lord has been given to me,
> for he has anointed me.
> He has sent me to bring good news to the poor,
> to proclaim liberty to the captives
> and to the blind sight
> to set the downtrodden free
> to proclaim the Lord's year of favor. (Luke 4:18–19)

She was so thankful that her dear father was set free and that
he no longer had to suffer and when she received communion
she knew Jesus as their savior and she wanted his liberation.
She was now fifty years old and her daughter married a
wonderful man who was in the Air Force and she liked him
so much and he was so handsome in his military uniform
when they came to Ketchum for a wedding party with their family.
And a new little grandson, Joseph Robert, was brought to visit
them by David and Wilhelmina. And the name "Robert" resonated
for her in so many ways for it was her brother's name and
her second son's name and her first grandchild's name and now
also the name of Bette Jo's new husband. And Grandpa Joe
was especially ecstatic with Little Joe. And one day they noticed
that both Grandpa Joe and Little Joe were missing and
then they discovered that Grandpa Joe had taken the little guy
who was only six months old down to the casino so he
could show him off to all his friends. And he knew that
Grandma would object if he would have said what he was up to.
But she too was mellowing and now that she was not bringing
up her children she did not have to worry about discipline.
She had learned from her priests to seek first the Kingdom of God
by practicing the spiritual exercises of the sacraments, prayer,
and spiritual reading, and her children had learned this with her.

I.6.7 How Sacred Confirmation Graced Their Physical Exercises

"Seek ye first the Kingdom of Heaven and all these things will be added unto you." And she did absolutely love the absolute and relatively love the relative. From her family and her community she did learn of physical, vital, intellectual and spiritual values. From the sacred priests she had learned to seek first the kingdom of God and she practiced the spiritual exercises of the sacraments, prayer and spiritual reading and she taught them to her children. From her Mormon Community she learned especially of the healthy values of vitality and its exercises of right sociality and politeness and of right eating and drinking and of a positive attitude. The quotation from Luke said: "The Spirit of the Lord has been given to me for he has anointed me." She pondered the anointed Christ and the gifts of his Holy Spirit especially in the sacrament of confirmation which each of her children received as they were reaching puberty. Her description of her prayer when saying the Rosary shows that having faith is all important for her and that only it can make possible a life of devotion. She felt a Catholic education would best cultivate in her children that faith and devotion which their confirmation nourished in them. Cliff and Tom went away to a Benedictine College in North Dakota. Cliff learned to become a medical technician and met Ruth who was studying to be a nurse and Tom studied to be a teacher and he met Annette and both the young ladies had all the virtue and the pure goodness of those Lawrence Welk folk and all the devout people of their Germanic culture of North Dakota. Bobby Brian also left Mt. Angel Seminary and went out to Loyola of Chicago to be with David and to study literature. His education took him from wanting to be a monk, to wanting to be a poet, to wanting to be a psychoanalyst, to finally becoming a lawyer and like his brothers and father he liked to run and practice regular physical exercises.

I.6.8 How Sacred Holy Orders Graced Their Intellectual Exercises

Mother was sincerely and deeply thankful to Holy Mother Church for all her sacred priests ordained with the Seven Holy Orders. Their offering of their lives in poverty, celibacy and obedience let Catholic education be available even for her poor family. She and her husband had worked very hard in raising their five children and seeing to it that they all would go to college. In the spirit of *The Imitation of Christ* Father O'Connor had helped her carry her cross with near constant friction over drinking, smoking, gambling, certain television programs, certain movies, over Bette Jo's dress code, over Ernest Hemingway, over some of my books, and over the question of my lust, anger, and swearing. All these evils were very real and were destroying her husband, her father, and were a great danger for at least David and Bette Jo. She prayed for the healing of the family tree and knew that the forces of heredity and environment tended to trap her children also in various kinds of determined addictions. Gramma Coates said to me that with my liberal education maybe I would even be able to help alcoholics and she and mother both believed in the intellectual exercises of reading, writing, speaking, listening, thinking, and even dreaming in a creative way so that one could become free to serve others. Bobby's journey from practicing the exercises of the monk, to those of the poet, to those of the psychoanalyst, to those of the lawyer prepared him to meet and fall in love with Genie, a wonderful young lady whose father was a doctor in Salt Lake City, and who studied literature at the nearby Northwestern. Gramma Coates said that Genie was of finest quality and Bobby and Genie were happily married in Salt Lake. Mother felt happily complacent with Bobby-Genie in the sense of being pleased with the character of both and she had hardly any concern that either of them would be negatively necessitated.

I.6.9 How Sacred Sacraments Graced Their Spiritual Exercises

As mother was becoming grandmother it was as if she were beginning more and more to discover The Holy Spirit's love. She would pray: "Come Holy Spirit of the Risen Lord Jesus, of the Holy Mother, and of the Holy Father, please pray through us now." She would pray: "Holy Spirit, please give us your Pentecost love, with your loving, forgiving, reconciling heart with its health, happiness, holiness, wisdom, good jobs, great grades, and wonderful lives for each of us." Mother and father worked together to see that their five children got a college education. For father this primarily meant the passageway to good jobs and to take advantage of the opportunities of living in America. For mother it primarily meant a good religious education so that her children and their children could be delivered from evil and could build up the Kingdom of love, justice and peace for all. The two sayings of Jesus about peace began to make her think: "I come not to bring peace but the sword." And "My peace, my peace I give unto you." By becoming a follower of Christ she did find the sword. Deep down she was a Republican and wanted good, strong family values. And very deep down dad was a Democrat and had been very stung by the Republican's Prohibition and the way they put him in jail for delivering whiskey. As time went on she even had to battle the liberal education atmosphere of the seminary in that especially her son, David, was beginning to be conditioned by worldly books and ideas. She was aware of the many evils that threatened her offspring and she fought for the mid twenty-seven years of her life to ward off the temptations of the world, the flesh and the devil. From the sacred priests and in the sacred Mass she learned the spiritual exercises of prayer, meditation and spiritual reading that let her reconcile the sword of law and the gospel of peace especially as she prayed Mary's Holy Rosary.

II. Søren Kierkegaard

II.4 Reconciling the God-Man and Plato

II.4.1 By Preserving Plato's Paradoxes in the Incarnational Leap

Like *Fear and Trembling*, *Philosophical Fragments* is an inspired and inspiring book which is an excellent introduction into Kierkegaard's existential world and its new postmodern approach to the questions: Does God exist? Can we be free? Are we immortal? What is the meaning of life? Why is there something rather than nothing? Once Kierkegaard was inspired by Regina into his new world of loving joy he then, in exploring his new world, wrote about the inspired visions of Socrates, Abraham, and Job to see how they too make a leap into a new love, freedom and immortality. Kierkegaard moved from his modern Lutheran world with its theology of the atonement with which his father's depression and guilt complex were connected into the premodern and postmodern world of the theology of the incarnation and its joy. In *Philosophical Fragments* he treats eight philosophical paradoxes which the inspired Plato used to explain how we can move up the ladder of love and the divided line of knowledge to get out of the cave into which we fell when we became embodied because of a double burden of forgetfulness and wrongdoing. Kierkegaard contrasts incarnational embodiment with Plato's recollectional disembodiment to show how helpful Plato's paradoxes can be if we but keep them open in faith. Concerning each paradoxical fragment Kierkegaard contrasts and relates the quantitative climb of Plato, written about by his pseudonym, John the Climber, with the qualitative leap which the disciple can make by following the incarnational God-man. *Philosophical Fragments* is beautifully organized into a) an *Introduction*, which treats 1) the learning paradox, and 2) the love paradox; b) a *Body* of the arguments, which treats 3) the Typhonic paradox, 4) the absolute paradox, 5) offense at the paradox, and 6) the temporality of the paradox; and c) a *Conclusion* treating 7) the paradox of the contemporary follower, and 8) the follower at second hand.

II.4.2 By Preserving the Learning Paradox in the Incarnation

Kierkegaard's main point concerning each of the eight paradoxes is that if we are to maintain the moment of truth in the leap of faith as momentous with a future and free choice then we cannot accept the Platonic solution to the paradox, but we must preserve its absurdity with the God-man's absurdity even as Socrates might. Kierkegaard makes an eight step analysis of each of the eight paradoxes.

1) The learning paradox is that a person cannot seek what he knows, and, just as impossibly, he cannot seek what he does not know.
2) Plato thinks through the difficulty by means of the principle that all learning and seeking are but recollecting for the truth is not introduced into the ignorant person but has been in him all along as forgotten and he merely needs but a reminder to begin to see it.
3) Thus in the Platonic situation the moment of truth is only an occasion with no decisive significance as something really new.
4) If the temporal moment is to have significance then the learner in the preceding state must be in the untruth and he must be given both the condition for the truth as well as the truth if he is to stop fleeing the truth.
5) Freely fleeing the truth in self deceit must be a sin and the teacher who gives both the condition and the truth must be the God.
6) The condition of the learner is like that of the child who bought the toy instead of the book and cannot later buy the book; or, it is like that of the knight who joined the army about to be defeated and then as a prisoner cannot join the victorious army.
7) The god who teaches such a learner is thus a savior, a deliverer, a judge, who in the fullness of time brings the learner to conversion as a new person.
8) If the moment is to have decisive significance then learning the truth is a transition from not existing to existing or a rebirth such as Paul's or Kierkegaard's conversion.

The first of the philosophical fragments shows that we should remain in objective uncertainty before complexity in the moment of truth.

II.4.3 By Preserving the Love Paradox in the Incarnation

Kierkegaard now goes back to the paradox of his love for Regina. 1) Not to disclose itself is the death of love; to disclose itself is the death of the beloved. 2) If the god who loves lowly man is like a king who loves a humble maiden then there is the question how the maiden can arrive at true love for the king in which she knows him as he is, or how man can come to know and love the god. 3) Now the god is like the king and unlike the Platonic teacher who learns and then teaches, for the god is unmoved though he moves all. 4) And the god is aware that if he discloses himself as unequal to the maid he may provoke the inclosing reserve of a secret sorrow that destroys happy love. 5) Therefore, since man is the object of God's love, the god wants to be his teacher and the god's concern is to bring about equality and understanding in a moment that is temporally significant. 6) The god could use the Platonic method of ascent and lift up lowly man and let him forget his lowliness, but such deceit would further concretize the non-being of self-deceit. 7) The god could use the Platonic method of the glorious apparition and let humble man forget himself in adoration of the god's glory, but again this would permit self-deceit. 8) So only by his descent in which the god becomes a suffering servant can he bring about the equality and understanding of true happy love. So we should be happy on this earth even though we are suffering servants for only happy love shows through its joy that we truly do love. Plato in having the soul ascend the ladder of love does have a happy love, but he does not love the humble maiden in her lowliness and in her body. All the values of the body and the singularity of the beloved are transcended by the lover. But the God-man gets beyond the erotic paradox to the paradox of *agape* which retains in repetition the loveliness of the humble maiden and her body and all her singularity which is the object of the humble God-man's love.

II.4.4 By Preserving the Typhonic Paradox in the Incarnation

The lover as a mix of opposites reveals the complexity of each single individual and Socrates is aware of this when he loves. 1) Socrates who tried his best to know himself and who has been eulogized for centuries as the person who knew man best still had to ask himself—am I a more curious monster than Typhon or a friendlier and simpler being, sharing something divine? 2) The paradox is the passion of thought, and the thinker without the paradox is like a lover without passion. 3) As Socrates asks if he is monstrous or divine he beholds the gentle and assumes it is divine, but do we not here encounter the most terrible spiritual trials and is it ever possible to be finished with all these trials and suffering? 4) If I experience the terrible and the monstrous within myself how could I suppose the existence of the god and trust in him? With his physio-teleological proof Socrates constantly presupposes that the god exists, and on this presupposition he seeks to infuse nature with the idea of fitness and purposiveness. 6) Against this Socratic assumption which idealizes nature Climacus poses the moment when one leaps into trust in the god and in one's own paradoxical being. 7) This leap by which one lets go of reason since one knows of the frontier of the unknown is made possible by the god. 8) Thus the paradox becomes even more terrible for it is revealed as the consciousness of our sin. So even though Socrates is a skeptic he makes dogmatic assumptions that the god is kind and gentle and that there is a monster like Typhon who is connected with all evil in a way that is analogous to the god being connected with all good. However, when I meet the God-man, I see that the very god suffers and is afflicted by the terrible and I see that I with my free decisions sin or that I am fleeing the god and it is not as if I can blame my sin on a monster like Typhon who in the *Phaedrus* is depicted as the Gnostic source of all our suffering.

II.4.5 Preserving the Absolute Paradox in the Incarnation

1) The Typhonic paradox (am I a more curious monster than Typhon or a friendlier and simpler being, sharing something divine?) involves the absolute paradox (How can I know the unknown god?) 2) If a human being is to come to know something about the unknown god, he must first come to know that the god is different from himself, absolutely different. 3) I cannot know the absolutely different god by proving his existence for I never reason to existence, but I reason from existence and thus do not prove that a criminal exists, but that the accused is a criminal.
4) Napolean's existence explains his works, but these works do not demonstrate his existence unless I have already in advance interpreted the word 'his' in such a way as to have assumed that he exists. 5) However, between the god and his works there is an absolute relation. God is not a name but a concept, and perhaps because of that his essence does involve his existence.
6) God's works, therefore, only the god can do. Quite correct. But, then, what are the god's works? The works from which I want to demonstrate his existence do not immediately and directly exist, not at all. 7) Only if I interpret events ideally can I say they are the god's works and then trusting in my ideal interpretation I must disregard all objections to such an ideal interpretation. 8) It is only when I let go of a proof that I indirectly and by way of a leap make my contribution to demonstrating the god's existence, as one lets go of the Cartesian dolls who then stand on their heads. In wrestling with the universal Abraham and Job could have taken offence at God because he seemed absurd and unjust. But they continued to trust and thereby became justified exceptions. They doubted in the face of the complex paradox but in their doubt they chose to trust instead of to be scandalized at the absurdity of God. Their paradoxical faith gave them anxiety and tranquility at once.

II.4.6 By Not Taking Offense at the Paradox in the Incarnation

For Kierkegaard our decisions as moments of truth are significant because they are either a leap into sin or a leap into faith and we make the leap of sin by taking offense at the absurd complexity of the paradox when before it we get trapped in anxiety without tranquility and despair. As Kierkegaard looks into the paradox he examines taking offense. 1) If the paradox and the understanding mutually understand their difference, then the encounter is a happy one, but it is possible for the understanding to be offended by or take offense at the paradox. 2) All offense is a suffering even if it is an active suffering and thus the discovery of the offense does not belong to the understanding but to the paradox. 3) Although the offense sounds from somewhere, indeed from the opposite corner, it is the paradox that resounds it, and this is indeed an acoustical illusion. 4) Offense is an erroneous accounting just as someone caricaturing another person does not originate anything himself but only copies the other in the wrong way. 5) The more deeply the expression of offense is couched in passion (acting or suffering) the more manifest is the extent to which the offence is indebted to the paradox. 6) All offense is in its essence a misunderstanding of the moment, since it is indeed offense at the paradox, and the paradox is in turn the moment. 7) From the Platonic point of view the moment of decision is foolishness and the offense remains outside the paradox. 8) But in Christianity there is such a bond between the moment and the paradox that the moment will be a fall into the snare of sin or a leap over the scandalon through faith. Thus Kierkegaard argues that Socrates is the greatest of philosophers but he and other natural thinkers tend to make things ordinary and trivial by not believing in freedom and the leap over the chasm of non-being. That something comes out of nothing is a wonder beyond the power of natural philosophy and the incarnation is such a wonder.

II.4.7 By Loving His Platonic Readers as More Important

How the truly new happens as a gift from the other that is freely received is the whole point of Kierkegaard's analysis and it brings him to analyze how the immediate followers of the God-man become believers in him. 1) Can an historical point of departure be given for an eternal consciousness? How can such a point of departure be of more than historical interest? Can an eternal happiness be built on historical knowledge? 2) The happy passion that allows the understanding and the paradox happily to encounter each other in the moment is faith. 3) Faith is made possible when the paradox as an historical event intends to interest the contemporary follower otherwise than merely historically, intends to be the condition for his eternal happiness. 4) If the paradox does not provide the condition, then the learner is in possession of it. But if he is in possession of the condition, then he is himself the truth, and the moment is only the moment of occasion. 5) Historians may know the historical but unless they see the paradox as uniting the contraries they do not have faith in the eternalizing of the historical and the historicizing of the eternal. 6) The follower is in faith related to that teacher in such a way that he is eternally occupied with his historical existence: he does not merely know either the historical or the eternal. 7) The object of the faith is not the teaching by the teacher who to give the condition must be God and to put the learner in possession of it must be man. 8) Faith is just as paradoxical as the paradox and is the wonder that the eternal condition is given in time. So Kierkegaard is a follower of the paradoxical God-man and through his pseudonym, Johannis Climacus, he goes out to Platonists in lowly humble praise of Plato who is the older brother. Plato beautifully described erotic inspiration in its enthusiasm and Divine Madness which Kierkegaard experienced with Regina. But Plato needs to see the whole paradoxical truth of eternal values plus temporal values which the God-man reveals by his incarnation.

II.4.8 Plato's Transition from The Symposium to The Phaedrus

Plato's student Aristotle brought Plato a long way toward appreciating the body and the temporal which Plato left behind on the climb up the ladder of love toward absolute and eternal Beauty. Aristotle argued that the forms have to be mixed in things for them to exist and Plato being open to this argument abandoned Middle Platonism and thus in the *Phaedrus* thought of the beautiful beloved as having a share in absolute Beauty itself. So an analysis of following the God-man in the eternal-temporal paradox involves considering the paradox of temporality or the temporality of the paradox. 1) Has the possible by having become actual become more necessary than it was? Or is the past more necessary than the future? 2) *Kinesis* (coming into existence) is distinct from *alloiosis* (a change within existence) and the non-being in *kinesis* that is abandoned by that which comes into existence would remain unchanged in its coming into existence. 3) A being that nevertheless is a non-being is possibility and a being that is being is indeed actual being and *kinesis* is the transition from possibility to actuality. 4) The actual is no more necessary than the possible for the necessary is absolutely different from both and all *kinesis* occurs in freedom and not by way of necessity. 5) *Kinesis* is historical and as coming into existence it can contain within itself a redoubling, that is, a possibility of coming into existence within its own coming into existence. 6) The past is no more necessary than the future for, by having occurred, it demonstrated that it was not necessary. 7) The past does not become necessary through apprehension of it for knowledge of the present or of the future or of the past does not confer necessity upon it. 8) We can only believe in *kinesis* because of the double uncertainty of the nothingness of its non-being and of its annihilated possibility which is the annihilation of every other possibility. Aristotle prepared the way for this.

II.4.9 *That They Might Love the God-Man as More Important*

Kierkegaard is called to witness to his generation about the God-man but he can only be an occasion or fishing fly that the God-man can use in giving the condition for the truth and the truth which the recipient can freely decide for or against. 1) Is the historical distance which allows for greater objective certainty an advantage for the faith of later followers? 2) Since faith is not a matter of knowledge but of decision the first generation after the event has only the relative advantage of being closer to the jolt of the paradox. 3) The latest generation is a long way from the jolt but it can romantically urge the probability proof in support of the improbable. 4) The first generation has the advantage of difficultly appropriating the difficult; the latest generation has the advantage of an ease which can give rise to a terror. 5) The report of contemporaries becomes the occasion for everyone coming later to become a follower by believing in neither a mere historical fact nor an eternal fact but in the fact of the absolute paradox. 6) The contemporary can be an occasion for someone who comes later by expressing his belief and by warning that it is folly to the understanding and an offense to the human heart. 7) Since the contemporary can only supply an occasion and the god must give the condition for the truth there is no follower at second hand for any disciple is an immediate disciple. 8) The faith that celebrates triumphantly ahead is ludicrous for one should never celebrate triumphantly ahead of time, what is, never in time. Thus, Kierkegaard argues that the skepticism of Socrates if it is held fast to, even by Plato, does not deceive itself with solutions to the paradox. I can thus prepare the way for faith, for faith and truth or the moment of truth are not matters of knowledge but of passion before objective uncertainty as the *Postscript* shows. John the Climber thus shows how climbers can be saved by the God-man.

II.5 Reconciling the God-Man and Hegel

II.5.1 In the Truth of the Existential Dialectic

Kierkegaard, a follower of the God-man, is like the prodigal son in relation to the older brother, Hegel, who with his dialectic sought to think through the history of love and personal growth in an objective way which saw truth as belonging to the whole. Hegel's idealism is quite like Plato's in that history moves as it were up the dialectical staircase in which the thesis of the first stair such as Platonism is negated by the antithesis of the next stair of Aristotelianism and then there is the synthesis in Neo-Platonism which in turn becomes a thesis that is further negated so that the ascent up the staircase of truth is like the ascent up the ladder of love and up out of the Platonic cave to the absolute whole truth. In Hegel's *Philosophy of Right* when he treats the ethical life beginning in the family and then moving to civil society and then the state he argues that: "The family, as the immediate substantiality of mind, is specifically characterized by love which is the mind's feeling of unity."[9] The affection of this familial love begins in the marriage of two persons and their free consent to become one person. So in his dialectic Hegel does not treat the single person as an individual and yet relational. Hegel's dialectic makes the great contribution of seeing persons as relational but he only treats personhood in general and does not get down to single individual persons. In seeing truth only in the whole development of the person in general, Hegel does not stay with skepticism as did Socrates. The heart of Climacus' *Postscript* in which he moves from Hegel's objective dialectic to the existential dialectic is thus the new definition of truth as "objective uncertainty held fast in the appropriation process of the most passionate inwardness." This truth is a new kind of passion for Kierkegaard.

II.5.2 In the Objective Uncertainty of the Historical Process

Hegel did think that in a man of genius one of the strongest passions is the passion for truth and Hegel always pursued truth. But Kierkegaard as a genius of creative illness did not want to give the human a divine power which could see the whole. In his definition of truth Kierkegaard stresses that we humans can never acquire objective certainty for certainty is a firm adherence of the mind to an idea without any doubt or any fear of error. However, as Socrates pointed out we can never connect all the dots. There is so much complexity in anything because of its unlimited relationality which Hegel has revealed that it always exceeds any concept or notion which we might try to form about it. Hegel works with the leap as a quantitative build-up within the historical process which is like a caterpillar, becoming a pupa becoming a butterfly but he does not have the qualitative leap. Hegel can treat mankind's movement from the aesthetic basement to the ethical first floor and then the quantitative leap up to the religious second floor, but the religiousness B of the leap back to living on all floors at once in imitation of the God-man Hegel with his objectively certain truth does not consider. That is because he only treats the person in general as an abstraction and does not think through the concrete single individual in the passionate inwardness of his objective uncertainty. The whole point of Kierkegaard's philosophy is to get a subjective certainty and that is why the *Postscript* concerns itself with the subjective thinker who like a prodigal son offends the elder brother by trusting in a world of loving mercy that knows that what the world of strict justice thinks is quite unfair. Kierkegaard's world of subjective certainty trusts that even the workers who arrive at the job at the last hour might be paid even as much as the one who worked all day long out of a duty that is fulfilled but takes offence at loving mercy.

II.5.3 In Holding Fast to the Uncertainty of the Single Individual

In order to make a case for subjective rather than objective truth Kierkegaard appeals to Lessing in saying that: "If God had all truth in his right hand and the striving after it in his left hand I would choose the left hand."[10] The task of becoming subjectively true to ourselves, God and each other is a life-long task and we should not be through with it until it is through with us. There is not a simple leap into an authentic relating for each single individual but rather the leap is always a leaping that to be true must hold fast to objective uncertainty that there might be instead the subjective certainty of following the God-man. Following Lessing Climacus argues that becoming a subjective individual is the highest task assigned to every human being. The point of the double movement leaping is to humble oneself under the divine and to serve the human and Climacus goes to Lessing who knows the distinction between speculation by itself and faith which can use speculation in service of others. Climacus expresses his gratitude to Lessing and works with four theses that help make the task of subjectivity clear.

The first thesis is that: "The subjective existing thinker is aware of the dialectic of communication."[11] This gets right to the core of Kierkegaard's entire strategy by which the prodigal can reconcile with the elder brother by deceiving the elder brother out of his self-deceit into the truth by indirect communication. All the writing of the pseudonyms is done for this purpose. So Kierkegaard is writing to Hegelians to deceive them out of their self-deceit and into the truth and we might consider how this worked with Heidegger and Sartre and Derrida and Deleuze and the many who have come to take Kierkegaard so earnestly. How did Kierkegaard succeed by using the dialectic of communication?

II.5.4 By Living in Fragments instead of the System

A system is held together by the laws of a logical necessity. Those laws can be intuited and agreed upon by everyone in their objectivity, but for the single individual person: "Only the truth that builds up is truth for you." We can easily be fragmented in many ways and subjective truth builds up a unity within the person. In Hegel's system history is a logical process that moves by means of negations that are also mediations. The thesis is negated by an antithesis which is a means toward a synthesis that on the stairway to truth goes beyond both prior stages. However, as Climacus has Lessing point out: "In his existence relation to the truth, the existing subjective thinker is just as negative as positive, has just as much of the comic as he essentially has pathos, and is continually in a process of becoming, that is striving."[12] So existential truth has to do with the striving after it that we might be built up into a unity of our fragmented relations according to a logic of mixed opposites so that we do not go through negativity to get to positivity but we are negative and positive at the same time just as Jesus was God and man at the same time and just as David was a great sinner and a great saint at the same time and just as Woody Allen, for example is both comic and tragic at the very same moment. So Kierkegaard has Climacus write a book on *Fragments* and then an *Unscientific Postscript* to those *Fragments* in order to communicate with his fragmented readers that they might appreciate the fragmented nature of their lives, and yet, by doing that build up a unity within themselves. We can be narcissistic aesthetes, or ethical altruists or religious deists, but there is something of the aesthetic in each of these unless we follow the God-man in living on all floors of our house at once insofar as we build up our interior dwelling place in a unified fashion.

II.5.5 In the Appropriation Process of a Postscript

The key word in Kierkegaard's philosophy of love and personal growth and the key word in this definition of truth is "appropriation." How do I become and make my own whatever comes my way? Kierkegaard's writings up to this point have themselves been systematic even though they have been treating live theory or the existential, postmodern dialectic of the double movement leap of a loving growth in which I follow the God-man in loving faith. Kierkegaard writes that Hegel builds up a great palace of thought but then goes out in the backyard and lives in the dog house. If Kierkegaard only wrote the writings we have been discussing he too would be living in the systematic house we have been explicating in terms of basement, first floor and second floor and then with the qualitative leap living on all floors at once. But each of Kierkegaard's existentially systematic works are accompanied by *Upbuilding Discourses* that have to do with his own appropriation of himself through all his writings. Each of his pseudonymous writings as aesthetic-ethical have religious-ethical counterparts which might best be thought of as prayers in which I am always reminded that to know the self is to know that I am capable of nothing by myself. They constantly bring out that to need God is my highest perfection. Lessing argued that "contingent historical truths can never become a demonstration of eternal truths of reason so that the transition whereby one will build up an eternal truth on historical reports is a leap."[13] Kierkegaard's *Upbuilding Discourses* work with building up eternal truths out of whatever happens to come my way in praise, repentance, thanksgiving and petition. This is why the strategy of reconciling love is one of always praising loving even if I cannot marry Regina and even if my brothers are dying and my father is suffering greatly and then I must appropriate even my dear father's death.

II.5.6 In the Inwardness of a Double Movement Leap

Kierkegaard's definition of truth as faith stresses the inwardness of the appropriation or upbuilding process for truth can be objective and outward as our minds conform to things or as ideas cohere together, but subjective truth has to do with putting into practice the truths that one works out and professes. Kierkegaard writes his first *Edifying Discourse* on a passage from Luther's criticized epistle, the Letter of James: "Every good and every perfect gift is from above and comes down from the father of Light, with whom there is no change or shadow of variation" (1:17). This *Discourse* is a secret love letter to Regina, who was the good and perfect gift for Kierkegaard and its inwardness has to do with grieving in its isolation, anger, self-pity, depression, and finally in acceptance. He knew that Regina read the *Discourse* and that it had the utmost passionate inwardness for her as well as for himself because it let her know that he still loved her as his dearest love who must live, alas, apart from him. She was the inspiration for his work of constant creative genius and all of his writing while being his gift to her was also her gift to him insofar as she opened for him the light from above. So what are these good and perfect gifts that Regina gives to him and that he hopes to be giving to her? Everything created by God is good if it is received with thankfulness and especially with praise. Even punishment can be a gift if it is received with thanksgiving. As Kierkegaard appropriates his life and all that comes his way he does it in prayer and thus all his writing is a praying. For Kierkegaard sees God in both the giver and the gift and the condition for receiving the gift for God gives not only gifts but most of all as the God who is love he gives himself with them. So in the depths of his inwardness Kierkegaard's truth sees that loving reconciliation is a receiving of God as gift from each other.

II.5.7 Loving Hegel as More Important with Climacus

Kierkegaard's definition of truth as becoming himself in the most passionate inwardness has to do with the passion of suffering. Climacus writes, "Whereas esthetic existence is essentially enjoyment and ethical existence is essentially struggle and victory, religious existence is suffering, and not as a transient element but as a continual accompaniment" (289). So what Kierkegaard did was to give up Regina whom he loved with all his heart in order that he might instead be with the likes of the Hegelians. He was called as one of three or four in a generation to witness to the God-man by following the God-man as a suffering servant. When he broke the engagement by choosing to be a witness instead of marrying Regina there was the suffering of loss, sorrow, and disappointment for both of them over Kierkegaard's choice for celibacy. Kierkegaard's strategy for loving in the best way imaginable or for a reconciling love of the most passionate inwardness brought him to writing his authorship and to writing the *Postscript* under the name of Climacus who is a kind of Hegelian climber who makes the movement up the stairway. Just as time for some is money so time for Kierkegaard is love and Kierkegaard spent a vast amount of his time or love with Hegel and the Hegelians so that Hegel is more important for him than himself in that he gave up his dear love, Regina, in order to spend his time thinking and writing in response to the great systematic theology and philosophy of Hegel's history. Climacus and the other pseudonyms are writings a kind of comprehensive system that has to do with archaeology, genealogy ecclesiology and eschatology even though they do not use that kind of technical language and all of this opens the system to being even more comprehensive than the Hegelian system. Besides this great subjective system there are the *Upbuilding Discourses* that speak directly to the single individual readers.

II.5.8 Hegel's History of Love and Personhood

Kierkegaard in following the God-man is like the prodigal son who left his father's house and got involved in self-destruction. Then, the good and perfect gift, Regina, was given to him and he was caught by God's love as if she were a fishing fly and then he became even more prodigal by breaking the engagement with her. In his authorship this prodigal who left Hegel, the older brother, comes back to him when he comes back to the father and loves Hegel also as more important than himself with a praising of love as God. What is it that this suffering servant so genuinely loves in Hegel? It is Hegel's dialectical history of love and personhood that is really so loveable that Hegel is picked out with Socrates, Abraham, Job, and Plato as the older brothers to be so loved by the prodigal. In order to best witness to love Kierkegaard has to work out his strategy of reconciliation with these key pivotal figures. Kierkegaard through the climber loves Hegel in his thinking in two ways for Hegel's thinking becomes Kierkegaard's thinking in the existential dialectic of climbing up from the basement to the first floor and then to the second floor just as Hegel would climb up. That is the first way that the prodigal loves Hegel, but then when as Anti Climacus he descends back down and keeps living in the whole house he is reloving in repetition each Hegelian stage. To understand how Jesus and his followers like Kierkegaard love all the older brothers like the Jews and all older cultures as more important by being their suffering servants we might consider how Sartre appropriated Hegel through Kierkegaard with his formula: "I am what I am not. And I am not what I am." All through modernity there was the exclusivist logic which said: "I Calvin and not Luther." "I Hobbes and not Descartes." But in following Hegel Kierkegaard says: "I am the Hegel that I am not." Just as Aquinas would say: "I am the Aristotle, the Augustine, the Boethius, the Avicenna, the Maimonides that I am not."

II.5.9 Loving the God-Man in the Most Passionate Inwardness

The strategy of Kierkegaard's existential dialectic which goes to Hegel with highest praise for his dialectic of the relational person which makes clear that "I am what I am not. And I am not what I am." seeks to win over all Hegelians and all humankind to loving and following the God-man who is the paradigm person for this love. In the love which is God, the Father loves the Son as the one whom he is not and as not the one who he is. The love between the Father and the Son which is the Holy Spirit is not the Father alone and is not the Son alone and yet all three are one in God. The person as relational has been dialectically worked out by Hegel and the paradox of the God-man is the core and seed of his dialectic. But Hegel only thinks objectively of the relational person and does not show how the religious ethical task calls persons to Christian love. Kierkegaard with his subjective systematic authorship as written by the pseudonyms comprehensively explains *agape* and personhood as revealed by the God-man in the incarnation and as revealing the trinity of persons in God as the basis of personhood for humans in their equal worth and yet also in their differentiated uniqueness. In his *Upbuilding Discourses* he no longer communicates indirectly with his reader but rather directly in working together to appropriate and make their own all the relations that come their way in their joy, in their sorrow and also in their glory. It is Kierkegaard's intent that Hegelians and all humans when they read his writings will be led out of the dog house of self-deceit and come to live in the palace of dialectical thinking which Hegel in the eyes of Kierkegaard so brilliantly explicated but objectively. Hegelians when they read Hegel through the authorship of Kierkegaard hopefully will come to appreciate Kierkegaard's existential dialectic of the single individual person in all of his or her unlimited relationships and also come to appreciate the task of the gift of the incarnation to build up loving personal relations.

II.6 Reconciling the God-Man and Adam and Eve

II.6.1 Adam and Eve's Leap out of Anxiety into Original Sin

In working out an understanding of Kierkegaard's theory and practice of love and personal growth we have treated his definition of love as reconciliation and his definitions of person, repetition, paradox and truth as faith and now we must fit in his definition of sin. If we contrast the qualitative leaps of faith and of sin and see how they interact we will much better understand true faith as holding fast to objective uncertainty in the most passionate inwardness. Sin for Kierkegaard has the three elements of anxiety, despair, and taking offense, and he wrote a book on each: *The Concept of Anxiety* by the Watchman of Copenhagen on anxiety, *Sickness unto Death* by Anti-Climacus on despair, and *Training In Christianity* also by Anti-Climacus on taking offense. So now we must begin examining his definition of sin as: "The qualitative leap into despair by taking offense because of anxiety." so that we can better understand the truth faith of true love and of true personal growth. Anxiety is a being threatened by something indefinite as was Abraham when he was asked to sacrifice his son, Isaac, in fear and trembling. Adam and Eve are anxious about the prohibition not to eat of the fruit of the tree of the knowledge of good and of evil and they are anxious about the threats of punishment concerning death and suffering which are possibilities that they do not yet really understand. So the early Augustine's theory in *De Libero Arbitrio* of how we sin is not completely correct because he argues that we need to have knowledge, freedom and consent before we can responsibly choose between good or evil, but Adam and Eve did not yet know of them. Milton's modern theory of their fall into sin does not work either because in *Paradise Lost* they are supposed to know the distinction between good and evil by knowing the story of the fallen angels. Because of the Anti-Biblical shortcoming of both Augustine's ancient theory and Milton's modern theory that posit knowledge before sin Kierkegaard explains sin in his postmodern way in terms of anxiety.

II.6.2 Hereditary Sin's Quantitative Build-up of Anxiety

Eve was more anxious than Adam because she had to think about not only the prohibition and the punishment but also because she was derived from Adam's rib she felt the threat of the unknown with more fragility and thus focused more on the fruit of the tree. She wanted to get rid of her anxiety and be like God in knowing good and evil and so her pride and prejudice lured her into sin. She ate the fruit of the tree of the knowledge of good and of evil and then enticed Adam to do the same and then when God spoke to them they became more anxious about sex and history or what they had done in the past as they began to know of these things. So after their fall or leap out of innocence into sin they now had five reasons for anxiety: 1) the prohibition 2) the penalty 3) their derived fragility 4) sexuality and 5) their history or past and this quantitative build-up of anxiety was the state of sinfulness that would be passed on to any of their offspring for it became programmed into them like any habit that we inherit from the tainted family tree. Each actual sin of Eve or Adam or any of their children is a qualitative leap into our anxiety which faith makes possible. If we do not have faith or make the leap of faith we cannot sin or take offence at God for we are threefold somatic, psychic and pneumatic persons and if we are only concerned with the body or even the ethics of the reflective soul we cannot yet sin against God but we can only be offensive to ourselves and to others. We can be anxious about our bodies and we can be anxious about our souls as we relate to ourselves in reflection, but anxiety that is religious or that we think might offend God is rooted in our being spirit and being more than only body or mind. So before we make the qualitative leap of believing in the God-man and living on all floors of the house at once we are not really free to make the qualitative leap of sin and we will only offend ourselves or another human or God but not take offense in anxiety.

II.6.3 Anxiety and the Leap of Faith into Actual Sins

In Kierkegaard's theological philosophy of anxiety there is
the distinction between the quantitative build-up of anxiety
and the qualitative leap into anxiety which is also the distinction
between the state of sin and the events of actual new sins.
Eve began with the threefold anxiety of being threatened by
the mystery of the prohibition, the penalty and her derived fragility.
Then she took offence at God and disobeyed and ate the fruit
and began to learn about good and evil, about the pain of
childbearing and about the death of her child, Abel, and the
state of her anxiety built up as she became anxious about
sexuality and the threatening events of remembered history.
This quantitative build-up of anxiety is the result of her sin
and it is inherited by her offspring and inclines them to also sin.
As sin gets programmed into Adam and Eve and their offspring
in the form of a quantitative build-up of anxiety it is all the more
difficult not to keep falling into sin and even to go mad.
Kierkegaard defines madness or demonic anxiety before the good
as an inclosing reserve that unfreely discloses itself all of a sudden
out of boredom.[14] We have the choice to live freely on all three
floors of our house at once or to enclose ourselves on one floor only.
If we only live in the aesthetic basement, or only on the ethical
first floor, or only on the religious second floor we will become
bored because that kind of limited existence is not enough
for a somatic, psychic, pneumatic person who is made for all.
Kierkegaard, the prodigal and Cain wanted to live only in the basement
and to get rid of all ethical and religious pressure, but fleeing
anxiety only increases it as Adam and Eve found out.
So how can you live anxiously in repose is the big question?

II.6.4 Anxious Leaping into the Inclosing Reserve or Repose

The more we grow as persons or the more we appropriate all that comes our way the more anxious we become or the more threatened we are by all kinds of complexity and possibility. In order to try to escape anxiety we might try to limit the pressure by focusing upon only certain values and disregarding others. Like the prodigal and Cain and Kierkegaard we might leave our father's house and all his rules and live only in the basement of our aesthetic inclination and not worry about consequences. We might lock ourselves up in the inclosing reserve of only our physical concerns and not worry about any psychic order. On the other hand we might grow out of the world of childish impulses and with the likes of Job and Judge William concern ourselves seriously with the good that we should do and with the evil that we should avoid as earnestly ethical. However, even if we are as good as was Job in inclosing ourselves on the first floor of the ethical there is anxiety. To escape the anxiety that haunted Job we might go to the religious second floor and enclose ourselves there by living out the neither-nor against both the aesthetic and ethical. In this realm of spirit, however, it is possible to go mad with anxiety by moving from: "The Lord has given and the Lord has taken away; blessed be the name of the Lord!" to "Let me get God in a court of Law and prove him wrong!" We can go into the inclosing reserve and unfreely disclose ourselves all of a sudden out of boredom. The whole point of life according to Kierkegaard is to grow through various levels of anxiety by learning to have repose in anxiety which is the leap of faith and of loving growth. When something very frustrating and anxiety-causing comes our way if we can reposition ourselves in loving faith and receive it with graceful joy then we will live in true love.

II.6.5 That Discloses Itself All of a Sudden or is Open to Disclosure

Kierkegaard thinks that whoever has learned to be anxious
in the right way has learned the ultimate for each person needs
to learn how to be anxious in order that he may not perish
either by never having been in anxiety or by succumbing in anxiety.
The whole point is to grow more and more in tranquility and repose
by growing in anxiety for the most passionate inwardness has
to do with transforming anxiety, pain, shame, dying and death
into a glorious love, joy, peace, patience, kindness and gentleness.
We should grow in repose through anxiety, without succumbing to it.
So how do we succumb to anxiety or avoid that succumbing?
Kierkegaard tells us we succumb by leaping out of anxiety into
the inclosing reserve of one of the three floors by ignoring the others.
As we are enclosed we begin to disclose ourselves all of a sudden
in a kind of a leap such as when a cat leaps upon a mouse.
On all the floors of our house we live in freedom but when we
limit our freedom in the inclosing reserve we then unfreely
disclose ourselves in a sudden leap with some unexpected outburst.
We succumb to anxiety which we try to flee in a self deceit when
we unfreely disclose ourselves as caught in that very anxiety.
The prodigal flees his home and encloses himself in his new
wished for aesthetic life without any rules and regulations whose
pressure make him feel that he just does not want them anymore.
But he is ambivalent for once he is out on his own the consequences
hit him and he is more anxious than before and he unfreely
wants to get back home and he discloses his great discomfort.
He is beginning to go mad and blurt out things that are contrary to
what he thought when he enclosed himself in the aesthetic.
Mad people can be of different types with bodily madness such
as with brain injury, or psychic madness such as with phobias
or with a spiritual madness when they are psychotic or neurotic.
This pneumatic madness expresses itself in out of control acts.

II.6.6 Out of Boredom or in Faith's Most Passionate Inwardness

So Kierkegaard explains how we succumb and why we succumb to anxiety for its pressure tempts us to go into the inclosing reserve and the reason why we go mad or succumb is because of boredom. An aesthete is always bored but never boring while the ethical person is never bored but always boring. Aesthetes are especially bored by moralizers and they seek fulfillment by bracketing out duties. Pure moralists are bored with religion and seek morality within the limits of reason alone. Religious devotees of infinite resignation are bored by impulsive aesthetes and moralities that let you down so they live in the pure Being, pure Bliss, pure Consciousness of being one with the One beyond the travails of body, mind or spirit. However, in the negativity of their not this and not that they reveal a mad negativity toward all differences as they seek only unity. If we go up to the second floor of our house and abide only there we will unfreely disclose ourselves out of boredom as we deny everything about the basement and everything about the first floor. These very denials of infinite resignation are unfreely disclosed outbursts which arise from thinking of body or mind or spirit as an absolute that can totally satisfy us apart from one another. But if we have faith in the God-man we will be able to get beyond any kind of boredom and self-deceit by absolutely loving the absolute and relatively loving the relative by living on all floors of our house without any inclosing anxious reserve. The God-man gives us the grace to be reposed in anxiety by his incarnation that can let everyday be Christmas, especially Good Friday because of Easter Sunday. Anything less will bore us and drive us mad because we are made for the infinite and the finite cannot satisfy us and once we live with the infinite then every finite person, place and thing is so lovely in its dearest freshness deep down things that we can sing *Yes* and *Amen* for all of existence in a love beyond any anxiety.

II.6.7 Loving Adam and Eve as More Important in Atonement

So we the children of Adam and Eve are born with the hereditary sin of our first parents because as a result of their loss of innocence we are even more anxious than they were before they succumbed to sin. As Kierkegaard will explain in *Sickness Unto Death* when we succumb to anxiety we fall into various stages of despair just as there are various stages of anxiety which can guide us to fulfillment if we receive a repose from the God-man who gives us saving faith. In his incarnation when God became man atonement for sin began as we were shown the worth of both the divine and the flesh. In the incarnation the God made the qualitative leap into the flesh so we can imitate him and learn to find repose in our anxiety and thereby be educated by anxiety rather than succumb to it. So God became man because he loved Adam, Eve and their offspring even more than himself and even went so far as to become a suffering servant that he might love us and help us to have the repose of faith that can save us from our anxiety. Dreadful evil haunts every person and imposes itself upon us right through our life as we go step by step toward our death. The God-man by his birth, life, death, resurrection and ascension taught us how to reposition ourselves in a much larger universe of love so that we can take any impositions and through repose become composed in a new composition of all life's complexities. The older theodicies that sought to justify evil all argued that God writes straight with crooked lines but Kierkegaard's new theodicy of following the God-man in suffering love is different. Objective thinking according to Kierkegaard cannot give us a fulfilling approach to the problem of evil that makes us so anxious. But the example of the God-man suffering for us out of love does grace us with a gift so that we can believe that all of our suffering and all of the suffering of all flesh is joined with God's suffering and makes up what is lacking in his suffering.

II.6.8 Anxiety through Faith is Absolutely Educative

The children of Adam and Eve have found wonderful ways to escape anxiety and build up a repose that is guaranteed in any situation. We can with our own efforts find repose in any sort of actual suffering as have the great mystics of Hindu, Buddhist and Taoist traditions. In modern mass society pain management can even be addictive. But Hegel began to see something else in a faith beyond our efforts. He thought of faith as the inner certainty that anticipates infinity. This has to do with the possibility of anxiety rather than actuality. Possibility can threaten us infinitely more than the worst actuality. If a person should be without anxiety Kierkegaard thinks he would be spiritless by going beyond the pneumatic or spirit as would the mystic or by not getting there as might the person with only actual bodily or actual psychic afflictions to trouble him. As the children of Adam and Eve meet with the God-man there is plenty of the beautiful, good and true that the God-man can love. He can love the family of man not only by stepping back and letting them be free and by stepping down as their suffering servant but he can love us as more important because we are so loveable. However, that the reconciliation between Adam and Eve and the younger prodigal Jesus might take place it is necessary to appreciate what is new about his message concerning anxiety. The individual through anxiety can be educated into faith, for possibility if we do not defraud it somatically, psychically or pneumatically it can teach us that we cannot lift ourselves up by our own bootstraps out of all the possibility that can get us. Anxiety before countless possible evils is a great good for Kierkegaard because it can bring us to a power greater than ourselves. Only when I leap into the arms of God who has taught me how to suffer with love for others by opening his arms on the cross can I have a faith that will make sense of all suffering without trying to get rid of it by coping with it as mere actuality.

II.6.9 Loving the God-Man in Body, Soul, and Spirit

We children of Adam and Eve can be either audidacts like Buddhists who find repose in our own efforts of coping with anxious suffering or we can be theodidacts who are given repose by the God-man. According to the watchman of Copenhagen audidacts are trained by the finite anxiety before actuality and theodidacts are trained by the infinite anxiety before possibility which can give them faith. The main point of Kierkegaard's philosophy of love and personhood is that we as persons should keep growing in the appropriation process. We can stunt our growth and be finished with life before life is finished with us if because of anxiety we go into an inclosing reserve and avoid the tensions of living for the eternal and temporal at once. If we live on all three floors of our house at once and keep building it up we will be able to keep growing in body, in soul and in spirit. It is the God-man who teaches us how to do this by being the mix of the eternal, infinite God and the temporal, finite man in balance. Attaining the balancing of this composition in repose no matter what impositions come our way can happen if we love our enemy completely. The ultimate task we have been given by our master, the suffering servant, is to follow him in loving others that they might have repose. The God-man comes to teach us of love and of the sin which works against that love and we learn of both by growing through stages of anxiety even the anxiety of being sinners which educates us. We can grow as persons by loving the God-man and all others especially those who are most anxious and in most need of love. We are motivated in a twofold way to constantly grow in love by the passion to seek the pleasant and the passion to avoid pain. Adam and Eve had a passion to eat the fruit of the tree of the knowledge of good and evil and the anxiety of their passion led them out of their father's house on the ethical floor of triadic garden repose. Then because of the pain of living in the basement of negative anxiety they were pushed toward the second floor of repose.

III. St. Paul

III.4 Paul's Second Love Letter to the Corinthians

III.4.1 It Was God Who Reconciled Us

It is in this Second Letter to the Corinthians that Paul finally has his breakthrough to the actual concept and word of *reconciliation*. As a Bible Concordance shows the concept is only treated in four Pauline Epistles and it is mentioned a bit in *Second Maccabees*. Outside of these few scant passages this notion of such importance is not explicitly developed or used in any other Biblical texts. The verb in Greek is *katallaso* and the noun is *katallage* and they are translated into Latin as *reconciliare* and *reconciliatio*. In 2 Corinthians 5:16–21 Paul writes:

> From now onward, therefore, we do not judge anyone
> by the standards of the flesh.
> Even if we did once know Christ in the flesh,
> that is not how we know him now.
> And for anyone who is in Christ, there is a new creation;
> the old creation has gone, and now the new one is here.
> It is all God's work.
> *It was God who reconciled us to himself through Christ*
> *and gave us the work of handing on this reconciliation.*
> So, God in Christ was reconciling the world to himself,
> not holding men's faults against them,
> and he has entrusted to us the news that they are reconciled.
> So we are ambassadors for Christ;
> it is as though God were appealing through us,
> and the appeal that we make in Christ's name is
> to be reconciled to God.
> For our sake God made the sinless one into sin,
> so that in him we might become the goodness of God.

So the theology and philosophy of reconciliation that is flourishing in our times first had its beginning in this very passage.

III.4.2 To Himself through Christ

On its visible surface Paul's life was not one of peace, but of enmity. Before he became a Christian he had many enemies and his enmities were rooted in the irreconcilable differences of religion and politics. The Roman Empire occupied Jewish lands and Jews were divided into Zealots, Sadducees, Essenes, and Pharisees and they argued about how to live with the Romans and to be loyal to God. The enmities were very violent and Jesus was crucified and Paul was engaged in stoning Christians. Paul experienced a new solution to the problem when he beheld Stephen loving his enemies. Paul came to believe that God reconciled us to himself through Christ. Paul became a totally committed missionary for this wonderful new truth that Christ's atoning death had reconciled us to God. But, now as he tells us especially in the last three chapters of this letter he is more caught up in enmity than ever and in chapter eleven he writes of archapostles and counterfeit apostles with sarcasm. He himself has been beaten and stoned for his enmity causing teachings which to some pious Jews look like fraternizing with Rome. And yet in spite of all his past enmity and his increased enmity in his new Christian life Paul believes that enmity has been overcome. As he is plunged deeper and deeper into the insurmountable enmity of more and more violent irreconcilable differences he is given in a moment of inspiration his new motto:

> It was God who reconciled us to himself through Christ
> and gave us the work of handing on this reconciliation.
> (2 Cor 5:18)

This new notion of reconciliation to God through Christ's atonement which he spells out right here for the first time is the crystal form of Paul's understanding of *agape* and of personal liberation. Even though Paul is in constant enmity with Cephas and such archapostles and Apollos and such counterfeit apostles he still believes that deep down in spite of temporal differences they are reconciled and that was the point of the council of Jerusalem in which they spelled out their different functions within Christ's Body.

III.4.3 And Gives Us the Work

This motto of Paul:

> It was God who reconciled us to himself through Christ
> and gave us the work of handing on this reconciliation.

is the seed idea that contains the story of his life and the life of Church tradition or the work of handing on belief in reconciliation. Once we see this logic of reconciliation everything in Paul's writing makes sense in terms of God's work who first reconciled us and in terms of the work we now have in handing on this Good News. There is the work which God has done or the *ex opere operato* and the work we have been called to do or the *ex opere operantis*. God has justified us through the cross and suffering of Christ and now we are called to suffer in telling others that they are saved. Thus Paul always lives a life of prayer in which he praises and thanks God continuously for the comforting peace of reconciliation. It is Paul's gift and task to live in the presence of God where there is the grace and peace of reconciliation even if there is strife. Thus Paul always begins his letters and preaching with the same prayer: "Grace and peace to you from God our Father and the Lord Jesus Christ." Paul prays constantly as a result of this grace and for this grace. Even if there are insurmountable factions and irreconcilable differences Paul believes that there is at the same time a deeper reconciliation. This Good News can be comforting and consoling for all who suffer for they can believe that all their suffering can be united with the suffering of Christ and be their work in revealing reconciliation. This letter is the story of the glory of Christ's death and resurrection which can call forth from the sorrow of factions and differences the joy that can let Paul and each of us experience reconciliation. This letter teaches the way of alienation, hostility and reconciliation and the point is that God has forgiven us so we should forgive others. God's love lets sinners be reconciled even though they still fight and even though they remain sinners while they are justified.

III.4.4 Of Handing on This Reconciliation

It is Paul's task to hand on the Good News of reconciliation.
He keeps stressing that everyone with a cultivated and sensitive
conscience should be able to hear and understand his message.
The word "conscience" like the word "reconciliation" is not a
Biblical term except in the Pauline letters and so they are both
part of the new logic of *agape* and personhood as Paul works it out.
Paul knows there are irreconcilable differences everywhere and yet
he says that persons of conscience have no eyes for things
that are visible but only for things that are invisible and eternal.
Paul writes that:

> It is the same God that said, "Let there be light shining out of darkness,"
> who has shone in our minds to radiate the light of the knowledge
> of God's glory, the glory of the face of Christ." (2 Cor 4:6)

Paul beheld the glory of the face of Christ shining in the face of Stephen.
Glory is the manifesting of the unmanifest in its unmanifestness.
What is most visible to our eyes of the flesh is the violence of factions.
But with the eyes and ears of our conscience the face of Christ
with his forgiving love can shine out even from our own faces
as we pray for and work for and serve others knowing that
the face of Christ shines out from all of their suffering faces too.
It is only when Paul's face shines out with love as did the face
of Stephen which revealed to Paul the glory of the face of Christ
that Paul's work and words will really bring reconciliation to others.
Paul lives and operates or works in this realm of glory which
is the realm that a sensitive conscience can understand
and thus even though he becomes angry at other apostles
who do not proclaim freedom from the law he knows
that they live in the reconciliation of the first council
of Jerusalem in which they agreed to disagree and to work
together and yet against each other with purity, knowledge,
patience and kindness insofar as the medium is the message.

III.4.5 Not According to Standards of the Flesh

In order to explain his religion of *agape*, that is: his creed of *agape*, his code of *agape*, his cult of *agape* and his canon of *agape*, Paul makes a distinction between the body as *sarx* or *carnis* or flesh and the new body as soma or corpus or the corporeal Body of Christ. Paul's creed begins with the belief that at the moment of the death of Jesus his *sarx* or flesh became *soma* or corpse and at the moment of the resurrection of Christ his soma as corpse became soma as corporeal. Just as the concept of reconciliation in Christ is new with Paul so is this notion of corporeal, corporation and incorporation. We are reconciled with God and with one another because by Christ's resurrection there is a new creation, for the old fallen creation is gone. We used to judge everyone according to the standards of the flesh but now we have a new standard of the corporation or Body of Christ which we can now see because the old creation has died with Jesus. In Paul's conversion he went through this very same double process. As Saul he lived in the flesh and according to the standards of the flesh. But he heard the call: "Saul, Saul, why do you persecute me?" He was persecuting Stephen, a member of the corporeal Body of Christ. Then Saul was knocked off his horse and blinded in a death of the old Saul and he was made to see and was baptized and he ate a meal with other members of Christ's new corporation and he was incorporated into the Body of Christ in which we all are reconciled in a new creation. Paul heard the Good News of God's work through Christ of atonement, of forgiveness and of reconciliation and with Ananias and the others in the soma Body of Christ he believed in the death and resurrection. He began to cultivate that seed of the corporation with them in the cult of baptism and the Lord's Supper as he explained this to the Corinthians in his first letter. And with the death of the flesh the old law code died also and now we are taken into a new law of love or *agape* with the gifts and fruits of the Holy Spirit of the risen Lord Jesus who guides Paul to the new canon.

III.4.6 And Not in Accord with Christ in the Flesh

This very letter of Paul that he is working out under the inspiration of the Holy Spirit and that was given him at the time of his conversion is the beginning of the new covenant written in the Body of Christ. The law was written on tablets of stone, but we have been freed from the law by the death of Christ's flesh so that now the law of *agape* is in his heart and in ours if we die and rise from the dead as did Paul at his conversion and baptism. Christ came into the flesh at the incarnation and he lived in the *sarx* or flesh by being subject to the law of the flesh in that he must suffer and die so that Paul writes:

> For our sake God made the sinless one into sin,
> so that in him we might become the goodness of God. (5:21)

To be in the flesh is to be subjected to suffering and death which are the result of sin and living according to the flesh by sinning. Christ was in the flesh but he never judged anyone according to the flesh, or acted according to the flesh. By the incarnation of God's Son into the *carnis* of the flesh we were already becoming the goodness of God and we knew the goodness of God by knowing of Christ in the flesh. But that we might fully become the goodness of God Christ had to die in the flesh and become a corpse. He was the flesh of the incarnation and the corpse of the crucifixion. By becoming flesh and by becoming corpse God in Christ no longer held the faults of humans against them. But there was still not reconciliation which came with the resurrection when the corpse became the corporation of which we are all members. That was the moment of reconciliation even though humans still have to hear of it to believe it and accept it in Baptism by which Paul turned away from Saul and his life in the flesh in which he judged according to the flesh. Paul calls each of us to be like himself and move from living in and according to the flesh, to becoming a corpse and thirdly a resurrected member of Christ's corporation.

III.4.7(a) But We Have Been Reconciled (Part One)

With this discussion of being in the flesh and not being in the flesh and of living according to the standard of the flesh or another standard we are taken into Paul's anthropology or theory of the human person. He has worked all of this out with a precise new vocabulary to explain his new notion of being justified and forgiven by God but still being in need of cultivating reconciliation or sanctification. Paul's concept of the ambivalent person has to do with what he calls *sarx* and *soma* which are two different words for the human body. In the Hebrew Bible there was one term for the human body and that was the term *basar* which was related to self, others and God through *nefs* or what was translated into Greek as *Pneuma* or *spirit*. The Semitic peoples unlike the Aryan peoples and thus the Greeks did not think of humans in terms of a soul in a body and thus the Jews like Paul do not think as dualists and think of the human as a soul that can exist apart from the body as did the Platonists. So Paul here writes about living according to the standards of the flesh and Jesus being born in the flesh. At 2 Cor 10:3 he uses the terminology of *kata sarka* and *en sarki* again in a clear contrast. To live *kata sarka* or according to the flesh is to live in a sinful way while to live *en sarki* is to live in the natural, fallen state that all humans are in since the Fall. What Christ's death and atonement have accomplished is that they have reconciled us to God in a new supernatural life so that we can now live according to a new supernatural standard. Paul's term for the crucified Body of Christ and for the resurrected Body of Christ is *soma* which is translated into Latin as corpus so that *Corpus Christi* is the Body of Christ. So the Christian who dies with Christ in Baptism becomes a corpse and yet rises up from the drowning but cleansing water in the body of the resurrected Christ. So *soma* has to do with the supernatural standard of being in Christ's Body.

III.4.7(b) But We Have Been Reconciled (Part Two)

Paul has discovered that Christ's *agape* is wider than any
irreconcilable differences and deeper than any insurmountable factions.
When he experienced Stephen's loving forgiveness and then saw that
it was Christ's loving forgiveness even for him, a stoner of Stephen,
he experienced humankind's highest affirmation with this new notion
of reconciliation with its new logic, anthropology and theology
that he is now beginning to work out to meet the challenges of
the factions and differences that are so obvious in spite of God's love.
We have been reconciled and yet may not understand it so we need
to keep the process of reconciliation going as we believe in it
in a glass darkly but do not fully practice or comprehend it.
Christ's death and resurrection planted the new seed of reconciliation
but the birth of the new person needs to be clearly proclaimed
and the new seed needs to be cultivated with the water of Baptism
and the constant nourishment of the fourfold prayer and the Eucharist.
The face of Christ in all of his suffering members is not always
evident so when Paul is in conflict with the archapostles and
the counterfeit apostles he must still smile upon them with
the loving and forgiving face of Christ just as he must
constantly pray for them that they might forgive him for
reconciliation goes beyond forgiveness in being a two way street.
If God has really reconciled Cephas and Paul and Apollos
unto himself then it is the God-given-task of Cephas, Paul,
and Apollos to be reconciled and know it with each other in God.
Just as there were four factions of Jews so there will always be
four factions of Christians or any political or religious group.
The Zionists had an exclusive logic of either us or the Romans.
The Sadducees were on the middle right and practiced
getting along with the Romans. The Essenes went off into a
neither-nor mysticism. Paul as a Pharisee was also a Roman
citizen and respected all four but still would stone Christians.

III.4.8 As Different Members of Christ's Body

As long as we are here in this time in between Christ's first and second coming we will be both in the flesh *en sarki* and *en Soma Christi*, in the Body of Christ, and if we live according to the flesh we will only war, but if we live according to Christ's love we will also forgive each other and be reconciled. This time in between the first and second coming is a time, therefore, of great ambivalence and we must live according to a logic of mixed opposites being in a contest as Paul, Cephas and Apollos are, but believing in a higher reconciliation. To live out this logic of mixed opposites we should see that we are suffering servants of each other just as was Christ. Thus Paul writes at 2 Cor 4: 11–12

> Indeed, while we are still alive we are consigned
> to our death everyday, for the sake of Jesus,
> so that in our mortal flesh the life of Jesus,
> too may be openly shown.
> So death is at work in us, but life in you.

While we are living in the flesh and in the Body of Christ at the same time one member might pain the rest of the Body as an aching tooth or a broken leg might make the whole person miserable, but the task is to heal the member because of the pain. Paul might be a pain to Cephas and to the whole Church in Jerusalem, but they can in council work out reconciliation. Insofar as Cephas and Apollos give Paul a difficult time they do press him forward to better understand his faith and to appreciate their worth even in their constant opposition. Paul gets the Corinthians working hard for the poor in Jerusalem where some will see Paul as not being a good Jewish Christian and therefore aiding and abetting the Roman invasion, a charge that is not too far fetched since he is proud to be a Roman citizen. But in the spirit of reconciliation he urges all to be cheerful givers.

III.4.9 That We Should Love Our Enemies

So Paul's task is to love his enemies, Cephas and Apollos,
and yet to contest them at the same time in the spirit of love.
In the Body of Christ they are each members who are reconciled,
but in the flesh until the Second Coming they can contest
each other as long as they do not do it according to the flesh,
or in the spirit of self indulgence rather than of service to the other.
Paul's peculiar logic of mixed opposites brings him to boast
of all his trials and tribulations and even of how he contests
the archapostles and especially the counterfeit apostles who,
of course, contest his theory of dropping the Jewish rules and
regulations even though he would not drop the Ten Commandments.
Of course, Paul must practice what he preaches for he knows that
the medium is the message and that others learn from our example
as well as through our words and theory that are often contradictory.
So who are Paul's enemies and how well is he loving them?
Paul is a very strange and contradictory character who is both
a Jew by birth and a Roman citizen and he takes both seriously.
He studied Judaism with the Pharisees and was such a serious Jew
that in his youth he was in the inner circle that killed Christians.
Jesus and his followers were insurrectionists who spoke out
against social injustice and both Roman and Jewish institutions
which did not appreciate that we are all equally children of God.
Of course, Jesus too practiced what he preached and he was as
innocent and loving as a child which Paul discovered in Stephen.
So Paul loved the Romans and all Gentiles and he identified
with them as a citizen of Rome. Thus his enemies were Jews
who wanted to impose the Jewish Law on new gentile converts.
The test case became circumcision and the many cultural practices
that went along with it as a sign of the covenant. Paul's enemies
were Cephas and Apollos who insisted on this in different ways.

III.5 Paul's Love Letter to the Galatians

III.5.1 Paul's Ethics of Reconciliation

Paul begins his letter to the Galatians with a shorter and harsher address than usual and you can see why the Lutherans and the Protestant Reformers like Paul so much because he got his authority directly from God and not from the eleven Apostles. Right away he points out that we need to be rescued from this present wicked world and he believes that we soon will be because he expects the Second Coming of the Lord very quickly and thus the Lord's conquering of Satan so that we will no longer live according to the flesh or in the flesh but in accord with *agape*. Just as God performed the works of reconciliation but gave Paul and the rest of us the task of working further to cultivate that reconciliation so now before Christ's coming it is our task to prepare for it by living an ethical life in the service of others. After his address which ends with a prayer of giving glory to God Paul then gives another warning that if other troublemakers want to change the Good News of Christ as he has taught it then they should be condemned even if an angel should teach it. Paul tells the story of his conversion and how he was chosen by God from his mother's womb and destined to be sent on his mission. He tells the story of the first council with Peter and James and how they all shook hands and agreed that Paul and his could go to the gentiles and not require that they be circumcised. Paul vigorously opposed Peter to his face for at first eating with the pagans but then ceasing out of fear of rebuke from James. Paul as a Roman citizen would always eat with pagans even before he became a Christian and he thought it only ethical to do so. Pagans too have a conscience and they too can follow it and be good. Pagans and Jews are equally in need of the freedom of Christ so that they can perfect their conscience just as Jews need to become altogether new creatures so that they too can be truly ethical. For to exclude others as the chosen people is no longer ethical.

III.5.2 Is Based on the Standards of Love

In Galatians 5:13–15 Paul writes:

> My brothers, you were called, as you know, to liberty,
> but be careful, or this liberty will provide an opening
> for self indulgence.
> Serve one another, rather, in works of love, since
> the whole of the Law is summarized in a single command:
> Love your neighbor as yourself.

This new *agape* ethics of Jesus Christ which was revealed to Paul during the double movement leap of his conversion as he was called to be reconciled to God and sent out to reconcile others is an absolutely new ethics unlike any ethics of the Greeks or Jews. The Jewish ethics of the Mosaic Covenant Theology recalled that just as God had delivered his people from Egypt and from so many empires so the people should keep his law which he gave them. But now Paul is explaining the new law of *agape* as based on the Davidic Promise Theology rather than the Mosaic Covenant Theology and he emphasized the renewal of the Davidic promise in that the promise is no longer so much concerned with the renewal of the promised land and a Jewish nation but for blessing for all persons of the earth. The emphasis is on serving others. All five kinds of Greek ethics were also types of self realization ethics which are here transformed into an ethics of suffering and service for others. Being called to live in the incarnated, crucified resurrected Body of Christ means that we are now to love all others humans persons as we love our self for now each and every single individual person has a unique worth as a member of the Body of Christ. Even though Christ has redeemed us the call must go out to each person so that he or she can begin to serve the neighbor rather than being caught up in self-indulgence. This new notion of the neighbor as including every human person takes us beyond the limits of living according to the law of the flesh.

III.5.3 Which Believes That We Have Been Freed

Just as Paul thinks that the new ethics of *agape* comes out of the Davidic Promise Theology rather than the Mosaic Covenant Theology so he explains it in terms of Stoicism rather than the other systems of Greek ethics. All five schools of the Greek ethics developed a virtue ethics of self-realization. The Stoic had the theory and practice of being freed from the vice of reactions of negative and enslaving passions and freed for the virtue of proactive positive and liberating passions. At Tarsus, where Paul grew up, there was a Stoic school and being a Roman citizen for him meant knowing and practicing the Greco-Roman Stoic philosophy with its universal law for all reasoning humans which Paul preferred to the Mosaic Law after his conversion. The Stoics explained how by cultivating apathy we can be freed from a network of concupiscible and irascible passions and freed for a life of reasoned calm and tranquility. That sort of tranquility could bring about self realization and the great Roman Peace. In a Stoic form but with a revolutionary new material list Paul writes at Galatians 5:19–23

> When self-indulgence is at work the results are obvious: fornication, gross indecency and sexual irresponsibility; idolatry and sorcery; feuds and wrangling; jealousy, bad temper and quarrels; disagreements, factions, envy; drunkenness, orgies and similar things . . .
>
> What the Spirit brings is very different: love, joy, peace, patience, kindness, goodness, trustfulness, gentleness and self-control . . . you cannot belong to Christ Jesus unless you crucify all self-indulgent passion and desires.

So Paul does state his new ethics in the Stoic form of becoming free from vice and free for virtues but the Stoic would still have a self-centered ethics of self-realization whereas the suffering servant will love especially the enemy with this new *agape*.

III.5.4 From the Law and Self Indulgence

Plato's self-realization ethics is also a natural law virtue ethics which pictures us as moving from the enthrallment at the bottom of the cave to the truth of wisdom when we again behold the forms which are outside the cave sending out heat and warmth like the sun. Plato thinks of human excellence in terms of the four cardinal virtues of self-control, courage, wisdom and justice. Self-control or temperance is the excellence of the vegetative soul of the black horse which controls greed, lust and gluttony so that we don't become enslaved and destroyed by addictions for possessions, sex, and food and drink. Courage is the excellence of the animal soul and the noble white horse. Wisdom is the excellence of the human soul or the charioteer. When each part of the tripartite soul is excellent then there can be justice or harmony or integrity both within the individual soul and in the city state. According to Paul these four cardinal virtues and the other virtues that are hinged on them have to do with living in the flesh. When we begin to live within the Body of Christ then there are also the three higher theological virtues of faith, hope and *agape*. The four cardinal virtues when they are uninfluenced by the three theological virtues all have to do with self-interest. But even they can become reoriented by *agape* or that love which absolutely loves God with one's whole heart, mind and body and then loves the neighbor as one loves oneself or as Paul loves all others as his children because they are God's children. Paul who has become freed in his conversion from the greedy center of the territory, the lusty display point of the territory and the power controlled boundary of the territory has given up wife and children and therefore territory for the sake of a universal, unconditional love so that he now feels toward all persons as if they are the children of God therefore his own children for whom he labors.

III.5.5 In Order to Serve All Others

So the person of highest excellence should be for Plato
the Philosopher King who because he has attained the integrity
of a virtuous justice is able to rule the city state with wise justice.
But instead of being the Philosopher King the person of ideal virtue
for Paul is the suffering servant whose virtues are charity
or *agape* and then joy, peace, patience, kindness, goodness, etc.
Plato in his *Symposium* and *Phaedrus* explained his ethics
in terms of a growth in a more and more excellent *eros* that
could let the soul and the city state be liberated through recollection.
Aristotle continued on with the same four cardinal virtues
but explained them in terms of an Apollonian friendship
rather than in the Platonic terms of a Dionysian *eros*.
Aristotle's ethics too is a self-realization ethics in which
the virtues are means to the end of one's own happiness
and also a happy and healthy city state which persons who
practice the four moral virtues and the five intellectual virtues
can attain by being good political animals for their highest good.
Paul's ethics of *agape* with its three theological virtues
as the primary structures of the new Christian attitude
radically differs from both the *eros* ethics of Plato
and the *Philia* ethics of Aristotle in aiming at the joy
and peace of reconciliation for all the creatures of the earth.
For Plato and Aristotle there were still the Greeks and
the Barbarians just as for the Jews there were Jews and Gentiles.
Paul sees Jesus as going beyond this self-realization ethics
of us and them to a new ethics of brotherly love of all humans.
Now the Stoics did think along those lines in that they thought
that the reason that all humans share in common is the
basis for a brotherhood of man. But their universality of
a brotherhood of all reasoning beings still depended on power
and setting up an empire of Caesar's power that could enforce peace.

III.5.6 Greeks as Well as Jews

Just as Stoic natural law ethics aimed at peace and tranquility
for both individuals and all of mankind so the Epicureans
put the emphasis on virtue as a joy that would not self destruct.
Each of the five Greek philosophies had a natural law ethics in
which right reason was the standard for activity as it would judge
thoughts, words and deeds in accord with human nature adequately
viewed in all of its essential relations and thus decide its worth.
Plato defined self-realization in terms of that activity which would
enable the soul to recollect the truth which formerly nourished it
and thus rise up out of the body to contemplate once again the Good,
the True and the Beautiful by ascending the ladder of love out of the cave.
Aristotle defined self-realization as the happiness which arises
when we actualize all of our human potentialities by means of
the four cardinal moral virtues and the five intellectual virtues.
The Stoics thought of the long chain of negative passions as
colliding with the long chain of positive passions and each of
the passions had a mechanism of self interested desire within it.
If we cultivated detachment from a small self interested desire
through apathy we could build up the good of the cosmopolitan whole.
Given its universalism you can see why of the Greek ethical views
Paul would build on Stoicism in thinking of his Christian ethics.
The Epicureans saw a long term pleasant joy as the goal of
life and thus pain and suffering were defined as evil and any
pleasure that implied pain was a vice and since only long term
pleasure in its tranquil joy was virtue so short term pleasure would
be judged as vice by sages who tended their gardens in friendship.
Paul's new ethics of the servant who would even suffer for others
was contrary to each of these Greek ethical systems which did
not emphasize the worth of being a humble servant of others
as was Jesus or of suffering in the Body of Christ with him
to glorify God by sharing in the goodness of atoning sorrow.

III.5.7 Women as Well as Men

Thus in their ethical and political thinking the Greeks would always put themselves as first and see Barbarians as inferior. So also the Jews as the chosen people of God would always because of their history of being subjugated by empires, see others as natural enemies rather than as members of Christ's Body. So Paul's new ethics of the agapeic imperative which says: "Love your neighbor as yourself" and included all humans as neighbors, especially our enemies and persecutors, turns the ethics of the territorial imperative of the natural law completely upside down. In the natural law ethics of the territorial imperative reason commands us according to Plato to sublimate the *eros* of the display point and rise up through Platonic passionate love to perfection. The materialistic Epicureans oppose the spiritualistic Platonists and argue that with a few good friends we should cultivate the center of the territory and not get caught up in the pain of the erotic display point or the golden rule of trying to get along with others out at the boundaries of the territory in fighting for more power. The Stoics are interested in securing the periphery of the territory and setting up social contracts so each have rights and duties. The Aristotelians look at the history of the three schools who emphasize one aspect of the territory and claim that as political animals we need to have an ethics concerned with working out the working together of the previous kinds of ethical emphasis. But even though Aristotle would stay away from Platonic love and condemn adultery, he, like all the Greeks, did not stress the equal worth of the sexes. The Greek culture like the Hebrew was patriarchal and in the hierarchy first worked out by the Pythagoreans women were imaged as being lower than men as dark was inferior to light and matter to spirit. So when Paul proposes an ethics which sees women and men as equal as well as Jews and Greeks he is a revolutionary.

III.5.8 Slaves as Well as Masters

Socrates considered the four different kinds of Greek ethics
and became a revolutionary himself by putting the emphasis
on ethical honesty, humility, humor, and health instead of
on claiming dogmatically that one theory is truer than another.
But when Socrates claimed that he was the wisest man in
Athens because he alone knew that he knew nothing he too
developed a noble ethics of self-realization and looked down on
slaves and the slavish attitude that is ignorant and ordinary.
Socrates clearly saw himself as wise and others as fools.
But Paul's ethics always stresses being a fool for Christ's sake.
As soon as the good of the other becomes the point of your ethics
and not the primacy of your own good then you stress serving
others and even being a slave so as to be equal to all slaves
who are not to be thought of as inferior but as equal members
in the Body of Christ. If one lives according to the standard
of the flesh then slaves, women and aliens will be inferior.
So the whole point of the new ethics is not only to have a theory
in which the inferior are seen as equal but also a practice
that accomplishes that ideal and such a practice begins by
seeing the folly of one's unnatural ethics and of being a servant.
Paul's ethics which he first learned by beholding Stephen
does not look upon suffering as an evil to be avoided but as
the way of joining Jesus in suffering and redeeming humankind.
In our present age before the second coming of the savior,
foreigners, women and slaves are made to suffer in a
special way and there could be nothing lower than a Jewish,
woman slave, but Jesus went out especially to the suffering
and with his love let them experience the value of their suffering.
He became a suffering servant to introduce a new ethics that
would bring about a new culture in which all sufferers could
see themselves as members of his Body in the agapeic imperative.

III.5.9 While We Prepare for the Lord's Coming

As both a Jew and a Roman citizen Paul appreciated both Roman law and the Hebrew Torah or law and when it came to push and shove he would rather be tried under Roman Law which he thought was more fair for he knew from the inside the dangers of stoning. Paul understood how Roman Law was more open to the foreigner than was Jewish law for it let the Jews govern themselves except when their laws and customs would conflict with Roman Law. But Paul's ethics was very Jewish in its apocalyptic context. The Jews believed since the time of the Babylonian exile and especially since the time of Daniel during the Hellenic Empire in the coming of a Messiah who would free them from subjugation. The coming of the Messiah was a major disputed question which divided Jews into factions just as it became a disputed question which divided Christians as they waited for the second coming. Even though Paul's ethics is revolutionary in his totally new approach to all humans being our neighbors whom we should love as ourselves and in his new belief in the equality of all persons be they Greek, Jew, female, male, master, or slave he was not an insurrectionist who wanted to fight the Roman State and its injustices. Because of his belief in an immanent second coming he thought Christ would come soon and bring about a new Kingdom of love, justice, and peace for everyone. So until then men and women should keep their traditional customs as should masters and slaves and Greeks and Jews. Jewish men could be circumcised but it was very important that Gentile men need not be. Women should still wear head covering in church and glorify men as men glorify God. A slave should go back to his master. Of course, we should all love each other as equals in the Body of Christ, but we should keep the old customs until Christ comes and establishes his new Kingdom.

III.6 Paul's Love Letter to the Romans

III.6.1 Paul's Anthropology of Reconciliation

Each ethical system of the Greeks differs because it is based on a different psychology or view of the human's place in the universe. Each great religion and ethical system has a view about origination, our fall and our deliverance. Many great stories equate origination with the Fall and thus the Hindus, the Babylonians and Plato think of our coming into being as resulting from a dream on the part of Brahman so that we dwell in *maya* or illusion, or a battle on the part of Marduk and Tiamat so that we come from the dismembered particles of the fallen dragon, or a fall from original bliss because of the double burdens of forgetfulness and wrongdoing. If we were fallen from our beginning as Gnostics claim then taking responsibility for a better future here is impossible because all we can do by good ethical living is to get back to the golden age we came from. In the Priestly creation story in the first chapter of Genesis it is reiterated after each day of creation that what comes into being is good and thus not fallen. In this creation story humans take responsibility for their fallenness and there is no excuse blaming it on a pre-human cosmic event. Paul takes this view that humans are responsible for their own fall. But then God redeems us just as he created us and after he has objectively reconciled us to himself we have the subjective task and ethical responsibility for giving glory to God by appropriating that reconciliation. Thus Paul writes to the Romans:

> When we were reconciled to God by the death of his Son,
> we were still enemies;
> now that we have been reconciled,
> surely we may count on being saved by the life of his Son;
> Not merely because we have been reconciled
> but because we are filled with joyful trust in God,
> through our Lord Jesus Christ,
> through whom we have already gained our reconciliation.
> (5:10–11)

III.6.2 Bridges the Gap between God and Humans

So, in the beginning God created things and saw that they were good. Then came the event of the Fall and all creatures had to suffer and die. Thirdly, through the death of his Son, God conquered death and brought about a reconciliation between himself and us and each other. Fourthly, through the graceful gift of his Son's death and then resurrection we are given the faith to take responsibility for not only our own fallenness but also for the future appropriation of our continuing subjective reconciliation until the Lord comes. The ambivalence of objective and subjective reconciliation lies right at the heart of Paul's anthropology and of his ethical task. We believe that God has closed the gap between himself and us and even between each of us and yet there is still strife between us. Paul describes the peculiar inward struggle at Romans 7:15, 22–23:

> I cannot understand my own behaviour.
> I fail to carry out the things I want to do,
> and I find myself doing the very things I hate.
> In my inmost self I dearly love God's Law.
> But I can see that my body follows a different law
> that battles against the law which my reason dictates.
> This is what makes me a prisoner of that law
> of sin which lives inside my body.

So by the death of the *sarx* flesh which Jesus accomplished in his death all flesh becomes a corpse with him and in his resurrection rises up into the soma corporation of his body. This has taken place for all living creatures and through the word of God or the Good News of this objective reconciliation we can come to have faith in it and to be baptized into it. So until the second coming we are in the flesh and in the body of Christ at the same time and it is our ethical task to live according to the law of love rather than according to the standard of the flesh even though we constantly fall.

III.6.3 Through a Gift of Faith Like Abraham's

Paul's very confession of his split personality and of the soma *sarx* war within himself is a practicing of reconciliation. Even thought he often blames Peter and James for the factions and lack of reconciliation he sees a bigger picture than that and he knows that his very enmity against them comes from the power of the flesh within him for even though he has faith and has been baptized, and is nourished by the Body of Christ and practices the sacrament of reconciliation by confessing his sins he sees that faith in the threefold promise of land, nation and name, for he believed that if he was faithful to God, God would be faithful to him and let him have a land flowing with milk and honey, and a nation-family more numerous than the stars of the sky and a name that would be a blessing for all the peoples of the earth. But every story in the Abraham cycle of stories in Genesis has been preserved because it is a key story about a threat against one of the three promises and, of course, the Abraham-Isaac story is the key one for how could all the promises be fulfilled unless Abraham were to have a child of promise through whom all three of the promises could be fulfilled in the future. So even though Father Abraham had great faith he also had great trials and tribulations and thus though Paul cannot understand the war within himself between the law of the flesh and the law of love he sees that Abraham even because of his faith had a similar anxiety. Abraham like David was a beloved of God and they both had faith in God and were loved by God as Paul says at the beginning of chapter four: "Irrespective of good deeds." The justification of the ungodly takes place through God's grace and though given the gift of faith in it we still have to work for it.

III.6.4 Which Believes That Christ Died for Us Sinners

Paul's anthropology or theory of our human journey is the
story of his own life, conversion and mission writ large.
He thought of himself as a pious Jew and a Roman citizen.
He wanted to kill Christians in order to nip an evil in the bud
so that such insurrectionists would not team up with Zionists
and provoke further strife with the Romans. In order to
reconcile Jews and Romans he wanted to curtail Christian
extremists who wanted a revolutionary change of the social order.
When Paul was called by the loving face of Jesus in the loving
face of Stephen he began to see that he was wrong and to repent
his evil ways. He believed that he and others were sinners
but that God loved them anyway and Christ's death for
sinners proved that love. Just as Paul experienced a love
in Stephen that he could not deny and a love unlike any
other he had ever known so he now had to go out and love
all others in that way for that was truly mankind's ideal.
But even though Christ died for us and we are justified
and reconciled we still remain sinners and have strife
between us as Paul clearly saw and confessed. He does not
overlook his sin even though he is a saint. He sees it, but
cannot understand it for his faith lets him see it even though
he cannot understand the strange contradiction he himself is.
Plato and Augustine like him can become saints and cease
being sinners by sublimating their sexual passion in
such a victorious way that they hardly have trouble with
sex any more. But Paul's temptations are not sexual
and even though he likes to confess his sins he hides
his sexual life by speaking of a thorn in the flesh.
So the law of the flesh is always a thorn in his side
and he has great trouble reconciling with his closest
associates, namely, Peter, James and John, and the eleven.

III.6.5 Which Proves That God Loves Us

So the pious and loyal Paul was called by the loving Christ
and in responding with faith that justified him he could see
for the first time that he was really a sinner. According to the law
of love he could see that he had been living according to the law
of the flesh and when in the Body of Christ he could now see
that he was also in the flesh just as Christ was before he died
for Christ was born of the seed of David according to the flesh.
As Paul says in Romans 1:3 Jesus out of love became born
kata sarka and thus Jesus, the sinless Son of God, out of
love was born into sin and death in order to become one
with us that we might become one with God and with each other.
Just as Jesus became mixed up with sin and death out of love
for us so now Paul freely confessed that he is mixed up with
sin and death even though he has been justified and reconciled.
Paul now is consistent with Saul of yesteryear in a certain way
insofar as he still wants to reconcile Rome and Jerusalem
and he believes that we do not have to be insurrectionists
to do that but God will do it by sending Christ a second time.
Paul is very upset with Peter and James and the Jerusalem
Church because he thinks they are not really working for the
reconciliation of the Greeks and Jews, of men and women,
and of masters and slaves because they still insist on
the old Jewish Law which is not required for the Gentiles
under the new law of loving. So Paul gets trapped by love.
In trying to love all he finds that he has enmity with his
closest brothers namely the apostles who won't do things
his way. Paul is basically saying with his view about
ethical urgency given the immanent coming of the
Parousia: "Take my way or the highway." He knows
that he is irreconciled with his fellow apostles and that
he sins in getting angry with them, but he is trapped.

III.6.6 Since before We Were Reconciled to God

So, Paul's very faith has brought him to a perplexity that his reason cannot understand in that in wholeheartedly and sincerely proclaiming reconciliation he is the source of much lack of reconciliation even with his closest brethren. In practice Paul seems to be caught in a very disturbing contradiction. He and the other apostles are sent to proclaim the Good News of God's love which is believed in because of Christ's death and resurrection. It is believed that this saving event has justified the ungodly and has brought reconciliation especially to believers. And yet Paul and the very apostles are not at all reconciled for even though in AD 48 they had the council of Jerusalem we still see that Paul is very angry with them and telling his converts not to believe them if their version of the Gospel disagrees with his. So there seems to be the contradiction that we have been reconciled and yet we are not reconciled with our enemies and even our closest associates can be those with whom we fight even about reconciliation. Paul could not understand his own subjective self that was reconciled and yet not reconciled so this challenge brings us to meditate more deeply with Paul into this question that his faith has revealed and his experience contradicts.

> What proves that God loves us is
> that Christ died for us while we were still sinners.
> Having died to make us righteous,
> is it likely that he would now
> fail to save us from God's Anger? (Rom 5:8)

This is the big question for Paul and his question seems to imply that God will save us all in the end because he is a very loving and forgiving God as the death of the Son of God has revealed. So before the second coming there is objective reconciliation: "My peace, my peace, I give to you." But no subjective reconciliation: "I bring not peace, but the sword." What is Paul to think and do?

III.6.7 By the Death of the Son

Now that we are with Paul thinking our way into this question which arises out of a collision of faith with both experience and reason let's look once more at Paul's belief in reconciliation and then see if we can understand his attempt at a resolution to the paradox.

> What proves that God loves us
> is that Christ died for us
> while we were still sinners.
> Having died to make us righteous,
> is it likely that he would now
> fail to save us from God's anger?
> When we were reconciled to God
> by the death of his Son,
> we were still enemies.
> Now that we have been reconciled,
> surely we may count on
> being saved by the life of his Son?
> Not merely because we have been reconciled
> but because we are filled
> with joyful trust in Christ,
> through whom we have already
> gained our reconciliation. (Rom 5:8–11)

So there are only these couple of passages about reconciliation in Paul's own writings and outside of the Pauline literature the Good News of the Kingdom and the Cross is not posed in this kind of terminology. Notice that Paul is making an argument in the form of questions. Is it likely that anyone would not be saved from God's wrath since he is such a loving God as Christ's death has revealed? Cannot we count on with joyful trust the salvation of all flesh since Christ died in the flesh for us that we might all love with him in his new life and as members of his resurrected corporation. Through God's weakness on the cross we can all be in his Kingdom.

III.6.8 We Were Still Enemies

Paul was an enemy of Christ and of Christians when he took part
in the stoning of Stephen and was persecuting the Body of Christ.
But God loved him even when he was still such a sinner and
called him to proclaim the love that God has for everyone of us.
Paul is here revealing the evidence that he has for believing that
God has reconciled us to himself through the death of his Son.
He is giving an argument to help his readers believe and better
understand what they believe concerning our own salvation.
St. Augustine developed a pair of ideas that can help us better
to understand what is happening in this questioning argument of Paul.
As Augustine pondered the relation between belief and understanding
he wrote: *Credo ut intellegam* ("I believe that I might understand").
and: *Fides quaerens intellectum* ("faith seeking understanding").
We might believe that God so loved us even when we were sinners
that he reconciled us to himself through his Son's death and
that it is now our task to explain this loving reconciliation
to others so that they can understand it and come to believe in it.
Paul wants to understand the best way to live and his belief can
help him do that for by believing that God loves us so much that
he even sends his Son to die for us and thus to reconcile us
is the greatest story of love that Paul can imagine and hope for.
How best to understand this belief and answer all objections to it
is Paul's task as he loves others by sharing his belief with them.
As Paul tries to prove that this story of loving reconciliation is
humankind's highest affirmation and no mere pie in the sky
and as he tries to show how we can hold it fast in the
appropriation process of the most passionate inwardness
he gives evidence for eight different kinds of convincing evidence.
If we look into his letters we can see that he is working with
evidence that is: (1) historical, (2) emotional, (3) literary, (4) ethical,
(5) psychological, (6) logical, (7) exemplary, and (8) metaphysical.

III.6.9 And Our Joyful Trust Is Proof of Our Salvation

Paul makes a distinction between being reconciled by the death
of the Son and being saved by the life of the Son for he writes:

> Now that we have been reconciled,
> surely we may count on
> being saved by the life of his Son? (Rom 5:10)

And earlier he does write about "Having died to make us righteous"
as distinct from "saving us from God's anger" so that this is the heart
of Paul's belief that by Christ's death we are reconciled or justified
and then by his resurrection back to life we are saved for eternal life.
We can believe in this eternal life

> because we are filled
> with a joyful trust in Christ.

So how does this proof work and what is the evidence for it?
Paul knew that Jesus was put to death and that was a simple fact.
But four points still need proof: (1) that Jesus is the Messiah
and Son of God, (2) that his death reconciled us to God, (3) that he rose
from the dead, (4) and that he will save us for eternal life also.
Paul's double experience of beholding Stephen's joyful love even
for those stoning him helped him to understand Jesus' loving death.
His experience of hearing the Risen Lord on the road to Damascus
was a miracle that let him belief the power of the resurrection.
But how can he prove this to others when they do not have the miracle?
He says that our being filled with a joyful trust in Christ is our evidence.
Stephen was filled with a joyful trust and that became proof for Paul.
Paul is aware that the heart has its reasons that the mind knows not.
There is an emotional cognition that can be aware of physical, vital,
intellectual and spiritual values and that can motivate to a new life.
The example of Jesus and of Stephen and of Paul can convince us
of new anthropological possibilities or of a new way of being human.
Paul's joy even in suffering for others as more important than himself
has a logic to it that lets sorrow be joy and that is the greatest story.

IV. Personhood

IV.4 To Defining Personhood as Three Persons in One God

IV.4.1 The Person of the Father beyond Judaism and Neo-Gnosticism

At the time of Jesus and the New Testament writings the Christian concept of personhood was not yet worked out and thus Father, Son and Holy Spirit were not yet referred to as persons. The term 'person' had only dramatic, grammatical and legal meanings. The notion of the incarnational God-man has been hotly debated through, we might say, nine periods of Western history, through conflicts with: Jews, Gnostics, Arians, the fall of the Roman Empire, the tribes of Europe, the Eastern Orthodox, the rise of urban Europe, the rise of modernity, and of postmodernity. In showing how the definition of personhood in terms of three persons in one God was worked out we shall now consider only the first two conflicts with Jews and Neo-Gnostics. Many Jews could not accept Christ because in calling God his father he claimed to be the Son of God and thereby seemed to contradict their monotheism and their holy God. Saul was a very loyal Jew until he beheld Stephen's love for his enemies, the Jews, who were stoning him and that love of Stephen which revealed the love of Jesus to Saul began to haunt him as the greatest love he could imagine. Paul's conversion brought him to believe in God as one who suffered out of love for sinners and Paul came to see all humans as now the chosen people of the God of love. Of course, the Jews were still special but in Christ there was neither Jew nor Greek, male nor female, master nor slave. Through Jesus Paul saw that all humans were created out of love and now redeemed by the suffering, death and resurrection of Christ. Gnosticism also was transformed once Jesus came on the scene. He was seen as a redeemer bringing the Gospel of knowledge (*Gnosis*) of supramundane things that could help higher humans become free from this material world which was evil and which the God of the Jews was thought of as creating in its materiality.

IV.4.2 The Work of the Father beyond Judaism and Neo-Gnosticism

There were many different Neo-Gnostic groups once Christianity started growing and the first point they shared in common was a dualism with an infinite chasm between the spiritual world and the world of matter which they regarded as intrinsically evil. Secondly, the Gnostics did not attribute the creation of matter to the ultimate Divine Principle of Goodness and Light, but rather to the Old Testament creator God who was seen by them as emanating from the Good and who then created materiality. So God the Father and his creative work were seen by Christians in a way totally opposite to that of Neo-Gnostics and in a way even different from that of their Jewish forefathers because once the childlike Jesus of the early Q sayings turned the *lex talionis* upside down God the Father became understood as creating out of love and all flesh was not only good as the priestly creation story urged against the old Gnosticism but it was lovely insofar as it proceeded from out of God's love. So the very work of the Father became even more positive once the Son revealed that all creation was not only good but also lovely in accord with *hesed* now revealed as *agape*. The belief in one God, the Father Almighty, creator of heaven and earth, was the main doctrine of Christianity which came from Judaism and it was opposed by pagan polytheism Gnostic emanation and Marcion's dualism even as neo-Gnosticism mixed emanation and dualism in a great variety of Gnosticisms. The main problem for theology was to integrate with this Jewish Monotheism all the fresh data that came from Christian revelation which made known the Father and his work through the person of Jesus, the Son of God and Messiah who offered a new understanding of suffering not as evil as the Gnostics would think of it but as a way of love. And that love implied a greater freedom against determinism.

IV.4.3 The Person of the Son beyond Judaism and Neo-Gnosticism

In Mark's Gospel at the significant points of the beginning, the middle and the end the Father says of Jesus: "This is my Beloved Son in whom I am well pleased." And thus there is the new revelation of God as being a Father and having a Son. This is an idea at which Jews would naturally take offense and which will call upon Christians to formulate conceptually and verbally. In the Primitive Period before Irenaeus the Apostolic Fathers (Clement of Rome, Ignatius, Polycarp, the author of *II Clement*, Barnabas, and Hermas) and the Greek Apologists (Aristides, Justin, Tatian, Athenagoras, and Theophilus) all wrote about the relation between God the Father, Son and Holy Spirit in terms of the Hebrew Prophets and the Apostles but without precision. Besides having to explain themselves to the Jews and the Pagans the Neo-Gnostics were always making new demands on them. A common source of both Christian and Neo-Gnostic thinking was Neo-Platonism, with this world of many changing things that are material and which can suffer, die and pass away. Purgation can take the inner worldly mystic to the inner and higher realm of Soul or the Life Force and then illumination can take the enlightened one to the realm of *Nous* or the Self-knowing knower and finally unification can let the mystic be one with the One Good Light from which all things emanate and to which they can return with right practice. While the orthodox Christians with their belief in the incarnation and resurrection of Jesus affirmed the eternal value of all matter, the Neo-Gnostics believed in a spiritual element in humans or at least in the elite which could be freed from matter and by the mystic way get beyond all ignorance in being one with the one. So the Neo-Gnostics did think that all matter was evil and that as long as you were connected with matter it was your fate to be enslaved and that being enslaved was a kind of fated punishment.

IV.4.4 The Work of the Son beyond Judaism and Neo-Gnosticism

Mathew's Gospel ends with the words:

> All authority in heaven and on earth has been given to me.
> Go, therefore, make disciples of all nations;
> baptize them in the name of the Father
> and of the Son and of the Holy Spirit. (28:18–19)

Right from the beginning in scripture and tradition the formula of Father, Son and Holy Spirit was used in the liturgy of baptism. This formula was commonly used in the *Didache* and in Ignatius and Justin and all the earliest orthodox apologists and teachers. But the question was how to understand the Son and the Holy Spirit in relation to God the Father and the Neo-Gnostics saw them as emanations that were less than Divine even though they revealed the Divine and had vital roles to play in the salvation of humans. The concepts of three persons in one God were slowly worked out down to the Council of Nicea in 325 and the formula of one God existing in three co-equal persons was finally ratified at Constantinople in 381 with its definitive creed. The Neo-Gnostics argued the word of God could suffer even to the point of crucifixion but that did not mean that the God-head would be crucified or in any way suffer for the God-head was absolutely perfect and that made suffering impossible. So the orthodox Christians argued that the Father would not be crucified for God the Father and God the Son are distinct in their personhood and in their work, but the Father could still suffer out of love for suffering humans and thus would send his Son for their redemption by way of his crucifixion and resurrection. Irenaeus summed up the treatment of the Trinity in the second century and became quite clear about what he called the Divine Economy and the nature and work of the Holy Spirit. Since God is rational he created whatever was made by his Word and yet God is still identical with his manifesting word.

IV.4.5 The Person of the Spirit beyond Judaism and Neo-Gnosticism

The Prologue to John's Gospel begins with the words:

> In the beginning was the Word
> and the Word was with God
> and God was the Word
> and this one was in the Beginning
> with God. (John 1:1–2)

This precise philosophical language indicates a plurality in the one God and was given an heterodox Neo-Gnostic interpretation as well as the orthodox Christian interpretation. Just how to understand the distinction between the Father and the Son is the problem that received a spectrum of interpretations. The Monarchianists or those who argue that there is only one source or *Arche* claimed that if the Son is God then he must be identical with the Father and thus the Father too was crucified in the Son and the Father must be flesh if the Son is flesh. Neither the Christian Neo-Gnostics nor the Christians agreed with this and the Gnostics went further than the Christians in radically distinguishing the Son from the Father. The Christians in working out the clear idea of three persons in one God had to avoid the extremes of total identity and a total difference that would see the Son as not original with the Father in one *Arche* or beginning but who emanated. Irenaeus applied the same logic to the Spirit that he applied to the Son for, if God was rational and therefore had his *Logos* so he was also spiritual and had his Spirit. In following Theophilus rather than Justin Ireneaus identified the Spirit with the Divine Wisdom of Proverbs 8:22. The Christian Gnostics used this notion of the Divine Wisdom in a number of ways and in seeing Lady Sophia as female they argued that God was both male and female and they also thought of a higher and a lower or fallen wisdom.

IV.4.6 The Work of the Spirit beyond Judaism and Neo-Gnosticism

In the Infancy Narrative of the first chapter of Luke we read:

> The Holy Spirit will come upon you
> and the power of the Most High
> will cover you with its shadow.
> And so the child will be holy
> and will be called the Son of God. (Luke 1:35)

The Holy Spirit performs many works throughout Hebrew history as the *Ruah Yahweh* who works with God and inspires the Prophets. Now this Holy Spirit who is known to the Jews but not as one of the three persons in the one God gets Christian history started by empowering Mary to conceive of the Son of God in the incarnation. The Christian Neo-Gnostics thought of themselves sincerely as Christians, but there were two fundamental points of difference. Insofar as they disparaged matter and were disinterested in history they did not appreciate the meaning of the incarnation and the flesh. In all the Gnostic systems redemption is brought about by knowledge and divine mediators such as Christ, the Holy Spirit, Lady Sophia and many types of angels help spiritual men see the truth. Humans are of three types: the material, the psychic and the pneumatic or spiritual and these last are the ones who are saved. It was as the father of Christian history that Irenaeus summed up the various views about the Trinity and prepared the way for Tertullian to more precisely define personhood. In creation and in redemption the threefoldness of God's intrinsic being becomes manifest and it is Origen who begins to define the distinction between the three persons for the tradition. Origen argues that the Father, the Son and the Holy Spirit are "three persons" (*hypostasis*) from all eternity and that the Son has been begotten, not created, by the Father so that each person is a substance and the union of the three persons is one in terms of their works of love, will, and action.

IV.4.7 Incarnational Origins beyond Judaism and Neo-Gnosticism

At Colossians 1:15 it is written by the Pauline School:

> He is the image of the unseen God,
> the first born of all creation.

This passage attempts to show how God the Father and God the Son relate to each other and it can be interpreted in Jewish, Gnostic and Orthodox Christian ways just as can the passage in Proverbs 8:22 which relates Lady Sophia and God. The great debate about personhood and the three persons in one God taught orthodox Christianity to be precise about the three attributes of the person, namely, equality, uniqueness and relationality. In holding that the three persons in God are all equal there was caution against the theory of subordinationism which held that God the Son was God but was less than or subordinate to God the Father and this passage could be read in that way since the image is subordinate to what it images and the first born is subordinate to the one from whom it is born. Jesus' statements about the Father and even "The Our Father" could be read as if Jesus himself saw himself as subordinate. The uniqueness of each person could be downplayed by stressing their identity in God and the Monarchians did this by arguing that the one God is the source of all things. The concept of the Trinity means that personhood is relational. There cannot be a Son without a Father and the Holy Spirit of the Risen Lord Jesus who is with us always could not be without Jesus just as the Holy Spirit let Jesus be conceived. When we think of Jesus loving the Father and praying to the Father it seems that the Father is greater than the Son, but if we were to hear the loving prayer of the Father for the Son or even for the Holy Spirit then we would see that the Father loves the Son and the Holy Spirit as more important than he is himself. Each person of the Trinity loves the others uniquely but equally.

IV.4.8 Incarnational Religion beyond Judaism and Neo-Gnosticism

Without the incarnation we would not know about the equality, uniqueness and relationality of the three persons in the one God. We could believe that God loves us with an everlasting, merciful love but we would not know that God is Love in accord with 1 John 4:8–9:

> Whoever fails to love does not know God,
> because God is Love.
> This is the revelation of God's love for us,
> that God sent his only Son into the world
> that we might have life through him.

The many voices of Judaism and the many voices of Neo-Gnosticsm speak primarily of an atonement theology of the *Lex Talionis*. The Jews are the chosen people of the covenant of the Law of Moses. They will be rewarded if they follow it and punished if they do not. According to Neo-Gnosticism there is also a predestined election in which spiritual people are saved and material people are not. What makes Christianity orthodox is that it is a religion of incarnation Theology in which the Son of God through the Holy Spirit became flesh for the salvation of all and especially for sinners. Both Judaism and Gnosticism have a rewarder-punisher God so that non-Jews are not the chosen people any more than matter and people connected with it can be anything but punished. The incarnation gets Christianity started by revealing that God is a loving Trinity of persons and giving human persons the task to also be equal, unique and relational persons by loving God as their absolute foundation and all others as themselves. So the incarnation is the beginning, the process and the goal of Orthodox Christianity as it steers between anti-incarnational Judaism and anti-incarnational Neo-Gnosticism with the first employing the process of physical history and the other denying it. While monotheistic Judaism denies the divine spirit in matter and polytheistic-pantheistic Gnosticism does affirm spirit in humans.

IV.4.9 Incarnational Eschatology beyond Judaism and Neo-Gnosticism

The acceptance or denial of the incarnation also has implications concerning the afterlife and ideas about judgment, heaven and hell. The First Letter of Peter 1:3 speaks of Christian hope:

> Blessed be God the Father of our Lord Jesus Christ
> who in his great mercy has given us
> a new birth into a living hope
> through the Resurrection of Jesus Christ from the dead.

Only because the Son was incarnated in the flesh by the Holy Spirit could he be raised from the dead by the Father and ascend to be with the Father and the Spirit through all of eternity with all flesh. All Christian prayer has to do with this hope for eternal life with the Trinity, with the Mother of God and with all the angels and saints. The Sign of the Cross with which we begin and end our prayer reminds the orthodox Christian constantly that the beginning and goal of all things is the God of Love who as Father, Son and Holy Spirit promises us an eternity of Love with them because the Son became flesh and died and rose for us that we might live forever. The Prayer: Glory be to Father and to the Son and to the Holy Spirit,

> as it was in the beginning, is now
> and ever shall be, world without end. Amen.

likewise takes us into the beginning with the Father, the present with the Son and the eternal future with the Holy Spirit. Amen.
The Nicene Creed defined in more detail The God of Love who as Father, Son and Holy Spirit gives us the gift and task of a love which itself is Divine and a faith and a hope in that Love.
Is the Divine who appeared on earth and reunited man with God identical with the supreme Divine, which rules heaven and earth or is it a demigod? The Gnostics held the latter position and thus the notion of three equal, unique and relational persons was worked out to defend the Christian notion of the three persons in one God against Judaism and Gnosticism and also Arianism.

IV.5 To Defining Personhood as Two Natures in One Person

IV.5.1 The Son is Fully Divine against Arian Subordination

Arians insisted that the Father was both creator and redeemer
but refused to think of the Son in the same way for they thought
it false to regard him as God in the fullest sense of the word.
Their pivotal proof text was Proverbs 8:22–31 in which
Wisdom is described as a created creatrix of playful delight.
God was first and then created her and as a derived creature
she played her special role in cocreating the universe and
since Jesus is the Wisdom and the Power of God he too is derived.
In order to fully respect the Monotheistic God both of
the Hebrew Bible and the Platonic philosophers the Arians argued
that the Son must be created and must have had a beginning.
Although he is God's Word and Wisdom he is really distinct
from that Word and that Wisdom which belong to God's essence.
Five General Councils were called to combat a series of
Trinitarian and Christological heresies of an Arian type
and in these Councils the concepts and terminology of personhood
were worked out and became the basis for Western Culture.
The five Councils we will examine one by one were:

(1) The First General Council of Nicaea in 325

(2) The Second General Council of Constantinople in 381

(3) The Third General Council of Ephesus in 431

(4) The Fourth General Council of Ephesus in 449

(5) The Fifth General Council of Chalcedon in 451

These Councils were each called by an Emperor beginning
with Constantine and were bitterly political and religious
at the same time and were a battle between Antioch and Alexandria.
The School of Antioch emphasized the Indwelling *Logos*
which it defended with a passion for a literal exegesis.
The School of Alexandria stressed a notion of the Incarnate Lord
and used a method of typological exegesis which proved to be
an invaluable weapon in the battles with Gnosticsm and Marcion.

IV.5.2 For the Three Persons Share One Nature (Homoousios)

The Council of Nicaea set out to clarify especially the relation between the Father and the Son in order to respond to the Arian challenges which diminished the nature and the work of the Son. The Nicene Creed which was worked out by the Council treated the Father, the Son and the Holy Spirit as equal persons within one God and especially stressed the Son by saying:

> We believe in one Lord Jesus Christ,
> the Son of God, begotten from the Father
> only begotten, that is from the substance
> of the Father . . . of one substance with the Father.

The words begotten not made begin to answer the Arian diminishment of Jesus and saying that he is of one substance with the Father shows that he and the Father are totally equal. The key term is *homoousis* and "homo" means "one" while *ousia* means "being" and calling it substance could cause problems. The Greek word for substance was *hypostasis* and *stasis* means "standing" while *hypo* means "under" so that for Aristotle this would have a technical meaning which will be much debated, for in Neo-Platonism the *hypostases* emanate from one another which could be like the Arian theory. At the end of the Creed it was stated that the Son was not created and that it is false to think of him as coming from another *hypostasis* or substance so that he did not emanate. *Ousia*, translated as being substance or nature, could signify that which is common to several members of a class, or it could refer to an individual thing as it must for God. Thus, the persons who share in it must be one identical being. The three hundred Bishops at Nicaea intended to underline their belief that the Son was fully God, in the sense of sharing the same divine nature as the Father and the Spirit. But, the main question was the Son's co-eternity with the Father.

IV.5.3 And the Son has Two Natures (Hypostatic Union)

As early as 352 Appollinarius invented a brilliant theory to explain the incarnation by claiming that when the *Logos* became flesh that *Logos* was the Divine soul and intellect which then animated the body which was called the flesh. This could make excellent sense to philosophers who saw living things and humans as made up of body and soul. But the Orthodox were quick to see that this solution was flawed and Gregory Nazianzus argued against it. If the divine *Logos* which became flesh was already the divine soul and mind then the human nature of Jesus would be diminished for only his body would be human and he would not have a human soul and mind or human nature. Appollinarius insisted against the Antiochene's theory of two natures that there is only one nature (*phusis*) in Christ since he is a simple, undivided person (*Prosopon*). So the Godhead and the flesh make one nature or person. The flesh comes from Mary but is united with the Godhead so as to form one person so that when we receive the body and blood of Christ we are receiving the soul and the divinity of God but the soul of Christ is not human. The Cappadocian Fathers, Basil and the two Gregories showed that this savior was not a real man, but only appeared as a man in that his soul and mind were not human. The orthodox fathers at the council of Constantinople 381 clarified that there have to be two natures, the divine and the human in the one person in a consubstantial union. During this controversy the term *Prosopon* became the technical term for person and thus made the qualitative leap from being only a dramatic, legal and grammatical term to become a full theological term meaning that the three persons in one God are equal, unique but also relational.

IV.5.4 His Divine Nature is Absolutely Perfect

Arius and Apollinarius were Alexandrians who limited the human nature of Christ by arguing that he did not have a human soul, intellect and will and thus they weakened the notion of two full-fledged natures in the person of Christ. At Nicaea all agreed that the Divine nature must be thought of as perfect and the Divine omniscience and impassibility were stressed against the Gnostics who diminished those in Christ. But after the Trinitarian concepts of three persons in one God were worked out Christology and the two natures of Christ became the leading problem and Apollinarius began to become Arian. It was Theodore of Mopsuestia who challenged the Alexandrians by focusing on the concept of a Divine soul in Christ to show that if that were true he would not have been able to suffer. Theodore looked carefully at the literal, historical Jesus of the Bible and showed that he learned things and hungered and had thirst. The Alexandrians were very philosophical and in stressing the absolute perfection of God did not do that from a literal Biblical point of view which did show God in suffering and anger. Theodore in trying to account for the full humanity of Christ as well as the full divinity stressed the divine indwelling rather than the divine incarnation and wrote of *homo assumptus*. God the Son assumed a human dwelling for himself even as he might put on clothes and thus the human nature is a temple or a shrine in which God dwells so in stressing these differences between the two natures he stressed their unity in one person. Theodore did call Jesus Christ a *prosopon*, but not yet in the full Chalcedonian sense, but he was moving toward that. With Theodore the dispute between the Alexandrians and the Antiochenes reached clarity almost as if the Alexandrian were like Parmenides stressing one being or *Logos* and the Heracliteans stressing process and an historical dialectic.

IV.5.5 His Human Nature Suffers, Dies, and Rises

The next major Antiochene Christologist was Nestorius who saw himself as a follower of Theodore of Mopsuestia. He set out to correct the Alexandrians whom he thought of with their word-made-flesh incarnation theology as involving the perfect God in change and human suffering. To correct Arius and Apollinarius they thought of God as being born and dying and they thought of Mary as *Theotokos* or as bearing the divine word and thus being Mother of God. Nestorius saw this as a confusion of the two natures and said that Mary was not *Theotokos* or God bearer; she should be called *Anthropotokos* or *Christokos* or the bearer of Christ as a man so that Christ's Divine nature remain perfect. Nestorius insisted that the two natures remain unaltered and distinct as the Divine Son of God assumed the nature of the human so that the God-head existed in the man; and the man in the God-head. Hence the two, Divinity and humanity, existed side by side, each retaining its unique properties and operations unimpaired. Each nature was an objectively real *prosopon* or *hypostasis*. Many were offended by Nestorius' denial of Mary as *Theotokos* and Cyril of Alexandria argued for the hypostatic union of the two natures as though they are united like the body and the soul. Cyril thought of Christ as one *prosopon* or person with two distinct natures or *ousiai*, Godhead and manhood. Nestorius uses the same terminology as Cyprian but with a different meaning for he claimed that Christ's manhood was a *hypostasis* or *prosopon* but in the sense of "objectively real". He thought of the unity as a concrete psychological mix but he failed to provide an acceptable explanation for how two really distinct objective beings could be one reality. He had good intentions but an inadequate philosophical explanation to unite the perfect God with the suffering Christ.

IV.5.6 Same Person before and after Incarnation

Nestorius and the Antiochenes could deny that Mary was the Mother of God because they thought of two natures that mixed. To correct this fault Cyril advanced the Alexandrian position by arguing that the divine nature made a transition from being only a divine nature to becoming also a human nature and this was the significance of the incarnation that let there be the hypostatic union of the one nature with two different stages. In emphasizing the union of God and man as one nature Cyril used the Platonic analogy of the body-soul unity between which there was a distinction on the part of the mind but not in reality for they are not objectively separable entities. The body would no longer be a living body without the soul. So also the human nature of Christ was not really distinct from his divine nature for they were two principles not two things. The Jesus of history was God himself in human flesh and this was a very strong religious and soteriological position that let Jesus be adorable and explained how his death could save sinners. But the language was not clarified yet for both Nestorius and Cyril, for Nestorius equated *hypostasis* and *prosopon*. He often asserted that Christ's manhood was a *hypostasis* or *prosopon*. The same was true for Cyril for he too used the term *hypostasis* and *prosopon* interchangeably however with different meanings. Both Nestorius and Cyril also used the term *phusis* which was translated into Latin as *natura* or nature and so they agreed on the same terms but they had opposite meanings and implications. Both Cyril and Nestorius appealed to Pope Celestine who called a synod at Rome in (August 430) which came down in favor of the *Theotokos* position but there could still be no agreement. In 431 the third general council was called at Ephesus and a statement of agreement was signed by the Antiochene group and then Cyril accepted it even with the word *prosopon* for nature.

IV.5.7 The Western Contribution from Tertullian to Leo

In the West already by the year 200, following Irenaeus and Hippolytus, Tertullian had worked out a mature Christology based on the three concepts of person, substance and nature which the Latins had translated from Greek as *persona* for *prosopon*, *substantia* for *hypostasis* and *natura* for *phusis*. Tertullian clearly argued for two substances in one person. He argued that the Word is in the flesh and was not transformed into the flesh but like the later Antiochenes was clothed in flesh. A transformation as Cyril would later conceive of it would not be compatible with the perfect immutable, impassible Godhead. While the flesh remains flesh and the Spirit remains Spirit they both belong to a single subject, not confused but conjoined. Side by side in that indivisible person can be seen Godhead and manhood, divine Spirit and human flesh, immortality and mortality, strength and weakness and thus *credo quia absurdan est*. Already we have here the unfathomable paradox which the mind cannot understand but which is the object of our Christian faith. In the West faith was sufficient and all the debating as it was between the Alexandrians and the Antiochenes was not practical. Hilary did develop Tertullian's solution with the Pauline imagery of self-emptying that must have happened in the incarnation and Ambrose stressed that the human nature had to have a rational soul so that it was not merely passive. Augustine also developed the concept of two natures in one person and because they are united like the soul and body the son of mod can come down from heaven as the Son of God and suffer and die. In summarizing the western approach to Christology Leo on June 13, 449, sent a letter to Flavian making his position against the one nature doctrine clear in four related theses. This letter helped prepare the way for the Council of Chalcedon where equal recognition would be given to unity and to duality.

IV.5.8 From Leo's Summary of the West to Chalcedon

Between the first council of Ephesus in which the dispute between Cyril and Nestorius was worked out in 431 and the second council of Ephesus in 449, Archimandrite Eutyches argued strenuously against the two nature theory and based his argument on the term *phusis* which meant concrete existence. Two natures in the mind of Eutyches meant two separate beings. Flavian at the Synod of Constantinople in 448 argued that two natures did not have to mean two separate physical objects. He argued for one Christ, one Lord in one *hypostasis* and one *prosopon*. His identification of *hypostasis* and *prosopon* paved the way toward Chalcedon even though Flavian, the local patriarch, could not convince Eutyches about *physis* as a separate being. Both Flavian and Eutyches appealed to Pope Leo and thus Leo wrote his summary to Flavian to try to bring peace. Leo's *Tome* set out the following four theses:

(1) The person of the God-man is identical with the Divine word. While it was a "self-emptying" omnipotence it was not diminished.
(2) The Divine and human natures coexist in this one person without mixture or confusion for the form of God and of servant must work together in order for the saving acts of Jesus to happen.
(3) The natures are separated principles of operation acting in concert so that the Word performs what belongs to the Word and the flesh in carrying out what belongs to the flesh in harmony.
(4) The oneness of the Person lets the Son of God be crucified and buried and also lets the Son of Man come down from heaven.

The second general council of Ephesus took this into account but still no agreement could be reached for while Antiochenes appreciated the affirmation of the duality in Christ, Alexandrians were still not convinced about the strong two nature language which had put in jeopardy for them in the past the immutability of God and the *Theotokos* nature of the Blessed Virgin Mary.

IV.5.9 Chalcedon's Unique, Equal, Relational Persons

The Council of Chalcedon in 451, brought together more than 500 bishops from the spectrum of the four great traditions: the left wing human stressing Antiochenes, the balanced Westerners, the balanced Cappodocian Easterners, and the right wing Divine stressing Alexandrians with their own mix. The bishops all signed a middle of the road statement agreeing to a formulation clarifying the divine and human nature in the one person of Jesus Christ who is the Son of God. This council crafted definitions and distinctions about the personhood of Jesus Christ as unique in a double way, as equal in a double way and as relational in a double way. Most of all the Council was careful to make clear how the personhood of Jesus was relational in a double way both to the other Divine persons and to all of us human persons. Correcting the Antiochenes the council declared that Jesus is consubstantial with the Father in Godhead and because of our salvation begotten from the Virgin Mary, the *Theotokos*. Correcting the Alexandrians the council declared that Jesus is consubstantial with us in manhood and that the two natures are such that Jesus has a body and a rational soul. So Jesus as a person is not a rugged individual but is essentially related in love with his Father and brothers and sisters. He is one *prosopon* and one *hypostasis*, the only begotten. Thus his personhood is also defined as unique in a double way by the Council because while He is God he is not the Father or the Holy Spirit and he is also the only begotten of Mary. Persons are also defined by the council as equal in worth for the Father is not greater than the Son for he could not be Father without the Son and Jesus as a person became man for all human persons who are equally created and redeemed. But how did this idea of Person become applicable to humans?

IV.6. To Boethius and Defining Human Personhood

IV.6.1 An Individual Substance of a Rational Nature

Boethius well knew the many problems concerning Christology. He wrote five treatises on Christian doctrine with a polemic against Nestorius and Eutyches and a treatment of the Trinity. He studied both Plato and Aristotle and he translated two of Aristotle's logical works with the aim of showing the harmony between Plato and Aristotle in spite of their many differences. Part of the great legacy of Boethius is his definition of personhood. He not only clarified the issues concerning the person of Christ but with Aristotle's precise concepts he was the first to clearly define the human person in a way that would be influential for both medieval and modern thinking down to the innovations of Hegel. Each of the four terms in his definition is very significant. If we understand the meaning of "The person is an individual substance of a rational nature," we will see how defining the individual takes us beyond Plato and Eutyches; how distinguishing substances takes us beyond Plotinus and Cyril; how knowing the rational soul takes us beyond Epicurus and Apollinarius; how an insight into a natural history of nature takes us beyond the Stoics and Nestorius; how seeing the autonomy of the natural sciences can reveal the consolation of *philosophy*; how going beyond Gnosticism can reveal the *consolation* of philosophy; how going beyond Arianism is possible with Lady Philosophia; and how the suffering servant can be serene, peaceful and gentle. We have seen how the term *prosopon* which was the mask through which the actors spoke in Greek drama became the key term for the early church Fathers in referring to the personhood of the Father and the Son and the Holy Spirit. In Latin it became *persona* or sounding through for Tertullian, Augustine and now with Boethius we can see how it came to apply to all humans uniquely and equally.

IV.6.2 Defining Individuals (beyond Plato and Eutyches)

Aristotle was a student of Plato for twenty years and he greatly
admired his master's genius but slowly it dawned on him
that Plato did not have an adequate metaphysical account
of the individual such as "this horse" or this individual soul.
Aristotle's fundamental metaphysical breakthrough was to move
from a metaphysics of forms and information to a metaphysics
of substance and causality which could explain natural individuals.
Plato's cave allegory helps to explain his metaphysics of forms
and how our natural world came to be through fallen information.
According to Plato we find ourselves to be living here and as
it turns out we are only simple cave men trapped in a cave
where we assume that the shadows we see on the walls are real
for our everyday communication and thinking fosters that illusion.
But then as we read great literature about the gods and goddesses
and about various so-called creation stories we begin to move
up out of the cave and discover a pool of water in which the images
of what we previously saw only as shadows become clearer.
Then science and mathematics reveal the things themselves
as we ascend further upward and find real things and people
that with a fire behind them have been casting the shadows and images.
But then as we climb higher and out of the cave we discover
the Sun by means of philosophy which is the form of the Good.
Things and people here are not matter but only forms which
are in turn but parts of the one true form which casts shadows.
So individuals are not real and Aristotle found that account
to be unacceptable so he set out to explain single individuals.
With his metaphysics of substance and causality he replaces
Plato's metaphysics of forms and fallen information so that
the substance is the real single individual horse or human.
This realism of Aristotle brings him to a new logic which
can define individuals in terms of genus and specific difference.

IV.6.3 Distinguishing Substance (beyond Plotinus and Cyril)

As Boethius worked out his definition of personhood it was
Aristotle's metaphysics of substance and causality that aided
him in becoming clear about each element within the definition.
In going beyond Plato and his metaphysics of forms Aristotle
developed his hylemorphic theory or his theory of matter and form.
Aristotle saw matter or *hyle* as the principle of individuation.
We might think about the species or form of horseness but that
which makes Northern Dancer an individual and distinct from
all other horses are all his material factors that individuate him.
Thus Aristotle defined a substance as a thing which exists in itself
and he thought of each substance or individual thing as having nine
accidents or material traits that inhere in it: quantity, quality,
relation, time and space, action and passion, situation and habit.
Aristotle's realistic metaphysics of the ten categories or substance
and the nine accidents led him to a logic of defining things
in terms of the five predicables: genus, species, difference, property
and accidents which became the basis for the Aristotelian science.
Aristotelians define something by putting it into its genus or
general class and then determining its species by locating
the difference between one species and another within the genus.
Thus in the genus animal there are brute animals and
rational animals and the definition of the essence of the human
is thus the genus animal and the specific difference rational.
A property as that which necessarily flows from the essence
as always, only and every further defines so that a human
can be seen as risible or having the ability to laugh which
every human, always the human and only humans are able to do.
Accidents refer to the nine categorical traits above that vary
accidentally in each single individual substance which is real.
So while forms give species and existence they do not exist
in themselves and thus matter and form are principles not things.

IV.6.4 Knowing Rational Souls (beyond Epicurus and Cyril)

As Boethius worked out his definition of the person the concept of a rational soul was central to his thinking and again Aristotle's proof for the existence of the soul and his treatment of the nature of the soul were of key significance for him. With his causal thinking Aristotle argued that every effect must have an adequate cause and thus action follows being. The actions of a thing reveal what kind of being it must have. So a living being must have a life force and that is the soul. The vegetative actions of nutrition, growth and reproduction prove that plants have vegetative souls with those kinds of powers. The added powers of animals for external and internal sensations and for self motion prove the existence of special animal souls. Humans have vegetative and animal powers in their souls but because they can reason they must also have a rational soul. Reasoning depends upon universal or immaterial ideas and so that part of the human soul must be immaterial and thus immortal for that which has no parts cannot break apart or die. So the person for Boethius is an individual substance with a rational soul which is the first act of its natural organic body. The rational soul activates the individual body with life and then enables it to perform its vegetative, animal and rational actions. Thus the substance is the hylemorphic union of its matter and form and that form for the human is the rational soul. The substance is the *hypostasis* or that which stands under and supports all the traits and actions of an individual. With his proof for the existence of an immaterial intellectual soul Aristotle went beyond the mere materialism of the Epicureans. Also he threw light on the problem that got Cyril in trouble, for two or three natures can exist in the same soul without one having to evolve out of the other as Cyril imagined. Boethius is most indebted to Aristotle's hylemorphic nature.

IV.6.5 A Natural History of Nature (beyond Stoics and Nestorius)

Aristotle's entire philosophy or way of thinking is to take the middle way between the extremes of Platonic spiritualism and Stoic, Epicurean materialism and Boethius did exactly that as he thought through the problems concerning personhood and proved his middle position at each step along the way, with arguments based upon the Aristotelian science of causality. Eutyches had argued that there cannot be two natures in one person because the notion of *phusis* or nature refers to a single thing which Aristotle defined as a substance and thus for Eutyches there would be two substances in one substance which is confusion. Boethius learned all about physics as he studied Aristotle's history of the various theories of physics and pondered the Latin translation of physics into *natura* or that which is born. Of course, Aristotle also clarified the meaning of physical substances by thinking about them metaphysically or from the viewpoint of potency and act, and matter and form which are the principles that explain physical substantial things. The Alexandrians from Origen to Arius to Apollinarius to Cyril with their one sided Platonic spirituality could not properly appreciate and account for the human, material nature of Christ. The Antiochenes from Theodore of Mopsuestia to Nestorius with their Stoic pneumatic but not immaterial spirituality could not properly appreciate and account for Christ's immaterial nature. As he thought through the two extremes in the light of Aristotle he could equate *hypostasis* or substance and *prosopon* or person and with Aristotle's hylemorphic theory of the way matter and form unite he could account for two natures in one substantial person. Matter without form which gives it species and existence cannot exist. And as the vegetative and animal natures are in a rational soul or just as a person can have vegetative animal and rational natures so it is easy to see how one person can have divine and human natures.

IV.6.6 Autonomy of Natural Sciences (*The Consolation of Philosophy*)

For Aristotle science is a certain knowledge of things through causes.
To understand things philosophically you need to know their
four causes: the material, the formal, the efficient and the final.
Philosophy seeks to know the truth about the becoming of all things.
That becoming is the *physis* or the world of physical things and
we seek to know it archeologically by grasping the efficient
cause of its coming to be and to know it teleologically by knowing
the final cause that finishes it and is its ultimate purpose.
We quest to know its *arche*-beginning and its *telos*-ending and all
that happens to it and all it does in between with historical,
descriptive, material definitions from the sciences such as
physics, biology, ethics, drama, psychology and sociology.
In doing this we seek formal definitions of each thing in accord
with its genus and specific differences and with proper distinctions.
Boethius learned from Aristotle to appreciate both contemplation
that went in a Platonic, Alexandrian spiritual direction and
science which could be appreciated by those who loved matter
be they Stoics, Epicureans or Antiochenes who loved Christ's body.
This let Boethius fully work with a totally optimistic attitude
that took no offence at either spirit or matter to give the science
of consolation and the consolation of science and the consolation
of contemplation and the contemplation of consolation to the
many others who would read his book *The Consolation of Philosophy*
which he joyfully wrote when he was imprisoned by an Arian Bishop.
The Bishop wanted to restrain Boethius from teaching others about
his dangerous orthodox views and thus took away his freedom
by locking him safely in prison where he could do no harm.
But Boethius wrote about the freedom of the will and how God
can know our future even in such a way that we can be free.
He lost his freedom neither to Divine Omniscience nor the Bishop.
Instead he wrote a great book for the liberation of future humankind.

IV.6.7 Beyond Gnosticism (*The Consolation of Philosophy*)

Gnosticism is a philosophy and religion that is very pessimistic about matter and about most of humankind who lack *Gnosis*. At the extremes Plato and Epicurus are both Gnostic pessimists. Platonists say: "purge yourself and be an ascetic and in denying the world, the flesh and the devil your extracted soul can rise up out of evil matter and with true Gnosis become one with the One." The Epicureans on the other hand say: "Eat, drink and make merry for tomorrow we die. And why should we torture ourselves over gods who do not exist for we should be Gnostic humanists." The history of the Hebrew people is a step by step combating of this Gnostic view and so was Aristotle's scientific philosophy. As Boethius sat in prison and wrote his *Consolation of Philosophy* in dialogue with Lady Philosophia he was totally consoled and very happy that he had such freedom to write his noble work. It brought consolation to many for manuscripts of the work are widely distributed throughout the libraries of Europe and it was translated by King Alfred, Chaucer and Queen Elizabeth I. It was a favorite of Dante and gave him great consolation when his beloved muse Beatrice died and became his Lady Philosophia. The ultimate root of our consolation is the greatness of God to whom true intelligence with full comprehension belongs which we with the force of our reason can apprehend but not comprehend for God's eternity is the simultaneous and complete possession of infinite life which lets God know all by knowing himself. Given this loving knowledge that God in his eternity has for the universe we can here and now more deeply apprehend the concept of nature for Aristotle and the Greeks and for Boethius as he takes it into this new Christian realm. Nature is pervaded by necessity and universality and there is no chance within it for causal laws govern all things and thus make possible science which can express these laws.

IV.6.8 Beyond Aristotle and Arius (with Lady Philosophia)

Boethius detected in Aristotle a serious contradiction which, however, he passed over in silence in his loving attempt to show the spiritual harmony between Aristotle and his beloved master. Aristotle most of all wanted to account for individual material things which he thought were real, but our intellect which is the agent for abstracting ideas out of material things has to be spiritual or immaterial because it performs immaterial actions which let it alone be immortal since as immaterial it cannot be destroyed. So what is most important about the human being is not individual. Our agent intellect which alone is immortal has nothing to individuate it and thus humans are not ultimately individual substances of a rational nature for their very rationality cancels individuality. Just as the immortal human soul for Plato becomes one with the world soul so for Aristotle it becomes one with the prime mover. As a Christian Boethius believes that the resurrected body of each person will achieve the primary goal of Aristotle which, however, his reasoning about the spiritual alone as immortal could not reach. Thus Lady Philosophia can reveal to him the ultimate aspiration of both Plato and Aristotle which, however, their assumption about the nature of the body as destructible could not demonstrate. Lady Philosophia in personifying the gifts of faith, hope and love can guide Boethius in so defining person and eternity that he can be totally consoled in believing in the resurrected immorality of each person and in uniting the aspirations of Plato and Aristotle. It is no wonder that an Arian Emperor imprisoned Boethius for the Arians began by interpreting Lady Sophia and the God-man both as derived creatures and thus in not fully appreciating the begotten and resurrected body of the Christ. But Arian Bishops lost their credibility as philosophers like Boethius showed them that a person can be an individual substance of a rational nature and that matter does individuate.

IV.6.9 The Suffering Servant's Serene, Peaceful Gentleness

It is in his *De Duabus Naturis*, his treatise on the two natures of Christ that Boethius gave us his definition of personhood. This definition inspired the whole of the middle ages and held good for the whole of modern ethics up to Hegel who went beyond a metaphysics of substance to one of relationality. In Aristotelian thinking the substance is an individual substance and relationality is only one of the nine accidents so that a third trait of the person besides its uniqueness and equality was not explicitly defined theoretically even though practically it was highly significant for Boethius and that can be seen in the voice of Lady Philosophia which is, of course, a key voice within Boethius as in dialogue with her, other voices within him question, doubt and explore and work out the rational nature of the person that is free and creative. It is noteworthy that Lady Philosophia is not only the key voice within Boethius dialoguing with his other voices but hers is a feminine voice serene, peaceful and gentle. Just as the person is a composite of body and soul or matter and form so Boethius shows in *The Consolation* that each person is a relation of the masculine and feminine even though that is not spelled out theoretically but only revealed in practice. So Boethius not only shows the deep unity of intention between Plato and Aristotle as they try to reveal the worth of the immortal spirit in each of us, but also in Boethius the noble Stoic and even the Epicurean ideals of peace and of a simple life which Boethius suffered in prison. Already with St. Francis the Spirit of his Lady Philosophia could pray with the Stoics: "O Lord grant me the Serenity to accept the things I cannot change, the courage to change the things I can, and the wisdom to know the difference." And with the Epicureans he could tend the garden of his soul with peaceful mirth and joy.

NOTES

1. St. Francis de Sales, *An Introduction to the Devout Life* (Rockford, IL: Tan, 1994) 80.
2. Ibid., 87.
3. Ibid., v.
4. Ibid., 213.
5. Ibid.
6. Ibid., 102.
7. Ibid., 97.
8. William Cullen Bryant, "Blessed Are They That Mourn," (New York: D. Appleton, 1876).
9. G. W. F. Hegel, *Hegel's Philosophy of Right*, trans. with notes M. Knox (Oxford: Oxford University Press, 1967) 110.
10. Søren Kierkegaard, *Concluding Unscientific Postscript to Philosophical Fragments*, vol. 1, ed. and trans. Howard V. Hong and Edna H. Hong (Princeton, NJ: Princeton University Press, 1992) 106.
11. Ibid., 72.
12. Ibid., 80.
13. Ibid., 97.
14. Søren Kierkegaard, *The Concept of Dread*, trans. Walter Lowrie (Princeton, NJ: Princeton University Press, 1969) 110 and 115.

Bette Jo and Bob come home after their wedding

Mother with her first grandson, Joseph Robert

Mother and her children at Cliff's wedding

The Coates family reunion

Mother and Daddy with Grandma Coates

Mother's five children at the time of Daddy's death

The Grandchildren at the time of Grandpa's death

Mother at eighty

Mother's Rebecca Lodge friends

Part III

Glorious Finishings

I. Mother

I.7 With her Son, Clifford Scott, and Father Waldman

I.7.1 Christmas is Everyday in Joyful Mystery Love

By the time Mother reached the age of fifty-five she had already
been praying the full Rosary daily for twenty-five years
as she would continue to pray it for the next twenty-five.
The first third of her journey took her through three stages of joy;
the second third through three stages of sorrow and now
her life's final third would be through three stages of glory.
Her childhood, her youth and her early married life were times
of relating outwardly in aesthetically new and exciting ways.
Her mid-life period of raising her family took her through
the worst of times and the best of times in which the sorrow of
her trials and tribulations became her way of uniting deeply
in the offertory, consecration and communion of the sacred Mass
with Jesus, the Good Shepherd and the Suffering Servant in his priests
in a new maturing of her most holy passionate inwardness.
Now that her family was raised she moved more and more
into the reflection of tranquility and giving glory to the glory
which is the manifestation of the unmanifest in its unmanifestness.
Her life of prayer in the Sacred Mass let her holy Rosary give
her the answers to those great questions of life: Why is there
something rather than nothing? Is there a God? Are we free?
And are we immortal? Mother's loving prayer increased her
faith in the God who is Love and who out of love created
the universe that all places, persons and things might share
in a daily and constant increase in the Divine Love's loving.
As Mother prayed the Five Joyful Mysteries day after day and
year after year she came to live everyday in the Spirit of Christmas.
Christmas which is the celebration of God becoming man
is the Divine event that revealed the triune God of Father, Son
and Holy Spirit who in loving each other is the God who is Love.
The present of making present to us the Divine Love is the Christmas
gift of gifts that gives all gift giving its eternal temporal worth.

I.7.2 In the Annunciation and the Hail Mary's Five Parts

By the time mother reached her fifty-sixth year in 1973,
her children were all married, had good jobs and were
giving her grandchildren at the rate of one or two each year.
David taught philosophy in Canada; Bette Jo was a social worker
and a wife and mother; Bobby was a lawyer in Elko, Nevada;
Cliff was a medical technician in the same hospital in Burley,
Idaho, where his wife, Ruth, was a registered nurse and Tom was
teaching at Hailey High School where her children had studied.
Father Waldman, her fourth parish priest, was from Idaho
unlike Fathers Dougherty, Heeren, and O'Conner who were
from Ireland and dad, Cliff and Tom liked it that he was
interested in sports and he encouraged Cliff who excelled
in basketball and Tom who excelled in wrestling and they
both went on to become coaches like dad in those two sports.
As mother prayed her 150 *Hail Marys* each day she slowly
meditated more deeply into the *Hail Mary* and saw that it
had five parts that paralleled the five Joyful Mysteries.
(1) "Hail Mary full of grace, the Lord is with thee." Those are
the words that the Angel Gabriel said to her at the annunciation
and when Mary said "Yes" the incarnation took place.
(2) "Blessed art thou among women,
and blessed is the fruit of thy womb."
Those are the words that her cousin Elizabeth said to her at
the Visitation when her child, John the Baptist, leapt for joy.
So mother would praise Mary in the words of Gabriel and Elizabeth.
(3) Then she would pray "Holy Mary, Mother of God" which Mary
became at the Nativity and mother saw that Christmas was
already there in the incarnation of the Annunciation and in
the Joy of the Visitation. And she prayed "Pray for us sinners."
And she asked Mary to pray for her and hers in the spirit of
Mary's Presentation prayer of offering. And mother prayed
"Now and at the hour of our death" for Christ's dear presence there.

I.7.3 In the Visitation and the Mystery's five parts

As mother prayed the Joyful Mysteries she came to see how
they fit together and especially the Mystery of the Visitation made them
so real for her because she knew the joy of her children's visits.
She loved the image of Elizabeth being so joyful to see Mary
carrying the child Jesus in her womb that the child in her
own womb leapt for joy for being visited by loved ones is like that.
She always remembered how one Christmas Cliff and Bim, that
is Ruth's nickname, came to visit her and Joe for Christmas
and all the Joyful Mysteries illumined each other in their visitation.
They announced that they were coming from North Dakota for
Christmas and already the joy began and increased as she
prepared to care for her Sunshine and his utterly lovely young wife.
And her husband who named Cliff after his best friend in High School
was always so proud of Cliff and how he was so good at Little
League Baseball and High School Basketball and he loved watching
his games and being congratulated by his own friends and dad
and Cliff loved hunting and fishing and just visiting together.
And Christmas was a joyful time of giving presents to each
other for as mother saw as she prayed the Mystery of the Nativity
that event of the birth of God's son in Mary's baby was the greatest
gift ever given after the gift of creation itself because it was
the moment of Grace that revealed and made manifest God
as the Trinity and the Divine Love which is the meaning of our lives.
There was the annunciation of the visitation at Christmas and
the Christmas love and joy was already there in the announced visit.
Forty days after the Baby Jesus was born Mary and Joseph took
him to the Temple and offered him to God in the gift of the doves.
And mother saw all of her prayer as the thank-offering for Christmas
and she had to be reconciled with all that it might be fitting.
And, yes, the Finding in the Temple when the youth was lost at
puberty was in its joy once again a Christmas present.

I.7.4 In the Nativity and Her Intention's Five Parts

Mother saw it as her sacred task to bring the joy of Christmas to everyone everyday as she prayed her holy Rosary for them. The purpose of her life was to love the Lord her God with her whole heart, mind and soul and to love her neighbor as herself. She had to really love herself and to make of herself as a result of God's Nativity Grace the best person she could become. When she prayed the Mystery of the Annunciation she prayed for humility that she might not be proud which is the root of all vice, and humbly realize her dependence on God for everything. Notice, the intention for the Annunciation and for the Nativity are but an expansion of each other for God's grace gives us all. As she prayed the ten *Hail Marys* of meditation on the Visitation she would think about the *Hail Mary* as it related to the Visitation. She would say the same words to Mary that Elizabeth said to her: "Blessed art thou among women and blessed is the fruit of thy womb." Mother felt that she herself was blessed among women to have been given the grace and the faith to pray the Rosary each day. She prayed the Mystery that others might be given what she had been given to come closer and closer to the love of God. She prayed the last two Joyful Mysteries for *perfect* obedience and for a more *perfect* understanding of God's Holy will. Mother had always believed in being excellent and seeking perfection. She was motivated to do her best in keeping in touch with "The dearest freshness deep down things," "Humankind's highest affirmation" and "Holding fast in passionate inwardness." Her quest for excellence brought her joy and joy moved her to always want joy for herself and others and nothing less. While praying the Rosary mother's mind was focused sometimes on the words of the *Hail Mary*, sometimes on the Mystery and sometimes on her intention and the three reinforced each other by being three aspects of the same thing.

I.7.5 In the Presentation and Her World's Five Parts

Mother's constant praying of the Rosary not only made Christmas present for her everyday, but also it made it present for her everywhere in everyplace in her inward shamanic world. As mother prayed with Mary, the Mediatrix of Grace, her five dimensional inner world opened outwards in humility (1) from herself and her family, (2) with Mary, Queen of heaven and earth, (3) to Jesus, (4) and to the Blessed Trinity, (5) and to the family of all the living and the salvation of all flesh. As mother prayed: "Hail Mary full of grace, the Lord is with Thee," she learned the humility that let the Lord be with her also in the fullness of his grace for what is grace but the Lord's presence? In her humility mother became "other centered" and with Mary she wanted to help other persons come closer to God and with Mary, "The Queen of the Angels and the saints" she learned how to do that. Mother lived on earth but also in the upper heavenly realm with the angels and the lower heavenly realm with the saints. Mother prayed to the holy angels like Gabriel who came to Mary and to her own Guardian Angel and she loved reading the lives of the saints and praying for their intercession especially St. Joseph after whom she, her husband, Bette Jo, and Tommy Joe were named. And mother's praying let her live constantly especially with Jesus whose Sacred Name was right at the heart and center of the *Hail Mary*. And Jesus revealed to her the inner love life of the Trinity in the Father's love for the Son and the Son's love for the Father which is the Holy Spirit of love for as male and female we are made in the image and likeness of God so that the Holy Spirit must be the female love between the Father and the Son. And thus: "The Holy Ghost over the bent world broods, with warm breast and with ah, bright wings." Thus in her prayer God's complacency and concern became hers and God's will for mother was to pray for the salvation of all flesh.

I.7.6 In the Temple Finding and God's World's Five Parts

The finding of the lost had always been for mother a key experience.
Her mother lost her mother when she was but a child of eight.
And yet Martha Mae remained for Leona Mae a presence that
lived on even in Joneva Mae like May Day for girl and for boy.
And her father lost his mother when he was but a child of five.
And maybe he attempted to fill the void of his lost mother with
his addiction to alcohol as perhaps did her husband, who
lost his father when he was but a boy of five and who continued
to suffer one loss after another through life as a winning gambler.
The bum lambs lost their mothers and mother as a little girl
loved to mother them and all this prepared her to fully appreciate
Luke's parables of the lost coin, the lost sheep and the prodigal son.
Thus, this fifth Joyful Mystery opened up for her the Mystery
of God's Mysterious world and His-Her Mysterious will that
she was motivated to obey by the joy that comes when
the lost one is found and she knew it was God's will
that her husband and her father and all lost ones should
be found and while praying the Rosary she came to say:
"Oh my Jesus, forgive us our sins and save us from the fires
of hell, especially those who have most need of thy mercy."
As she tried to understand God's Holy Will that willed love
for every single individual she knew that in God's world
there must be many mansions where God is present
to his different dear ones each in their own unique way.
And those mansions must be open to one another for she
would certainly want to be with her father in his and with
her husband in his and with each and every dear one in theirs.
As she prayed the Mystery of the Finding in the Temple she
saw that Mary was the temple of the Lord for she was
the sacred Holy of Holies in which dwelled the Lord God Yahweh.
Mary is the Mediatrix between cosmos, angels, saints and God.

I.7.7 In the Johannine School's Incarnational Joy

Mother knew the joy of the Beloved Community from the Mormons. And yet outsiders were excluded as was she when she wore her cross to school and was cross-examined by those cross with her. The Johannine School whom the Holy Spirit inspired to write the three letters of John and the book of *Revelations* was just as shamanic as was the Gospel of John which was organized first around the seven signs and then the seven moments of glory. For the book of *Revelations* is organized around seven sets of seven letters to seven churches with seven seals and seven trumpets and seven visions and a violent seven headed dragon. The first three letters before the Apocalypse have to do with those who are getting lost by not being true to the Beloved Community. They are not true to the incarnation and the law of mutual love. If we do not love each other how can we love God who is Love? God is Love and is so loving that he became man and suffered and died for his Beloved redeeming her from world, flesh and devil. But according to this doctrine of tough love which mother found to be valuable when raising teen-agers her own dear father and most others would remain lost forever and this did not meet the higher criterion of love that Christmas joy is a gift for everyone in every place so that there is no hell and all are found. In her life mother lived through the tension of an incarnation love in Luke's sense that let all be found and an incarnation love that was swayed by an Apocalyptic atonement justice so that in the book of *Revelations*, *Agape* is no longer present. By praying the Rosary daily mother matured into the theology that let there be the joy of Christmas everyday for everyone in every place for she deeply believed the lost would be found. Mother's prayer did let her fully believe that God is Love but she with the grace of Mary's mediation saw that love as all inclusive rather than lacking in joy because of exclusivism.

I.7.8 In the Holy Joy of the Sacred Liturgy of the Word

At the heart of mother's life was the interplay between the
Sacred Mass and the Holy Rosary for they were the best ways
of loving with which she had been gifted and she was thankful.
When she met her husband and was given the grace to be a Catholic
she was so joyful to learn how to love in this new way that she
just grew and grew in adoration, repentance, thanksgiving and petition
throughout the rest of her life without ever slowing down for a minute.
With the qualitative leap into the sacred realm of the sacred priests
she knew that it was really the Sacred Mass that let it be Christmas
everyday for her and all of her loved ones and that the Rosary
continued to nourish that Christmas joy in them through each day.
The sacred priest, Father Waldman, her fourth pastor also was
her special, spiritual friend because his vow of sacred celibacy
set him apart to be free to love her and each person as if
they were at the center of his heart as would be his family.
He also enjoyed the physical exercises of athletics as well as
the vital, intellectual and spiritual exercises mother liked.
It was wonderful for her to see the affection and camaraderie
between him and her husband and Cliff and Tom for it was
filled with *agape* and he came from a Benedictine area of Idaho
and he knew of the Benedictine Assumption College in North
Dakota and helped Cliff and Tom so much there and at home.
He told mother about the four stages of the liturgy of the word:
the Confiteor, the Gloria, the Readings and the Creed and how
they all led up to the Kingdom of the crib and the Kingdom
of the cross and how the Kingdom was one of love which began
when Jesus was born in the Manger which as a sheep girl
she knew so well with the smell of hay and the animals.
And the first part of the Mass led up to the liturgy of the Eucharist
and the Eucharist which means well graced in joy is
the prayer of thanksgiving for the gift of Christmas everyday.

I.7.9 In the Holy Joy of the Sacred Liturgy of the Eucharist

The focal point of the Mass and of mother's life was the Sacred Consecration when the *Sacerdos* of the Messiah in the Sacred Temple in union with Peter and his church transformed the bread and wine into the body and blood of the Sacred High Priest, Jesus the Christ. This was a repetition of the incarnation when the Son of God became a child of flesh in the temple-womb of the virgin Mary. The priest raised the body of Jesus and her altar boy son, Clifford, rang the little bell as mother in adoration worshipped the God-man as she would when praying the Joyful Mysteries of the Rosary and as she would at the manger-crib when Jesus was there to be seen. The priest raised the chalice with the blood of Jesus and again Clifford rang the little bell, and mother's heart was overflowing with the thanksgiving of the Eucharist for all of this love was a great Christmas gift to her when she became a Catholic. Love for her was not first of all something she did but it was the gift that she received and simply receiving the gift of the Eucharist was the best way she could love this altar boy and this priest and her family and all of God's sacred creation. And she walked up to the altar with her head bowed in adoration and she knelt there with her eyes shut in worship and Cliff came to her and put the paton under her chin and she opened her mouth and received the body of Jesus with all the love which he had given her and she went back to her pew and she and Jesus made love in her heart and mind and body and soul and she could continue to do that throughout each hour of everyday as she said her Rosary and did her work and loved all whom she met. Christmas was everyday but mother never knew the deep joy of Christmas until she felt that Joy in her communion with the Sacred Heart of Jesus right within her inner being and right between her and all of hers and all of theirs.

I.8 With Her Son, Tommy Joe, and Father Denardis

I.8.1 Especially on Good Friday in Sorrowful Mystery Love

Each morning mother prayed the Joyful Mysteries of the Rosary.
And each day in her increasing joy she received new Christmas gifts.
As she performed the spiritual exercises of her spiritual reading
and spiritual direction from the priest and her weekly confession
and her Rosary three times a day and Mass three times a week she
did receive a richer and richer love life that let her in her heart
love more and more each one for whom she prayed as she connected
their names and problems and gifts with the names of Jesus and Mary.
But each afternoon she prayed the Sorrowful Mysteries of her Rosary
and by the time she was sixty-three in 1981, her sorrow too
grew in massive leaps and bounds with new terrors each day.
Her son, David, who had been spiritually nourished in seminary
for nine years was now a sexually addicted adulterer and while
still married to Wilhelmina now had a pair of twin daughters,
Angela Joy and Charity Marie with a very beautiful lady, Carolyn.
First her father ruined himself and his family with his
alcoholic addiction and her husband tortured himself with his
and now this ruinous and monstrous enemy had become the
sex addiction in her first son whom she named after *Just David*.
All of this broke her heart as she prayed fervently for Wilhelmina
and Josje and David Scott and for Carolyn and the little girls.
It would be terrible for all of them and David didn't even see it.
She couldn't believe what a callous heart her dear son had.
She just didn't know what to do so she took it all to Jesus and Mary
and begged Mary to intercede for them and begged Jesus to be merciful.
As she prayed the five Sorrowful Mysteries each afternoon
she began to see that everyday is Christmas especially Good Friday.
She spent the Agony in the Garden with Jesus as she
agonized over her son and his loved ones who would all be punished.
She saw that Wilhelmina and the boys and Carolyn and the girls
would suffer far more than David and that would punish him.

I.8.2 In the Garden Agony and the Hail Mary's Five Parts

Mother's prayer had prepared her well for her new garden agony over David and his tortured loved ones, for thirty years ago she began to learn to be tranquil in her anxiety as she worried about not having enough room in the house for her new baby. And then only seven years ago her dear husband was told that he had skin cancer and would have to have his ear removed. He was a tough and joyful gambler and tried to comfort her. He still said his prayers each morning as he had his cup of coffee and a cigarette and he too trusted in God's Holy Will. He told mother that he was going to quit smoking and drinking and he had his operation and never had another drink or smoke. He became more relaxed and joyful than he had been since youth. Each afternoon while praying the sorrowful mysteries mother said the *Hail Mary* one after another and in this Good Friday context they were very different than they were in the Nativity context, for now as she prayed: "Hail Mary full of grace, the Lord is with thee;" she saw the tortured and suffering and the crucified Christ there gracing his mother with his loving sorrow so that henceforth all suffering could be a loving and the Sorrowful Mother was suffering with Him. When she prayed "Blessed art thou among women and blessed is the fruit of thy womb," she knew Mary was blessed in her loving of her son and of us in her son's suffering and now she saw that the destiny of her son was to teach us to suffer in love's joy for others. Mother prayed: "Holy Mary, Mother of God," and she knew as she beheld Mary beholding the God-man that our sufferings became the very suffering of God and mother knew that there was hope no matter how much suffering David inflicted on his loved ones. And mother pleaded with her time and time again "Pray for us sinners." And her closest loved ones were terrible sinners. And she prayed: "Now and at the hour of our death. Amen." And she and hers needed help now and she knew that she was getting it now.

I.8.3 In the Pillar Scourging and the Mystery's Five Parts

Tommy Joe and his beautiful wife, Annette, and the children,
Paul and Kali, were now living close by and Tom was teaching
biology and wrestling in the local high school and Tom and
Annette were such a pair of kindred spirits that mother felt free
to discuss anything with them together in a friendship for three.
Tom asked why it was that David had gone so far astray and
mother said that the addictions of a family tree are strange things.
She thought of her grandfather Abbot marrying such a young girl
and grandmother, Martha Mae Hart, being so unhappy and
running away and then having had her baby taken away and
her early death and she thought of her dear father's alcohol addiction.
They tried hard to understand and since David had had the best
of upbringing and education his odd lust was even more mysterious.
Had his nine year attempt at celibacy somehow over-sexualized him?
And each afternoon as mother meditated on the Agony in the Garden she
saw the Sorrowful Mother there with her agony and she prayed
with Mary for her anxious Jesus who was now in dread because
of her own son, David, for his family's anxiety was Christ's anxiety.
Mother well knew the five moments of sorrow: in (1) their anxiety,
(2) their pain, (3) their shame, (4) in dying, and (5) in death and in his
Garden Anxiety Christ was threatened by the known and the unknown.
But soon the pain was very real as Pilate had him scourged at
the pillar and Mary beheld all of this and mother joined in Mary's prayer.
Mother prayed with and for the suffering Jesus that her loved ones
might be delivered from their suffering because of the suffering of Jesus.
Mother prayed with Mary and to Mary as they both beheld
the Crowning with Thorns. Mother prayed with Mary and to Mary
as they beheld him on his Way of The Cross. And mother prayed
for his help that hers could daily carry their cross and rise up
when they fell. And mother with Mary watched him die and pray:
"Father forgive them for they know not what they do."

I.8.4 In the Thorn Crowning and Her Intention's Five Parts

Daddy and Tom and Annette talked about a new home for
Tom and Annette and he wanted them to build a very nice one.
So to help them he got an outlaw poker game going at the Casino
and within a couple of years had saved forty thousand dollars
so he could give each of his five children eight thousand apiece.
And mother was thrilled that Tom was doing so well and yet
still each afternoon as she prayed the Sorrowful Mysteries she
was especially sorrowful over the sorrow in her own dear family.
David told her that he and Carolyn had been excommunicated
and yet they still went to Mass each Sunday without communion.
Mother could imagine Carolyn's shame even though David
was so nonchalant and complacent she could hardly believe it.
She earnestly prayed the Garden Agony Mystery that each
member of her family be truly sorry for their sins.
And with Father Denardis, the priest after Father Waldman,
she had learned to be especially earnest and devout for
though she always was so he and his devout spirituality
confirmed hers as they were total kindred spirits in loving
God and in dedicating themselves to the things of the Lord.
And she knew how large sexuality loomed in David's life
and at the Scourging of the Pillar she prayed especially that
each in her family might obtain purity and with the Virgin she
was pure of heart and it pained her terribly that her son
paid no attention to his marriage vow and it was her
own son whose sins were causing Jesus to be beaten so.
At the third Sorrowful Mystery she prayed again for purity
and her own thoughts were troubling her so that she prayed
that none have suspicious or uncharitable thoughts and thinking of
David's families she prayed that each be able to carry their cross.
And she prayed with all her heart that the Lord's crucifixion
not be in vain for any of her family and that they be saved.

I.8.5 In the Cross Carrying and Her World's Five Parts

Every day was filled with Christmas peace for mother as each morn
she prayed the Joyful Mysteries all centered on the birth of Baby Jesus.
All of her fourteen grandchildren were thriving in school and in church.
She and Joe sold their dear, little, old home in Ketchum for eighty-five
thousand dollars and they had paid for it only thirty-five hundred.
Daddy sold his trash-route and they were able to buy a wonderful
home in Gooding where daddy was born and raised. And Gramma
Coates was in a near-by nursing home and they could visit her
frequently and she was so happy to see them and as they laughed
together Joe's dark brown eyes still shined and danced as they did
when they first met sixty years ago and she was so happy that he
quit his smoking and drinking and that they were both doing so well.
And yet each afternoon as mother prayed the Sorrowful Mysteries
she realized that she was also always in her Good-Friday world
of sorrow and each day she did have to carry her cross and help
her mother and her husband in carrying theirs. And Gramma
Coates passed away and she was buried in Carey next to her dear
estranged husband whom she always loved so much and daddy
said a few words at her grave-site about how she was such
a good and strong lady and how she raised such wonderful children:
Joneva, Mildred, Robert, and Elwin and the older generation in Carey
all knew and loved mother's mother, that community minded woman.
And Joseph began to get pretty bad emphysema and mother took
special care of him and they even bought a cemetery plot for the
two of them there in that cemetery where many of dad's friends
were buried and where he had watched so many burials.
And mother lived in sorrow with the suffering and the dying with
(1) her sorrowful family with the Sorrowful Mother, (2) queen of the
angels even the fallen ones, (3) and queen of the saints even those in
purgatory, and (4) with the Blessed Trinity even the suffering Jesus,
(5) and with all the living everywhere who were always dying.

I.8.6 In the Crucifixion and God's World's Five Parts

In October of 1984, mother told David, Bette Jo, Bobby, Cliff, and Tom
that they should come and say goodbye to their father for the doctor
said he would not live much longer and she was preparing his funeral.
As she prayed the Mystery of the Crucifixion and that it would not
be in vain for anyone in her family she knew it was not in vain
for her husband for even though he had always been a sinner he
was also a saint in his simple faith and his daily prayer and
in the way that he repented so that his story had such a happy ending.
And on January 16, 1986, when he was exactly seventy-five years old
and all the family was there to bury him except for Wilhelmina
and Carolyn and her children and by now David and Carolyn also
had Jonathan Luke and Carolyn Crystal and mother in her sorrow
as she thought about being alone after nearly fifty years with Joe
could actually pray for him in the peace of Christmas and the glory
of the Resurrection but her heart was broken for Carolyn and her's
and for Josje and David Scott whose mother had to be absent too.
And mother had the funeral perfectly arranged and buried her husband
with dignity and one of dad's high school sports friends gave a eulogy
and said that he was the state champion in the Four-Forty but that
he was not the fastest man coming out of the backfield on their state
championship football teams and Tommy too praised his father.
Mother's prayer took her into God's world daily more and more.
As she prayed for her blessed dead: for Uncle Tony, for baby
Mary Theresa, for her father, for her mother, and for her husband
the other dimensions besides this world of time and space began to be
more real for her as she started to think more about the nine choirs
of angels, the nine realms of purgatory and the realms of heaven.
Father Denardis had told her about Dante and his conception
of heaven, hell and purgatory and mother hoped there was no hell.
And mother wanted her will and her world to be just like God's
and as her heart became more like his she wondered about eternal hell.

I.8.7 In the Catholic School's Love That Cancels Sin

Mother knew in the wisdom of her prayer which taught her so much
the alienating power of sin and the sorrow for all of that alienation.
David, Carolyn, and the children came to visit her and by now she
had all seventeen grandchildren and Angela Joy and Charity Marie
were as beautiful to her as their names and Jonathan Luke was
named not only after Carolyn's father, whom David told her was a most
loving man, but after Jonathan, David's friend and as mother
prayed for him each day she thought more of David and Jonathan.
And little Carolyn Crystal was a crystal child and was as cute as her
mother was beautiful, and yet for all this, mother knew that sin's
alienation was right around the next corner just as it had been
for the children of the adulterous King David and mother's sorrow and
her hope were in that promise God gave to David through Nathan.
For your sins you will be lashed with the rods of men and yet
my Kingdom of everlasting love will not be taken away from you.
And as mother listened to the readings at Mass and as she looked
further into her Bible the Catholic epistles began to direct her best
as she prayed the Sorrowful Mysteries with such sorrow for
David and his family and as she saw that the parental alienation
syndrome was so necessary if her son were to be delivered.
And St. Jude's Epistle was suited to her needs for he was the Patron
Saint of hopeless cases and her son's family was a hopeless case.
And the Epistle of St. James became a favorite of hers as he
warned against the dangers of gossip and as he argued that faith
without works is dead. And she saw the wisdom of the both-and
and by doing her daily works of prayer and of all her good deeds
her faith increased and increased faith made for better works.
And Peter wrote, "Above all, keep your love for one another at full
strength, because love cancels innumerable sins" (1 Pet 4:8). And
mother's sorrow over David and his family and all their broken
hearts led her to pray more fervently that their sins be cancelled.

I.8.8 In the Holy Sorrow of the Sacred Liturgy of the Word

Once mother moved to Gooding she could walk to daily Mass and
even pray the Joyful Mysteries on the way there and on the way back.
The Rosary was her way of living out the Mass throughout the day.
For the Offertory was the source of Holy Joy, the Consecration
the source of Holy Sorrow and Communion the source of Holy Glory.
The first part of the Mass was the preparation for the Sacred Eucharist.
Mother lived out the Liturgy of the Word in each of the Mysteries.
Now that the Mass was prayed in English mother began by saying
with the priest: "I confess to almighty God and to the Blessed Mary ever
virgin and to all the angels and saints that I have sinned exceedingly."
Mother prayed with sorrow for her sins of omission and commission
and she prayed that all her family be truly sorry for their sins.
As she prayed: "Lord have mercy on us! Christ have mercy on us!
Lord have mercy on us!" she pleaded for the much needed purity,
the lack of which had been the scourge for many in her family.
She prayed for the grace each needed in order to love and serve God.
During the praying of the Gloria she prayed that love and praise
and worship and adoration for God would come into each of her
loved ones and build up an attitude within them that would replace
all impure, suspicious, uncharitable thoughts and get rid of
any pride and selfishness which are at the root of sin's alienation.
She prayed that they love the other and the alien rather than be alienated.
During the reading of the Hebrew Bible and the Epistles and the Gospel
she listened with attention and patience and she prayed for patience
for all of them for in the big picture of God's wisdom not a sparrow
or a sinner would be lost and sorrow and patience must work together.
And in the Credo she prayed: "And I believe in his only Son, our Lord,
who was conceived by the Holy Spirit, born of the Virgin Mary,
suffered under Pontius Pilate, was crucified, died and was buried."
She prayed in the depths of her joyful and sorrowful heart that
that Christmas peace and Good Friday passion not be in vain for hers.

I.8.9 In the Holy Sorrow of the Sacred Liturgy of the Eucharist

The Sacred Event that the Sacred Priest performs in the Sacred Place
of Sacred Places there on the altar is the Liturgy of the Eucharist
with its joyful offertory, sorrowful consecration and glorious communion.
Mother always remembered how Father Dougherty explained to her
why a Catholic priest is so different from any other holy minister.
In the Catholic world the sacred *sacerdos* and the sacred sacrifice
of the Mass are not just another holy man and another holy event
but they are really distinct from any other type of prayerful worship.
The holy is not really defined in turns of its opposite but all
things can be hallowed and made holy. However, the sacred
is defined in terms of its opposite, the profane, which is that
outside or opposed to the *fanum* or the temple. So the priest is
set aside in sacred celibacy from the profane in order to offer
the sacrifice of the Mass in order that all might become holy.
And that interplay between the sacred and the holy was the secret
of mother's life for the sacred liturgy of the Eucharist inspired
her and gave her the grace that she might always hallow her life.
And the Holy Rosary was her way of bringing the sacred Eucharist
into her morning in joy, her afternoon in sorrow and her evening
in the glory that could transform sorrow into joy even though
it remained that fermenting sorrow with its sacred Passion.
As mother came down toward the end of her life she was
so thankful for her husband, her six children and her
seventeen grandchildren and she did feel her life had been blest.
Even though she knew great sorrow was coming for David's
children she did live in a spirit of gratitude for them.
The four younger ones were born in sin and that hurt
even the two older ones but still she was glad that they
existed and they were all such beautiful children.
Even out of her son's adultery and the sorrow it would bring
God through his Son's suffering it could bring a greater good.

I.9 With Her Grandchildren

I.9.1 In the Glorious Mystery of the Resurrection

Everyday was Christmas for mother and especially Good Friday because of the Resurrection Glory that transforms Good Friday Sorrow into Nativity Joy even though it remains a holy and loving sorrow. As mother prayed the ten *Hail Marys* of the Resurrection she was lost in wondrous thanksgiving at the difference it made for humankind. Before the Resurrection some philosophers did argue for the immorality of the soul but now that Jesus was born in the flesh at Christmas and risen in the flesh at Easter every human being could also rise with the Lord so that none of their lovely singularity would ever be lost. God made the starry sky above and the moral law within, but mother was more in wonder at the Resurrection of all flesh than she was over any other of God's mysterious wonders in the universe. Her father, her husband and now her son, David, brought sorrow to many and she was always in her Garden Agony because she knew David's children would suffer so much because of their father's sin. And yet when she prayed her *Hail Marys* and meditated on the Glorious Mystery of the Resurrection she believed in the promise given to David that the Kingdom of merciful and everlasting love would be there forever for David, his wives and all her dear grandchildren. The Resurrection that was made all the more poignant by Good Friday is so glorious because it manifests the unmanifest in all its unmanifestness for no one could ever have guessed what God is like without the Incarnation, Good Friday and then the Resurrection for God is a loving God beyond all comprehension. But even though we will have all eternity to keep knowing what God is like at least we can believe now that this God of love is. This all powerful God is yet as little and as sweet as Baby Jesus and suffers for us and with us as did Jesus on Calvary and rises from the dead to let us live forever in all that we are. In mother's constant giving of Glory to God she was glorious herself in manifesting for all who knew her how God loves even sinners.

I.9.2 In the Resurrection and the Hail Mary's Five Parts

As mother prayed the Glorious Mystery of the Resurrection she tried to envision how Mary must have been feeling now when mother prayed to her with the words of Angel Gabriel: "Hail Mary, full of grace, the Lord is with you." As Jesus departed from her in his terrible death she not only felt wild with anguish for him but she felt forlorn and forsaken and wondered if his beautiful birth and life were to be only for this ignominious death which would be the end of all. But, then he rose from the dead and was with his mother again and these words: "The Lord is with you" meant more now at this miracle of the resurrection than they did at the moment of his incarnation when she responded to these words and at the moment of the nativity when she gave birth to God's one and only Son. When mother prayed, "Blessed art thou among women, and blessed is the fruit of thy womb, [Jesus]" (Luke 1:43), she knew that Mary felt even more blessed than she had when John the Baptist leapt in Elizabeth's womb at their visitation for now John the Baptist had leapt to life again when the Resurrected Lord descended to the dead when he was dead and brought him to a resurrected life again. Mother knew her prayer would be answered even for the most impossible of cases as she prayed: "Holy Mary, Mother of God pray for us" for already all the sorrow of the afternoon was seen as a blessed event now that Jesus resurrected it in glory. Mother could now love all her sorrow and suffering and all the suffering of her loved ones because she experienced how the Resurrected Jesus turned it into glory-love and it now was the potent fertilizer that would become beautiful flowers forever. "Pray for us sinners now." How different this "now" was from what it had been in the afternoon and even in the morning. This "now" was an everlasting "now" that contained every "now" that had ever been in a resurrected and reconciled eternal Glory-Love. "And, at the hour of our death, Amen." Death where is now thy sting?

I.9.3 In the Ascension and the Mystery's Five Parts

As mother prayed the Glorious Mysteries day in and day out for
fifty years she came to see how the five mysteries each revealed
five different types of Glory that made Glory more comprehensible.
The Shekinah Yahweh was a sign of the divine Presence and would
appear as a cloud by day and a guiding pillar of fire by night.
When Jesus made his Resurrection appearances he was a sign
recognized only by those who loved him in the way he broke the bread
at Emmaus and in the way he said her name "Mary" to Magdalene.
In his resurrected body he manifested the unmanifest Divine Love
and that made manifest his own unmanifest incarnate body.
But both the Divine Love and his incarnate body still exceeded
the appearing sign that they could palpably hold fast in their hand
even though he would at the same time say: "Don't hold me."
Even though he ordered the Doubting Thomas to put his fingers
into the wounds of his crucified body that seemed unglorified.
Mother then saw that just as his resurrected body appeared so
his ascending body disappeared and there was not only glory
in his ascension but there was glory in his absence for forty days.
They huddled together in the upper room in fear and trembling but
united by his glorious incarnate, crucified, resurrected ascension Love.
Then at Pentecost the Holy Spirit of the Risen Lord came upon them
in tongues of fire that empowered them with those shamanic gifts
some of which some exercised and others of which others exercised.
As mother prayed the fourth glorious mystery of the Assumption
of Mary into Heaven she became especially fond of the special glory
of that mystery for though her glory was not that of the Son of God
it let mother know that even non-God flesh would be glorified.
The fifth glorious mystery was that of the Crowning of Mary
as Queen of Heaven and Earth and mother was so happy to have
Mary as her glorious queen whose *Hail Mary* she could pray all day
knowing that Mary would intercede for her with Christ her King.

I.9.4 The Descent of the Holy Spirit and Her Intention's Five Parts

Carolyn, David, Angela Joy, Charity Marie, Jonathan Luke, and
Carolyn Crystal came to visit mother and the family and it broke
mother's heart that these adorable grandchildren were born out of
wedlock and that their lovely mother was not David's true wife.
She loved them so much that she prayed for them more than for
anyone for where the greatest sorrow is the greatest prayer is.
Each evening when she prayed the Glorious Mysteries her intention
for the ten *Hail Marys* of the Resurrection was that David and his
receive true faith and might grow in sorrow for their sins.
And soon her prayers began to be answered for Carolyn read
a love letter from another woman and after five years of anguish
told David in September of 1993 that he was no longer welcome
to be with her and the children and he moved out to live with Josje.
Mother knew the sorrow of Carolyn and the children and she prayed
that that sorrow would move her son, David, to sorrow for his sins.
She prayed the beads of the Ascension for her grandchildren and she
put the emphasis on grace that they might be graced with the help,
protection and faith each one needed. And as she lived through
the Church's year of Grace there was the Resurrection at Easter and
then the Ascension about the time of David's birthday forty days later.
Then ten days after that there was Pentecost and the long season
of the gifts of the Holy Spirit until Advent and Christmas time.
And at Pentecost on her Rosary she prayed for her Godchildren
and they greatly profited from her prayer and care as Bobby Jr.,
Denise McDermott, and Michael MacPheters can attest today.
And when she prayed the Mystery of the Assumption she was so happy
to bring her brothers and sisters and all their families into her
heart and into the heart of the Blessed Virgin Mary. And finally
as she prayed the last Mystery each evening before going
to sleep she prayed for her parish and all parishes especially
the one in Ketchum that the Queen of Heaven protect all priests.

I.9.5 In the Assumption and Her World's Five Parts

Mother always felt especially close to David's wife, Wilhelmina, for she was a fun loving, kind, and loving nurse from Holland who always took the best of care for David, Joseph Robert, and David Scott. Wilhelmina loved the Charismatic Movement and also constantly prayed the way mother did and had Rosary prayer meetings at her home and she became the Godmother for Carolyn's daughters. When she saw Angela Joy and Charity Marie playing in her back yard she decided to move with Josje and David Scott that the twins might be with their father and it was a time of sorrow for all. Then in 1995, Wilhelmina passed away with cancer and mother prayed for her and with her for mother believed that now Willie, as she called her, could intercede for them with Mary and with Jesus. And mother prayed not only for her own Godchildren but for Wilhelmina's too, and it was all so complicated and confusing, and mother knew that Wilhelmina prayed especially to Mary as *The Star of the Sea* and mother prayed that that Star shine for them. As mother advanced in age, grace, and wisdom she lived more and more in a world of Glory for Jesus has ascended into that realm and his mother was taken up there too and many of her loved ones had also been called to their everlasting home with their God. Her prayer even when sorrowful was now always touched by Glory. Her prayer be it joyful, sorrowful or glorious let her always abide in (1) the Glory of the Father, Son and Holy Spirit, (2) the Glory of the Blessed Virgin Mary and all the Angels and all the Saints, (3) the Glory of her family and all of her friends and relatives, (4) the Glory of her parish where with the sacred priest for fifty years now she had been receiving her glorious communion, and (5) the Glory of Holy Mother Church who had been so good to her in helping raise and educate her family and who was so good for all the needy of the earth and now Priests were coming to Idaho from Mexico as before they came from Ireland.

I.9.6 In the Coronation and God's World's Five Parts

The whole point of mother's life was to conform her will to God's and that meant to conform her world to God's world insofar as the Father created it, the Son redeemed it and the Holy Spirit now sanctifies it. As mother continued to meditate on the five Glorious Mysteries she saw how they fit together to reveal God's world structurally. Just as the third Joyful Mystery, the Nativity, held together the five Joyful Mysteries so also the third Glorious Mystery, the Descent of the Holy Spirit upon the Apostles, held together the Glorious. The Holy Spirit does come as the Holy Spirit of the Risen Lord Jesus. The Holy Spirit is also changed by the Christmas Incarnation for she came first in the flesh of a dove with warm breasts and with, ah bright wings and now fifty days after the Resurrection she comes as tongues of flaming fire for one of the gifts of the Holy Spirit as Wilhelmina and mother knew is to speak in tongues. But what is this fire? When Jesus descended into hell for three days did he even redeem the fire so that now it is Holy Spirit fire. So God's world is that of the Father who is the Spiritual Source but once Christmas came God the Son is forever incarnate in his Resurrected Body and the Spirit of the Risen Lord Jesus is also forever incarnate in the animal dove and in the fire. And Mary as Queen of Heaven and Earth has been assumed into heaven in her glorious flesh also so that God's world is made up of the Spiritual Father and all his Spiritual Angels who probably also got redeemed if they were fallen when Jesus descended into hell. Then there is all the flesh that will see the salvation of the Lord, for Christ will be forever the Christmas King and Mary will be forever the Christmas Queen for the lowly Babe and the lowly Mother by the Holy Spirit are revealed as glorious to the likes of mother who in conforming to God's world shows us God's Love which until the incarnation was thought of only as justice but now forever must be mercy.

I.9.7 In the Pauline School's Glorious Battle

As mother approached her last days in the preglorious flesh
she saw that we are here to learn to love for unless there are
crucifixions there cannot be resurrections and Christmas eternally.
Mother beheld the merciful hand of Jesus touching Carolyn
and moving her to punish David by telling the children to stay
away from him for only then would he wake up and begin to see
how sinful and hurtful adultery is in hurting all concerned.
As she fervently prayed with greater and greater love each day
for Carolyn and the four dear children she saw that Carolyn
was a strong warrior as described in the Pauline School's
letter to the Ephesians and that she had the right strategy for David.
Mother was happy that Carolyn knew just how to battle David's
dark and demonic forces with "the belt of truth" and "the shield
of faith" that can halt the "Devil's flaming arrows" that crazy
David could only see as cupid arrows in his lack of insight
concerning the world of the flesh and its serious implications.
Mother noted that the devil's attack will not be part of a final
apocalyptic conflict for the glorious Mysteries reveal God's mercy.
Mother especially loved the Pauline School's letter to the Colossians.
Her praying of the Glorious mysteries prepared her to appreciate:
"The secret is this: Christ is in you as the holy of a glory to come" (1:27).
As she wondered about glory and its transforming of sorrow into
joy she loved to read Paul because he too was always thinking
about the glory of *agape* and even the Pauline School kept up
the meditation on self-emptying as the sorrowful way
of becoming sorry for our sins which is the transition from
suffering sorrow to sorrow for sin which is the secret of
Christ in you who comes at Christmas and at Pentecost.
And Carolyn seemed to know just that secret in divorcing
David from a marriage that was never a marriage and
in freeing herself and her children even in order to free him.

I.9.8 In the Holy Glory of the Sacred Liturgy of the Word

On each Sunday and special Holy Day the sacred priest at the
sacred Mass recited the sacred Gloria and mother continued to
meditate on that mysterious Glory that let every Mass be Christmas:
"Glory to God in the highest, and peace be to humans of good will."
And mother saw how Christmas could be everyday because Jesus
had given with his incarnation a new meaning to the law of
like for like. She could see how for those without Christmas
everyday there could only be the like for like of an eye for an eye
and a tooth for a tooth, but while that law of justice still held she
saw a great meaning in those words: "And peace to humans of good will."
She knew that her father and her husband and her first son even
though they were great sinners still were loving persons of good will.
She was so happy to know that God still loved them as did she
and that there was this new law of mercy that especially went
out and saved the lost sheep and even the most prodigal of sons.
Mother's children and grandchildren were living without
habitual mortal sin and they were greatly at peace but the world
did seem to be becoming more and more self-centered and there
were fewer and fewer priests from Idaho serving the Diocese.
However, the ways of God are miraculous and mother learned
that when her grandchildren Jody and Tobby were confirmed
that more than half the class for sacred confirmation were
of Mexican background and mother prayed for the constant
renewal of Holy Mother Church and her family by the Holy Spirit.
And she was so thankful that David was no longer excommunicated
and she was anxious that he would get mixed up with a divorcee.
But, lo and behold, a most beautiful and saintly lady, Johanna,
who was also a Doctor of Philosophy rescued him and they married.
And they came to visit her and she could hardly believe how
merciful God was because Johanna was utterly pure of heart
and had never been married and had the joyful peace of good will.

I.9.9 In the Holy Glory of the Sacred Liturgy of the Eucharist

They brought mother holy communion and she prayed her Rosary
each day of her last year in the Beehive Nursing Home in Gooding.
Its atmosphere was that of a Beloved Mormon Community and she
felt right at home as she prayed: "Holy Mary, Mother of God,
pray for us sinners now and at the hour of our death. Amen."
Now it was the hour of her death and she knew that Mary was
with her as she had been with Mary for every minute of her
last fifty years and she knew that her family and the parish
were praying for her too, just as she had always prayed for them.
And their visitations to her were as joyful as was that one
between the incarnation and the nativity and they came often.
Bette Jo and Bob and Lynn Marie and John and Ritchie and Tracy,
Bobby and Genie and Amy and David and Jesse and Tom,
Cliff and Bim and Jody, Tobby and Heidi,
Tom and Annette and Paul, Kali and Cory,
David and Johanna.
Josje and Scotty were not brought to say: "until we meet again."
Carolyn, Angela Joy, Charity Marie, Jonathan Luke, and Carolyn Crystal
were absent, but in their absence they were present in that sorrow
that mother's mother knew and her father and her husband knew and
as she prayed especially for them it left her heart weeping to know
that these dear grandchildren of hers had a father but no daddy.
Then they brought her communion for the last time and she prayed
her last *Hail Mary* and she was taken into the communion of saints
and she was no longer separated from any of her blessed dead.
And I was not able to be there for her funeral as she was buried
next to her husband but I said then in my heart that I would
write for my mother dear a Eulogy-Lament and this is it.
And so Mamma, I pray the Rosary with you and with Wilhelmina
each day as we say: "Oh my Jesus, forgive us our sins and save us
from the fires of hell, especially those who most need your mercy."

II. Søren Kierkegaard

II.7 Reconciling the God-Man and Luther

II.7.1 In the Agapeic Synthesis of Faith and Works

The title *Works of Love* is significant for it has to do
with Luther's exclusivistic logic by which he initiated
the modern world of nation states and rugged individualism.
With his formula of *Sola Fidei* or "faith alone" Luther
emphasized one element of Paul's letter to the *Romans*
against Paul's universalism and against the Gospel for all.
By arguing that we are justified and saved by faith alone
and not by works Luther expressed his either/or attitude.
In order to reconcile Luther and Modernity with the God-man
all of Kierkegaard's works as they culminate in *Works of Love*
make explicit the reconciliation of faith and works in love.
Kierkegaard received the gift of faith as a child but he fell
away from that faith and then was saved by loving Regina.
That Socratic-Platonic higher *eros* that transformed his life
let him clearly see how we are saved not by faith alone.
By loving Regina Kierkegaard was greatly gifted with grace.
But, his conversion was more like that of Socrates—Plato
than that of Paul or Augustine who were not saved through *eros*.
Freedom and asceticism are central to the faith-works dialectic.
Kierkegaard together with Paul and Augustine experienced conversion
as a becoming free to serve others with the works of love.
They see God in the incarnation as stepping back to free us.
Together with James they believe that faith without works is dead.
They each experienced faith as freeing them to help save others.
Luther and modern individualists say: "Here I stand!" saved
by God and the do not think of their works as saving others.
Kierkegaard was saved by God's grace through Regina and
his breaking of the engagement was meant to save her
from his thorn in the flesh until he could make faith's
second movement of the leap and come back to her with
the works of love that could be fitting to her as his wife.

II.7.2 In the Agapeic Synthesis of Scripture and Tradition

With logical consistency Luther devalued our human tradition
as well as all human works by seeing them as corrupted by sin.
The *Sola Scriptura* doctrine is intimately connected with the notion
of *Sola Fidei* and thus all philosophy is thought of as paganism.
For Luther the Scholastic tradition of Augustine, Aquinas, Bonaventure,
Scotus, and Ockham could have no merit insofar as they used
Plato, Aristotle, the Stoics and Socrates in their *caritas* synthesis.
Luther thought of all other religions as trapped in fallen falsity.
On the other hand Kierkegaard thinks constantly with Socrates,
Plato and Hegel while working with the Hebrew Bible as well.
With the both-and of his double movement leap of faith Kierkegaard
can love other philosophies and religions in his *caritas* synthesis.
Other traditions can be *Praeparatio Evangelica* or preparation
for the Gospel and thus can be fulfilled by the revealed Word
and can aid us in better appropriating Scripture's good news.
Kierkegaard's model of the prodigal son as loving the elder brother
as more important lets Kierkegaard approach Socrates as well
as Abraham by loving each of them as more important.
In his first book on *The Concept of Irony with Constant
Reference to Socrates* Kierkegaard's view of the Incarnate God-man
lets him love not only Regina but also Socrates as more important.
He really loved the ironical love of the white horse as more important.
A further point for Kierkegaard is to imitate the God-man
in loving Luther and the Lutherans as more important than
himself and the ones he loved, even though Luther rejects them.
The God-man's saving love already begins its works of love
for all persons as the creator becomes creature out of love
for all creatures and reveals the worth of each in an apotheosis.
As the God-man steps down and back out of love for his
creatures all flesh is seen as now possessing Divine worth.

II.7.3 In the Agapeic Synthesis of Law and Gospel

The Lutheran theology of Law and Gospel is intimately
connected with their understanding of faith and works.
With their exclusive either/or and not both-and logic
they latch on to (Romans 11:6):

> But if (salvation) is by grace,
> it is no longer on the basis of works,
> otherwise grace is no longer grace.

They put (salvation) in parenthesis because the word is not
in the text and the text refers to the God of Israel telling Elijah
that in spite of all the sins of his people a remnant is saved.
The issue has to do with the relation between Law and Gospel
which the Lutherans want to keep separate to show that Christ
has fulfilled the Law for us and that imitating Christ in order
to receive salvation changes the Gospel into Law or it implies
that our works and human works can help to save persons.
But we can make up in ourselves what is lacking in
the suffering of Christ and our works can help others realize
their salvation which Christ initiated by becoming flesh.
Law according to the Lutherans shows us what we do and
cannot do and Gospel shows us what God does for us.
Law is our S.O.S. for it shows us our sin and it can
give us a guilt complex unless the Gospel removes the complex.
Law is a rule, a curb and a mirror for it tells us the rules
of right and wrong and it is a curb that keeps us on the straight
and narrow and it is a mirror that shows us our sins.
The Gospel of Good News is that Christ has died for us
and atoned for our sins and if we have faith in him
as our Lord and Savior we are saved by his grace alone.
Faith alone in Scripture alone with its Law and Gospel alone
saves us and any works by anyone without faith is worthless
and even the works of believers only sanctifies but does not save.

II.7.4 In the Agapeic Synthesis of the Universal Community

As Kierkegaard pondered his beloved Lutheran world and modernity he saw that at its core was a rugged individualism implied by its faith alone in scripture alone and in its grace alone. When Luther said: "Here I stand!" against the church of Peter and the succession of the authority of the Petrine line, against the asceticism of the Monastic tradition, against the philosophy of the scholastic tradition, against the community of saints who can pray for us as we pray for all the blessed dead, against Mary as Queen of the Angels and saints, against the seven sacraments with their double work *ex opere operato* and *ex opere operantis*, and against the seven Holy Orders he became a rugged individualist with a direct relation to his God alone. His rugged individualism is a denial of any community in which love is primarily for others and of any universalism in which all of God's creation is wonderfully good as it is revealed by the God-man in his flesh that saves all flesh. Indulgences made no sense to Luther for given the denial of the works of love for others my offering and prayers can be of no merit for the blessed dead in their purgatory. Luther not only set up the attitude of rugged individualism but also of a self-centered nationalism in which he did not want any good German money going to Rome for Renaissance art. Modernity was already beginning in 1492 when Columbus sailed the ocean blue and the colonizers were getting wealthy. The politics of *cuius regio; eius religio* became a great rationalization to take over Catholic Churches wherever princes wanted to go along with Lutheran individualism and nationalism. The Lutheran state church in Denmark promoted excellence in its culture's physical, vital, intellectual and spiritual exercises. Even though Kierkegaard did not agree with the exclusivistic logic of Luther he greatly loved his Lutheran culture that gave him all.

II.7.5 In the Synthesis of Eros and Agape

To work out in detail his own version of the *caritas* synthesis
Kierkegaard comments on the hard saying of Luke 14:26

> If any man comes to me without hating
> his father, mother, wife, children,
> brothers, sisters, yes and his own life too,
> he cannot be my disciple.

In all the natural loves of affection, friendship and *eros*
Kierkegaard detects a preferential love that is self love.
So to get to a universal love of all persons and love our
neighbor as ourselves we need to first hate and get rid of
the preferential self love that prevents a *caritas* synthesis.
With the asceticism of self denial we can imitate Christ
if we step back and love family, friends and beloved as neighbor
and then with the second movement of the leap of faith we can
come back and love them relatively rather than absolutely.
Kierkegaard agrees with Luther that the natural loves can
be a self-deceptive, egoistic, self love rather than genuine
altruistic loves in which we love our neighbor as ourselves.
But with Luther he does not condemn Platonic *eros* and
think it has nothing to do with the Christian love of *caritas*.
Kierkegaard experienced for himself a transforming sublimation
that Luther never did experience and thus Kierkegaard like Paul
and Augustine with their conversion experience believes in a logic
of the both-and and of faith and works, scripture and tradition and
of a mix of law and Gospel that can grace all loving flesh.
Caritas is the Latin translation of *Agape* and Lutherans get
very defensive with anything like Augustine's *caritas* synthesis
because they think it goes to the other extreme with Pelagius.
Pelagius thought that with our effort alone and without grace
we can be totally self-sufficient in love and personal growth.
So Paul, Augustine and Kierkegaard harmonize Christ and Pelagius.

II.7.6 In the Synthesis of Affection and Agape

Kierkegaard's father greatly loved his youngest, hunch-back child
who was a short little fellow who compensated with witty genius.
As the father lost his children one by one his Lutheran conscience
made of him a melancholic Dane with whom Kierkegaard identified.
And the little boy reciprocated his father's heartfelt affection
and was gifted with his father's values and received from
his father and his father's theological friends the beloved Lutheran faith.
As his father carried the cross of losing his children
one by one he became more and more Lutheran in the melancholy
mood of the solitude of *sola fidei, sola scriptura, sola gratia*.
In his early twenties Kierkegaard who was bonded in affection
with his beloved father and his beloved Luther went also into solitude.
Then he became alienated from his father and his beloved faith
and in his solitude he was estranged from all existence
in the black *melanie* and the seething *cholia* of despair.
He could not even take solace in wine, women and song
as a little misfit and pervert in the secret shame of his
thorn in the flesh which linked him with pagan Greek homosexuals.
Then he met Regina and began to see the power of her dear love
and the solitudinal mood of *sola fidei, sola scriptura, sola gratia*
became transformed for him by the works of her dear love alone
in a new world of works alone, tradition alone and law alone.
Now he could follow the law with the ease of the white horse
submitting as a disciplined disciple to the charioteer.
The great tradition of Platonic love that through Neo-Platonism
came into Origen, Augustine and the mystics of monasticism
and Bernard of Clairvaux and John of the Cross and Teresa of Avila
now spoke to him without that bit of scripture selected by
Luther and used against the scripture of the incarnation.
Regina's works of love began to gift Kierkegaard with
a new erotic affection that was beginning to save him.

II.7.7 In the Synthesis of Friendship and Agape

Regina's affection bonding with his mother's affection gave to S. K.
a great new security and confidence in his own abilities and that
combined with the security to be with others that his father's
and his father's friend's affection gave to him in that world of
Lutheran Patriarchy in which pastorship passes from father to son.
The double security of Kierkegaard's new double affection gifted
him to stand side by side with friends exploring all together
and to stand face to face enraptured with each other in *eros*.
Kierkegaard knew of all these works of love from experience
and it was now his task to synthesize each of them with *agape*.
Each of them did have a preferential self-love within it.
Even in the natural world without the supernatural *agape* that
Jesus revealed in his incarnation and self-sacrificing love
for others a detachment from first attachments was necessary
that could then open them to higher affection, friendship and *eros*.
That was the point of the Greek philosophies and world religions.
Kierkegaard loved his Lutheran Bishops, pastors and professors
who taught him so much even about the Greeks and Hegel.
So when he came to write his *Works of Love* which broke
with Luther he was afraid of offending his beloved friends
just as he offended his dear father when he left home
and as he feared offending Regina by breaking their engagement.
He knew that standing side by side and face to face was
outlawed by Luther's "Here I stand" as a rugged individual.
By hating the preferential egoism in his affection,
friendship and *eros* Kierkegaard discovered how to come to
a universal love of all God's children as unique individuals.
Against the rugged individual but also for that individual
Kierkegaard worked out his primary concept of the single individual.
With this concept and the works of love of his authorship
Kierkegaard is working to reconcile the God-man and Luther.

II.7.8 In the Synthesis of Incarnation and Atonement

The dialectic of the four loves in *Works of Love* is the dialectic of Kierkegaard's entire authorship with its pseudonymical writings that deceive us out of the egoism of our self deceit. Luther deceived himself by making only the first movement of the leap of faith and then insisting on that faith alone. He did not make the second movement of the leap by living on all the floors of his interior castle and coming back to love relatively all aesthetic affection, ethical friendship and religious *eros*. He saw the egoism of affection, friendship, and *eros* but could not leap into Platonic Love with Augustine and into the higher loves of all the other great religious traditions which he negated. He denied them all with his *sola scriptura* and as a rugged individualist he basically denied the incarnation and its love for any kind of fleshly love anywhere as having some goodness. Luther was not primarily a lover and considered only his fellow Lutherans to be his neighbor whom he should love. Luther like all the religions of religiousness A stressed an atonement theology with faith in a rewarder-punisher God rather than in Jesus who does not live for self alone but as the God-man was the Good Samaritan for everyone and the suffering servant for all especially his persecutors. Luther had no love for other no-saying protestors like Zwingli and Calvin and as they got going you begin to see in their religious wars the war of all against all a la Hobbes. The task of Kierkegaard's theological philosophy is to balance Incarnation and Atonement theologies in the way that was first revealed in the Davidic promise in 2 Samuel 7. The Kingdom of David's everlasting, merciful love or *hesed* would last for all the house of David forever even though for any sin he and they would be punished with the rods of men. Incarnational love for all is eternal and punishment is temporary.

II.7.9 By Loving Lutherans as More Important

Kierkegaard's theology of the Incarnational God-man argues that
Jesus loves Luther and all Lutherans as more important than himself.
Jesus performed all his works of love beginning with the incarnation
and his works do not exclude even those who exclude works.
Kierkegaard naturally identified with all Lutherans who did
so much to make their own modern world so much better.
But he must hate his own with their exclusivistic preferences
and hate his preferential love for them that he might love all
and especially all those whom Lutherans declare to be enemies.
Once he loves all his neighbors in the flesh he can come back
and have faith in the lovability of all protesting Lutherans.
Luther had good intentions when he posted his ninety-five theses
and his ninety seven theses in order to show what was wrong
with Holy Mother Church and all the Holy Spirit did for the church.
The Holy Spirit was directing Luther too for God writes
straight with crooked lines even when they protest God's writing.
Kierkegaard and Nietzsche were both the best of good Lutherans
in initiating the beginning of the existential-postmodern movement
that went back and reclaimed the rejected pre-modern with
a fresh vitality that the great Luther experiment made possible.
No wonder Kierkegaard was happy to imitate the God-man
in loving Luther as more important than himself for Luther
certainly merited through all of his good works a great love.
And the Lutheran tradition as it developed the excellence of
the atonement line of scripture was also worthy of great love.
Kierkegaard by imitating the prodigal God-man and his
prodigal Catholic Church was happy to love the older brother,
the great protesting and reforming Luther as more important
than himself for continued reformation is always necessary.

II.8 Reconciling the God-Man and the Desperado

II.8.1 By Giving Spirit to Those Ignorant of Being in Despair

The Father, Son, and Holy Ghost by themselves were not desperados but once the long drama of human history began to unfold they decided for the Son to become a desperado out of love for their desperate children. Jesus became a prodigal desperado by leaving his father's house to go live with desperados and become a street kid whom they killed. Jesus became a desperado to reconcile desperados with God by loving each desperado as more important than himself. In *Sickness Unto Death*, his book on despair, Anti-Climacus gives a thorough analysis of the kinds of despair and in what way each can help us grow in love but can also destroy our hope. He explains it with his analogy of the house:

> Imagine a house with a basement, first floor, and second floor planned so that there is or is supposed to be a social distinction between the occupants according to the floor. Now, if what it means to be a human being is compared with such a house, then all too regrettably the sad and ludicrous truth about the majority of people is that in their own house they prefer to live in the basement.
> Every human being is a psychical-physical synthesis intended to be spirit; this is the building, but he prefers to live in the basement, that is in sensate categories. Moreover, he not only prefers to live in the basement— no, he loves it so much that he is indignant if anyone suggests that he move to the superb second floor that stands vacant and at his disposal, for he is after all, living in his own house. (43)

Living in the basement alone is the despair of aesthetes, while living on the first floor alone is the despair of the merely ethical and living on the second floor alone is the despair of the religious. To live on all floors of the house at once is the Christian ideal of religious B and Anti-Climacus is against only climbing up to the second floor because he wants us to come down to all the floors.

II.8.2 By Giving Hope to Desperados of Finitude with Infinitude

Like Anti-Climacus the God-man came down from his realm of infinite, eternal, absolute perfection into the realm of finite, temporal relative imperfection to teach us how to build up the houses of our lives. The first great cosmic event was God's creation of the universe as an overflow of Divine Love for us and the second great cosmic event was the incarnation in which out of love the Son of God became flesh that we might love the God who is the love between the three persons and each other with an ever growing love within our house of love. God the Son came down to live in the sensate categories of the basement and also in the ethical categories of duty on the first floor of our house in such a way that he might reveal to us the possibility of freely living in all the rooms of all the floors of our many possibilities. We are anxious about possibilities and when we venture out into new possibilities with growing pains we feel threatened by possibilities. But, if we succumb to that anxiety then we fall into despair by inclosing ourselves in certain programmed actualities and by taking offence at moving out into other, better ways of living. So on that same page of *Sickness Unto Death* Anti-Climacus writes:

> No, to be in error, is, quite un-Socratically, what men fear least of all. There are amazing examples that illustrate this. A thinker erects a huge building, a system, a system embracing the whole of existence, world history, etc., and if his personal life is considered, to our amazement the appalling and ludicrous discovery is made that he himself does not personally live in this huge, domed palace but in a shed alongside it, or in a doghouse, or at best in the janitor's quarters. Were he to be reminded of this by one single word, he would be insulted. For he does not fear to be in error if he can only complete the system— with the help of being in error. (43)

So how does Kierkegaard differ from Hegel on anxiety and despair?

II.8.3 By Giving Hope to Desperados of Infinitude with Finitude

If we only live on one actual floor of our house and do not consider other possibilities which offend us we are in the despair of finitude for the actual is finite and the possible is infinite. On the other hand we might never get serious about an actual ethical committed way of life and only play with possibilities and then we are in the despair of infinitude without actual finitude. Hegel considers the history of all kinds of aesthetical, ethical and religious possibilities but he does not actually start living in the palace of those possibilities for his actual life is not interested in living out the paradox of the finite and the infinite at the same time and if anyone mentioned it he would take offense. Hegel always wrote objectively like Johannes Climacus and he never wrote and lived like Anti-Climacus in anxiety. Hegel's writings are concerned with the march of progress up the stairs of history but they do not concern his unique life or any single individual's growth in faith, hope and charity. The writings of Anti-Climacus and Vigilius Haufniensis are concerned precisely with our own personal growth out of anxiety into faith, out of despair into hope and out of taking offence with love. Anxiety and its variety of stages can help us or halt our personal growth. Despair and its variety of stages can help us grow in hope and its motivation to constantly move forward on our journey, or it can fixate us in an exclusive value and sap our energy. Taking offence and its variety of negativities can prevent us from loving all of existence as good, true and beautiful and thus from giving us the faith and hope we need to live on all floors of our house. A desperado is one without enough of love's affirmations and positivity to keep from falling more and more into anxiety and despair. So the desperado lives in a doghouse and not his interior castle.

II.8.4 By Giving Hope to Desperados Not Willing to Be Themselves

The very seed of despair is self-rejection and Kierkegaard knew
this well from identifying with his father in a reflective way
and with his mother in a silent but perhaps disguised way.
Already the child in the womb is deeply identifying with the
physiology of the mother's attitude, mood and feelings and
perhaps his mother was very cheerful and happy to have been
a mere maid servant who was loved by her master and got
to bear his children and marry him and make his children happy.
But Kierkegaard is obviously a complicated mix of opposites and
his father as a boy out there on the Jutland heath cursing God
seems to have been a rejected child who became self-rejecting.
As a youth who willed not to be himself he thought of suicide
and he was so relieved to be cared for in Copenhagen.
Kierkegaard must have identified with his father's feelings of being
rejected and as a hunchbacked, little fellow he must have
been often rejected by his peers so that he too willed not to be
or at least not to be himself as he experienced melancholy despair.
The paradox of faith that Kierkegaard insists on has to do with
how we encounter eternity in time and Regina must have enabled
him to feel his eternal significance so that he could find hope.
She motivated him in such a way that he wanted to be for her
a poet and a philosopher and he wanted to be his God-given self.
He went from wanting to get rid of and of getting away from himself
to loving himself and wanting to build himself up out of love.
We humans can despair over something finite, temporal and
earthly because a blow might come our way and take away
our health or happiness or our job or our wonderful life.
But to despair over the self happens to the person who has
become ethical such as the Stoic who resigns himself to
the failure of external things and then commits suicide
when he comes to see that his malady implies self-rejection.

II.8.5 By Giving Hope to Desperados Who Will to Be Themselves

Desperados can go in a Hindu-Buddhist direction and will not to be themselves or they can go in the direction of enlightenment humanists and will to be themselves without thinking as thanking. Hindu hope is rooted in the eternal Brahman of Pure Being, Pure Bliss and Pure Consciousness into which this finite self or *atman* will someday flow and in getting beyond the self get beyond any pain or sorrow which is really only illusory. The same is true for the Buddhist who bases his four noble truths upon the idea of *anatman* or no self, for by becoming detached from the self and any of its attachments one can in getting away from the self get away from reasons for despair. Socrates unlike the Stoics or the Hindus or the Buddhists with his logic of the paradox never willed away the self nor did he will the self for in his skeptical honesty, humility, humor and health he was not resigned to his death penalty but he took the real middle path between not willing the self and willing the self or between resignation and the self made man. Socrates did not succumb to the despair of feminine weakness by not willing to be himself nor did he succumb to the definite masculine despair of thinking that he could save self and others. Those who only will to be themselves are also in despair according to Anti-Climicus for even though they have rejected the eternal as being given to them they trust in their own self-reliance and think they can build up a better life here on earth for themselves and others with their own effort alone. Religion within the limits of reason alone is in despair because each person and each project will die and come to nothing in spite of how much power these deceive themselves into having. Desperados of weakness in willing not to be and desperados of defiance in willing to be both miss the logic of mixed opposites of the Socratic paradox and of the paradoxical God-man.

II.8.6 By Giving Hope to Desperados Who Are Sinners

Despair or the sickness unto death has most of all to do with
facing death for maybe in despair we want to die or we are
in despair because a beloved has died or perhaps we are dying.
Philosophies and religions find repose in these kinds of despair
and the anxiety felt before their emptiness by universalizing.
So that any particular suffering can be overcome if we think
that we can become one with the Good or World Soul or Pure Being.
With Promethean Power we can overcome individual problems
by getting beyond individuality and seeing it only as a pathway
toward the universal that will do away with all evil appearances.
The one who goes to the God-man sees the despair in that
universalization that gets rid of solitude for he believes
that by the incarnation and resurrection of the flesh each
single individual can continue to exist without despair
forever and that no loving relation will ever have to end.
However, it is still possible for the believer to leap into
the despair of sin because of one's many sins and come to
the despair of taking offence at the God-man which is
a worse despair than that of the sins that lead to it or come
from it as omissions or commissions rooted in taking offence.
Mere aesthetes, mere ethical people and people of religousness A
do not really sin for they only think of themselves as offending
self, others and God, but the believer can take offence at God
and thereby with its greater anxiety and despair have an
opportunity for a greater passionate inwardness than the others.
Anti-Climacus who teaches against the universalizing ascent
and reveals the values of climbing back down into our inner house
has in mind loving the God-man who so loves desperados
that his whole reason for becoming man and for suffering
was to bring hope that for God everything is possible
and so we should not take offence but put all trust in the God-man.

II.8.7 By Loving Desperados as More Important with Anti-Climacus

The God became flesh out of love to give us the gift and the task of loving that we might all be saved from our anxiety and despair. But as we practice Christian loving we are led into more anxiety and despair as our concern for others develops our inwardness. Jesus whose name means savior came to save sinners and for that to happen according to Kierkegaard we must become aware of sin and even become anxious about our own guilt. Part Two of *Sickness unto Death* is entitled: "Despair is Sin."

> Sin is, before God, or with the conception of God, in despair not to will to be oneself, or in despair to will to be oneself. Thus sin is intensified weakness or intensified defiance; sin is intensification of despair.[1]

Sin is a concept that is revealed and thus neither paganism nor the natural man knows what sin is and for Socrates sin is ignorance and as ignorance it cannot really exist. For the Greeks immorality was a missing of the mark as if an archer shot his arrow and missed for one reason or another. For Kierkegaard sin is not as aesthetic offence against one's self nor an ethical offence against another person nor an offence against God but in anxiety to despair by taking offence at God. Jesus became man to love these desperados as more important than himself and his Good Samaritan and Suffering Servant love precisely for sinners who sinned against him was the purpose of the incarnation with its everlasting, merciful love for sinners. Even those who are not capable of true sin are so loved by Jesus that he became flesh and suffered and died and rose for them. But mere atonement theologians take offence at sinners and see only the good like themselves as being saved for if sinners do not have faith in Christ then they are doomed. The Hellfire and Brimstone Preachers of the law do not see the Gospel of the good news that especially the lost are found.

II.8.8 Hope for Desperados Despairing over Their Sin

Despair as the *Sickness Unto Death* can eat from within those who suffer; but *The Gospel of Sufferings* is that by sharing in Christ's suffering for others the greater our hope can become. Hope for a better future comes through the promise given to David and to all through the Son of David and his resurrection. Our faith in eternal and infinite love gives us the hope that we can share with others and thus Kierkegaard can write so passionately. His entire authorship is his way of bringing hope to desperados. For him to suffer for the true doctrine of Christ is true imitation. Sin is not willing to love oneself in the right way by loving ourselves as our neighbor and every person as ourselves. "Only when it is a duty to love, only then is love eternally secured against every change, eternally made free in blessed independence, eternally and happily secured against despair."[2] Natural, spontaneous love jealously says that if you will not love me I will hate you, but love that follows the duty of the two great commands says that if you hate me I will still continue to love you and in this way it gets beyond despair. Duty-love protests against natural love's hatred, jealousy and despair. Despair is not the loss of the beloved—that is unhappiness, pain and suffering—but despair is the lack of the eternal. Kierkegaard's loving task calls him to explain clearly the difference between true love and despair and thus he wrote three books that he might clarify sin in terms of anxiety, taking offence and despair. His message is that sin is not a matter of ignorance instead of knowing, but sin is a matter of not willing to love according to duty and that not-willing leads to greater and greater despair. Once Christians are not willing to love their enemies they begin to rationalize and procrastinate and to explain away their duty. That is how our Present Age moved away from incarnational love to that atonement theology that punishes rather than loves enemies.

II.8.9 Loving the God-Man in Faith, Hope and Agape

When Christians love desperados as more important than themselves Kierkegaard's belief is that they will be won over to loving the God-man as more important than themselves. But even if they never know of the God-man that God-man still loved them as more important than himself and thus they and all desperados will be eternally saved by the Christ who descended into hell and arose to take all out of hell and destroy it. Desperados at all four levels of despair will suffer here for God has made us for himself and our hearts are hurting until they hurt with the God-man out of love for desperados. Aesthetic desperados who live for the here and now do hurt because without reflection they do not avoid painful consequences. Ethical desperados suffer even more with their empathy for others. Religious desperados as they think they themselves must atone for any flaw of theirs against the beautiful, good, true, and holy suffer even more because of their awareness of the eternal infinite. Christians who suffer with the God-man might suffer the most but theirs is the blessed suffering of the five sorrowful mysteries. Their practice in Christianity trains them to suffer the anxiety of the agony in the garden, the pain of the scourging at the pillar, the shame of the crowning with thorns, the dying of the cross carrying and the death of the crucifixion done for love of others. The Kierkegaardian follower of the Incarnate God-man is a disciple because he practices the discipline of the double movement leap of faith. His double movement faith is a double movement love that follows the duty to love God absolutely and all others as himself. The double movement faith in the double movement God-man's love lets there be a double movement hope for this life and the next. When the God-man is for us who can be against us? And thus all suffering of all desperados whether they know it or not and whether they accept it or not is one with the suffering of Jesus.

II.9 Reconciling the God-Man and Our Modern Age

II.9.1 By Loving Those Who Are Guilty of Taking Offense

After writing *Works of Love* under his own name Kierkegaard
finished his authorship with the two books by Anti-Climacus.
Climacus climbed up the ladder of love through the three floors
of the Interior Castle and Anti-Climacus climbs back down
with the gift of God's grace and reveals how we leap into sin
by taking offence at the God-man through anxiety and despair.
Throughout *Training in Christianity* Anti-Climacus shows
how our training in physical, vital, intellectual and spiritual
exercises primarily aims at developing an attitude that
does not succumb to the negativity of blaming and taking offence.
The God-man often said:

> *Blessed is he whosoever is not offended in me.*

To take offense is to see the glass as half-empty rather
than as half-full and rather than affirming all of existence
as good, taking offence at it is the major fault of humankind.
Right away as soon as you meet people you can begin to
size them up as affirmers or as offence taking resenters.
Atonement justice thinkers focus on the negative side of things.
Incarnation love thinkers focus on the paradox of both
the spiritual and the material in loving the God become flesh.
Kierkegaard sees modernity from Luther and Calvin to Descartes
and Hobbes and up to Leibniz and Hegel as dominated by
taking offence either at the high side of spirit or at the low
side of matter since idealists and realists did not have
a logic of the both-and which let them love mixed opposites.
Modernity took offence at the threefold notion of personhood
in which each person is of equal worth, each person is unique
and all persons are interpersonal as related in the Body of Christ.
Leibniz and Hegel did begin to love all persons as interpersonal
and by loving modernity in their thinking and by stressing
the single individual Kierkegaard loved all of the moderns.

II.9.2 At This Actual Incarnate God-Man

Modernity began by taking offence at the paradox of the God-man.
Luther got modernity going religiously by affirming scripture
alone and not philosophy, faith alone and not works and grace
alone and not any merit of ours that could justify us.
He started the rugged individualism of modernity by standing alone
before God without the Pope and the hierarchy, without philosophy
and the tradition, without purgatory and thus without prayer
on a constant basis for the blessed dead and their intercession.
But Luther was not only a rugged individualist psychologically
but also politically he set up the nation state with his doctrine
of *cuius regio, eius religio* which set up state religions and
warring states which are no longer admired in our postmodern age.
Luther with his atonement justice theology which had little of the
incarnation love theology denied that we are all members of Christ's
Body and denied that key trait of personhood as being interpersonal.
Luther beheld the God-man in his church and denied the
human side of the paradox by taking offence at the worth of any
works of love or philosophy and even those ideas in scripture.
Descartes got modern philosophy going by concluding from doubting
that "I am a thinking thing" even in such a way that he could never
prove that I am at the same time an extended or material thing.
So just as Luther took offence at the lower side of the paradox
so did Descartes philosophy by not philosophically loving our body.
Just as Descartes by doubting reached the *cogito ergo sum*, so
Augustine had already done that with his *si fallor sum*, so
Augustine in his philosophy also kept the both-and of the
credo ut intellegam—I believe that I might understand and
then he kept philosophy with his *fides quaerens intellectum*
a faith seeking understanding so with faith Augustine unlike
Descartes believed in the God of the God-man and with philosophy
his faith did not deny the human side as did Luther.

II.9.3 In His Lowly Temporality

It was natural for Kierkegaard to want to reconcile Luther
and Descartes with the God-man because he was both a Lutheran
and a philosopher and he knew the danger of exclusive opposites.
But the spirit of modernity was even more strongly influenced
by Calvin and Hobbes than it was by Lutherans and Cartesians.
Calvin's doctrine of double predestination led directly to
the Protestant work ethic and the spirit of capitalism while
Hobbes' social contract set up a police state to protect
the predestined elect and their wealth from predestined criminals.
According to Incarnation love theology Jesus became one
with the lowly and as a suffering servant suffered the death
of a criminal but Calvin and Hobbes took offense at such
low life and never thought of redeeming but only condemning it.
According to the traditional conception of the person both in
the Trinity and for all humans all persons are of equal worth.
But that idea is extremely offensive to Calvin and Hobbes
and with their rugged individualism their major distinction
is between the good and the evil which is connected with not only
a rewarder-punisher God but with a God who makes them such.
Of course, Hobbes as a materialist is the opposite of Descartes
who is a spiritualist whose method cannot prove the material.
So Hobbes' method does take offence at the existence of the God
and of thinking of the human in terms of immaterial spirit.
So philosophy started out with a methodic denial of
the low side and a methodic denial of the high side, but
Calvin and Luther had much in common in denying the low side.
For the first fifteen hundred years of Christianity the church
had been seen as the continuation of Christ and as his Body.
But Calvin and Luther stressed a transcendent God with Christ
as the only mediator and his Body as made up of Mary and
the blessed dead and of the living was imminent and not divine.

II.9.4 Or in His Lofty Power And Wisdom

Like Luther and Calvin Henry VIII was a maker of the modern mind
just as the modernity of Descartes and Hobbes evolved with Locke.
Henry VIII contributed greatly to the Anglican Church of England
by breaking from Rome and the Pope who found fault with his
many wives and the murder of his wife, Anne Boleyn.
Henry did not stress the logic of exclusive opposites as did
Luther and Calvin who initiated their atonement justice models.
Like King David, Muhammad, and Brigham Young he was more
concerned with the battle of the sexes, as he sought power alliances
through marriages, rather than with the battle of all against all.
Within the Anglican world there can be conversation between
high, middle, and low voices that cooperate rather than battle.
Within this religious, cultural context Locke with a new version
of the social contract did not put emphasis on the police force
and moved from a conservative attitude to a liberal democracy
in which the executive, legislative and judicial branches of
government can peacefully act as checks and balances on each other.
Each individual man as long as he had property could vote.
Henry and John were like the continental modernists in breaking
away from the Body of Christ, the Pope, and Holy Mother Church.
In their rugged individualism they thought of themselves as
saving their own souls rather than being members of the human
family who would never feel saved unless all loved ones were saved.
But whereas the continental rationalists took offence at the
lower side of the God-man the British Empiricists took
offence at the higher side for Locke argued against Descartes'
innate ideas and thought all knowledge began with experience.
The English as materialists, realists and empiricists
fully appreciated the flesh and are scandalized with those
who go from the top-down rather than from the bottom up.
Anti-Climacus goes down to the basement with empirical materialists.

II.9.5 By Loving the God-Man as Our Contemporary

Our training in Christianity begins when we respond to an invitation which calls us to

> Come hither, all ye that labour
> and are heavy burdened
> I will give you rest. (Matt 11:28)

We can be caught up in fear and trembling or in anxiety and
if we do not take offense at the God-man but love him in faith
we will be able to have the rest of a deep joy and tranquility.
Joy can be ours in sorrow even unto death because we believe
that by suffering and dying with Jesus we too can be resurrected.
In his own day many did not believe that Jesus was the only
Son of God and thus they took offence at the high side of the paradox.
Some like Peter who believed him to be God took offence at the low
side of the paradox when Jesus said that he must suffer and die.
Suffering and death are a heavy burden but if one uses the possible
offence as an occasion to believe then the burden is made light.
To be a contemporary of Christ the follower has to believe in
his divine eternity and his human temporality and the believer
can do that in Kierkegaard's day 1800 years after Jesus' life.
Kierkegaard's message for us bears witness to the Good News
by showing us why faith in the paradox of mixed opposites
lets us believe that we might understand and affirm this life.
Kierkegaard's two books by Anti-Climacus further explain
The Works of Love by showing us how we can absolutely love
the absolute and then relatively love the relative when we do not
take offence at the absolute high side or the relative low side.
Modernists like Spinoza sought to find rest and happiness
with a good ethical life, but Spinoza was a Pantheist and
never worked with the concept of personhood because he took
offence at the God-man's claiming to be both God and man.
It is infinitely noteworthy that God lived here on earth as a man.

II.9.6 By Loving Him as That Unique Single Individual

As one thinks about modernity one might say with Kierkegaard

> Christendom has done away with Christianity
> without being quite aware of it.
> The consequence is that
> if anything is to be done,
> one must try again
> to introduce Christianity into Christendom.[3]

This is Kierkegaard's project and the project of postmodernity with its logic of mixed opposites and its threefold notion of personhood both of which were gotten rid of by modernity. Jesus as God is that perfect being of ineffable sovereign glory. As man he became flesh out of love for all created flesh. He suffered and died for us very creatures in our sinfulness. When we recognize our sinfulness and the heavy burden we have brought upon ourselves and our loved ones we can begin to love him and to appropriate him in our lives with our praise, repentance, thanksgiving and petition for self and others. Jesus is absolutely unique for the believer for he is the only son of God with no other living being remotely like unto him. But, this uniqueness and how I as a single individual might appropriate it in my most passionate inwardness is lost on the moderns and their Christendom which is lacking in love. Rousseau with his third version of the social contract is a good example of a modernist in Christendom for he does point out that before the great agricultural breakthrough no social contract was needed by the hunter-gatherer tribes with their shamanism. But as he ponders the human condition he thinks that no prayer is required except for gratitude because we have been given so much. So he pays no attention to Kierkegaard's loving believer who meets the God-man in repentance for sinfulness and in petition for further mercy from the all loving God-man.

II.9.7 By Praising the Love in Our Modern Contemporaries

Even though Kierkegaard was very clear about how modernity
worked with a logic of exclusive opposites and denied either
the low side or the high side of the unique God-man paradox
he still saw that there was much of value in each modernist.
He could appreciate and love Spinoza who would say: "Even if
I am an atheist, I would at least like to live like a saint."
Kierkegaard learned from the God-man to always praise love
whatever kind it was even though it might need to be cleansed
of its self-preferentiality so that it could become truly universal.
Hume like all the empiricists did believe in experience alone
and deny with Locke any innate ideas as a ground for rationalism.
But Hume still had a wonderful ethics which was based upon
a moral sentiment that could intuit values and their hierarchy
even in such a way that they would motivate us to passion for them.
In Kierkegaard's language Hume developed a theory of ethics
in which the heart can intuit the aesthetic, ethical, religiousness A,
religiousness B hierarchy and then with that subjective certitude
proceed to appropriate them in accord with the value of the
healthy, the happy, the holy and the wise in the most passionate
inwardness that would be a proper training in Christianity.
Kierkegaard saw that the modern protestants protested the
both-and of faith and reason, of grace and the works of love.
He saw that the modern philosophers especially the empiricists
and the social contract theorists lost faith in the other world
and in the day of judgment that could begin our reconciling
journey through purgatory and that loss could decrease passion.
But Hegel made a great synthesis of the material being in-itself
and the spiritual being-for-itself and he put the empiricists and
the rationalists together in a dialectical rational pattern.
When Kierkegaard took up and praised the love in Hegel's dialectic
in his own existential dialectic he praised the love in each.

II.9.8 By Praying for Their Blessed Dead When They Do Not

Training in Christianity has to do with the imitation of Christ by seeing the high side of the God and the low side of the man as possibly offensive but then leaping beyond that offence with a faith and hope in love as it appeared in *Works of Love*. Kant as a continental rationalist explained how Hume's experience could work by arguing that we already have within us as the make up of our mind the twelve categories built around quantity, quality, relation and modality and these innate ideas as it were let us organize into concepts our experience in time and in space through the mediation of our imaginative powers. In this way Kant got rid of truth as a realistic conformity of the mind to things in accord with either Plato or Aristotle. Truth for him became a coherence of ideas rather than a conformity of mind to the form of things and that worked for the sciences. Kant followed Luther and all the thinkers of exclusive opposites by arguing for religion within the limits of reason alone. But that enlightenment understanding of religion lacks any vital force and the passionate inwardness of Kierkegaard and so it died almost as quickly as it was born because in taking offence at the God-man and having no real faith Kant also was lacking in a philosophy of love with all of its power. In Kant's ethics he did recover the notion of personhood and argue that we should never treat a person as a mere thing. He did see persons as having an equal worth and as being related in a stoic way in that they all have reason and will. He asked (1) Why is there something rather than nothing? (2) Am I free? (3) Am I immortal? and (4) Is there a God? In order for there to be justice in the world reason dictates that the answers to the last three questions be a "Yes" otherwise an ethics within the limits of reason alone makes no sense. But praying for the dead with Kierkegaard makes no sense for Kant.

II.9.9 By Loving Modernists as More Important than Ourselves

Kierkegaard's existential dialectic is deeply indebted to Hegel's
rational reading of history which could see the modern reformers
as men of faith excluding reason and the modern philosophers
as men of reason excluding faith and out of that thesis and
antithesis Hegel would point out a synthesis coming together in himself.
Kierkegaard studied deeply Fichte, Schelling, and Hegel and he saw the
whole modern age which Hegel could account for so brilliantly
as being that Christendom in which he would become a Christian.
He could love the Christendom as more important than himself
in its aesthetic obstacle and its speculative obstacle which
pushed him on to living out his own existential dialectic as he
did not take offense at the aesthetic low side or the speculative
high side but found his way to love both in loving Jesus.
Kierkegaard's religious philosophy as he explains it in
Training in Christianity is to focus on both sides of the paradox
and so love one and so love the other so as not to exclude
either but to love God and to love all flesh as did the God-man.
Modernity took offence against the God who is love and who
became flesh that we might know persons as equal in worth,
as beautifully and complexly unique and as all related in the
family of the living even so that we might all live together
in an eternal love which each and every modernist forgot.
Kierkegaard could love Descartes, Hobbes, Locke, Rousseau,
Spinoza, Leibniz, Hume, Kant, and Hegel just as he could
love Luther, Calvin, Menno Simons, Wesley, and all of theirs.
As a Postmodern follower of the God-man he could come to
them by imitating Jesus who as the creator came to the creatures
in a love with which he would suffer for them and love
them as more important than himself which as Kierkegaard shows
is rooted in the logic of reconciliation in which one first
has to go and be reconciled with his brother before he praises God.

III. St. Paul

III.7 Paul's Love Letter to Philemon

III.7.1 Paul's Politics of Reconciliation

In his letter to the Galatians Paul argued that the *agape* of Jesus would so bring us to love all persons as equal that there would no longer be Jew nor Greek, male nor female, master nor slave. *Agape* implied a politics in which all persons are equal under the law and in which every person has equal opportunities. But, here Paul is going along with and condoning the politics of his day. According to Roman law and even Jewish law slavery was totally acceptable and was practiced without any qualms of conscience. So it seems that Paul is caught in a dilemma in that while he was in prison he met a runaway slave, Onesimus, and he befriended that slave and converted him to Christianity. However, Paul recommended to him and arranged it that he would go back to his master Philemon and serve again as slave. So is this not a contradiction right at the heart of Paul's *agape*? Should he not be a revolutionary and fight for the slave's freedom? If he believes in a love for all that implied no slavery for any how can he recommend, condone and promote this slavery? What are the factors that brought Paul to his decision to send this slave, Onesimus, whom Paul loves, back to his master? Paul's belief in the imminent return of Christ was the major factor that let him be content with Roman and Jewish politics. He strongly believed that God's grace and not our works would bring about the new world order that would let all be treated equally. He thought that Christ would return even in his own lifetime and renew the face of the earth and bring about the Kingdom of love. Also he wanted the most loving option for the slave, Onesimus, and he could have thought that returning to Philemon could be the best thing for him and at the same time also please Philemon. If Philemon would treat Onesimus as a dear brother in Christ even though he was also a slave there could be a reconciliation for all and both Onesimus and Philemon could be truly happy.

III.7.2 Begins with Affection and Agape

The introduction in *New Jerusalem Bible* to the Letter to Philemon says:

> A note from Paul carried back to his master
> by a runaway slave who has become
> a Christian and one of Paul's helpers.
> It is an affectionate expression of
> Christian fellowship and humanity.

So Onesimus is returning to Philemon with this letter from Paul. Paul knows and loves Philemon and all his good Christian works. But most of all it seems that Paul is concerned about Onesimus for he writes to Philemon:

> I am rather appealing to your love,
> being what I am, Paul, an old man,
> and now also a prisoner of Christ Jesus.
> I am appealing to you for a child of mine
> whose father I became while wearing these chains. (9–10)

This seems to be the focal point of the love letter, namely, that Paul is very fond of the slave and feels as if he is the child's father. Onesimus must be quite young, perhaps in his teens, and Paul is concerned that he have the best life possible with Philemon. So Paul seems to have done a lot of reconciling and is now in the midst of more for he helped Onesimus become reconciled to God and to his own life as a slave and now he wants him to become also reconciled with his master and live happily ever after. When Paul first met Onesimus the young man must have been quite bitter and that is why he ran away and was arrested and put in jail which must have seemed to be more terrible yet. Paul's love must have been very strong to turn Onesimus around. Paul wrote about the slave boy in his letter how he is

> especially dear to me, but how much more to you,
> both on the natural plane and in the Lord. (16)

How do these two loves reconcile to bring about further reconciliation?

III.7.3 For the Slave Boy, Onesimus

Paul thought that on the natural plane Onesimus must have been
even more dear to Philemon than he was to himself and thus Paul
must have seen a great deal of good in the runaway slave boy.
Paul's natural affection must have been felt with love by Onesimus
and that must have already begun to win the youth's heart
and help him start to become free from his negative offense-taking
and become free for a much more positive view of himself
and of his whole situation, especially of being a slave forever.
You can imagine how the free kids might taunt him and
how he could have already begun to develop an inferiority complex.
But with great love Paul must have taken him through the talking
cures and he must have started feeling a pride in himself.
With natural affection alone Paul could have won the boy's affection
and got him to love himself with a new sense of worth and hope.
But Onesimus knew what life had been like back home as a slave
and he did not like it and thus he ran away and was jailed.
So how could Paul ever convince him to go back there and
be a slave and be reconciled to that as a good life for himself?
Onesimus became especially dear to Paul both on the natural plane
and in the Lord and it was Paul's *agape* that was the miracle worker.
Because Paul's love of the Lord brought him to serve others in his
poverty, celibacy and obedience which freed him from self-interest
to be free for totally working for others such as Onesimus
God was able to work through Paul to convert Onesimus to *agape*.
His love for Jesus and the God who is love let him rejoice, even
in being a prisoner himself where he could minister to prisoners.
Paul with his natural affection could convince Onesimus that
Philemon would love him with an equal affection, but it was
Paul's *agape* for him that loved him and all others as brothers
and sisters that could convince him to go back to Philemon
and know that Philemon would love him even as a dear brother.

III.7.4 Whom Paul Is Sending Back to His Master

Once Onesimus truly believed that he was a brother in the Lord with all humans as brothers and sisters he could return also as a slave. After all Paul claimed to be a slave too that he might serve others. Paul was in prison and his words about Christ's love going out to all persons equally was convincing to Onesimus because Paul walked the talk and practiced what he preached as a prisoner. Onesimus even came to greatly love his master, Philemon, because the way Paul loved him taught him to love him likewise. In the letter to Philemon which Paul showed to Onesimus and with which Onesimus came to totally agree Paul wrote:

> To our dear fellow worker, Philemon,
> our sister Apphia,
> our fellow soldier Archippus
> and the Church that meets in your house,
> grace and peace of God our Father
> and the Lord Jesus Christ. (1–3)

Onesimus was a member of this household even as a slave. And he came to see how Paul loved Philemon, whose name meant friend, and perhaps Apphia was his dear wife, and Archchippus, maybe their son, must have been a fellow missionary with Paul out there fighting the good fight for love. Their home was a little church where Christians could meet and pray together and even, perhaps, partake of the Eucharist. Onesimus must have learned a great new love of them from Paul. Paul must have explained grace to Onesimus and helped him to see the peace that can come from the love given to us by grace. Onesimus must have wanted to become a dear fellow worker. Onesimus might still be a slave but with this grace and a love like Paul's he knew he would be free in a new charity and peace. Paul brought him to greatly love his master, Philemon, and his former household and now he knew he would be loved there.

III.7.5 With an Appeal to Philemon's Agape

Apparently Paul had not met Philemon for he writes:

> I always thank my God,
> mentioning you in my prayers
> because I hear of the love and the faith
> which you have for the Lord Jesus
> and for all God's holy people. (4–5)

In this short, one page letter Paul's love becomes especially clear.
He prays frequently and long and hard for many Christians
like Philemon and his prayer for them increases his love for them.
Paul's love for Philemon lets him know even better of Philemon's love.
With his prayer and this letter Paul is building up Philemon's love
and at the same time coming to love and trust in Philemon even more.
Paul's focus is on Philemon coming to greatly love Onesimus.
If Philemon truly possesses and is possessed by Jesus' *agape*
then Paul knows that he will love Onesimus as a dear brother.
And with confidence in this love Paul appeals to him:

> I suppose that you have been deprived
> of Onesimus for a time, merely,
> so that you could have him back for ever,
> no longer as a slave, but something
> much better than a slave, a dear brother. (15–16)

Paul has come to love Onesimus as a dear child and brother
and now that Onesimus also is a Christian living in this love,
Paul is confident and has even brought Onesimus to confidence
that Philemon will now love him even as he knows that Paul loves him.
Paul puts the argument of love very clearly:

> So if you grant me any fellowship
> with yourself
> welcome him as you would me. (17)

Paul believes that in Christ's love Philemon, Onesimus and he are
all equally brothers so that they should each love each other equally.

III.7.6 That He Will Treat Him as a Dear Brother

When Paul beheld Stephen praying with love and the joy of an angel
on his face for his brothers who were stoning him he was amazed.
And when the Risen Lord Jesus appeared to him his life was changed.
He knew that this Jesus had taught them how to pray *The Our Father*.
As Paul prayed daily for his brothers and sisters in the Lord
he prayed for them with the same joy that he saw on Stephen's face.
Paul learned what a dear brother in the Lord is first from Stephen
who died with the prayer of his brother Jesus on his lips:

> Father, forgive them for they know not what they do.

And now Onesimus knew of Paul's love and forgiveness and he knew
that God had forgiven him too for being a resentful runaway slave.
He did feel that Paul was like a father to him and yet he felt
even more that he and Paul and Philemon too were brothers.
Being dear brothers even with Stephen in the Lord gave to him
a total confidence that he could take this letter of Paul to Philemon
and that Philemon would forgive him because he didn't know
what he was doing when he ran away, but now he knows so clearly.
He didn't know this brotherly love before but now he does.
And he Onesimus the former slave also prays for Philemon
and in the love of his prayer he comes to know of Philemon's love.
When Onesimus read the words of Paul's letter:

> a dear brother, especially dear to me,
> but how much more to you,
> both on the natural plane and in the Lord. (16)

he almost burst into tears of joy because he knew how Philemon
would be so glad to see him and to see how he had matured.
Onesimus and Philemon had known each other for a long time.
It was true that he was more dear to Philemon than even Paul
on the natural plane and now that this new plane was there
Onesimus loved Philemon more than ever with a new kind of love.

III.7.7 And with a Guarantee That Paul Will Pay

Onesimus felt especially loved and safe and secure because in Paul's politics of love he was not only looking after right love but also right justice and thus he was sending Onesimus back. Surely that would greatly please and impress the wise Philemon. But even more, it seems that perhaps Onesimus stole something from Philemon or owed him something because of not working. But if Philemon should want it Paul was willing to pay for that. Thus Paul wrote in his letter to Philemon:

> If he has wronged you in any way
> or owes you anything
> Put it down to my account . . .
> I, Paul, shall pay it back. (18)

So to protect Onesimus and totally satisfy Philemon Paul was carefully thinking of any possible offence in order to rectify it. Onesimus must have felt totally fathered and mothered by Paul. Paul had completely dedicated himself to Jesus and all the members of his body, the church, with his celibacy, poverty and obedience. Paul was free from any concerns for himself and his own family and free for serving all others, even lowly slaves as if they were his own children and thus Onesimus learned of Holy Mother Church. Paul loved him with all the care and attention of a loving mother. And Onesimus came to believe that Philemon would love him also in this way and that even he could come to love in this way too. Paul finishes his letter by writing:

> Epaphras, a prisoner with me in Christ Jesus,
> sends his greetings, so do my fellow workers
> Mark, Aristarchus, Demos, and Luke. (23–24)

Onesimus must have felt that he too could become a fellow worker with Paul and with Philemon and his household and thus help bring about a loving family of all persons as brothers and sisters in that Christ Jesus about whom Paul taught him.

III.7.8 For Anything Owed to the Master by the Slave

Paul wants Philemon to welcome home his slave even as he would welcome Paul and Paul mentions a debt that Philemon owes him:

> I make no mention of a further debt,
> that you owe your very self to me! (19)

So Paul mentions what he will not mention and, of course, we do not really know what he is talking about for it might be that Paul somehow saved either his physical or spiritual life. Apparently Philemon understands what Paul is writing about but it is all rather complicated for Paul is making several arguments that can reassure Onesimus and convince Philemon. Philemon should welcome home Onesimus with agapeic affection:

(1) because Jesus has taught us to love everyone as brother and sister
(2) because Onesimus can be trusted now given his conversion
(3) because Philemon in welcoming him will pay a debt to Paul.
(4) Also Paul would like to keep him but he thinks he should
 send him back because he belongs to Philemon as he writes:

> I should have liked to keep him with me;
> he could have been a substitute for you,
> to help me while I am in the chains
> that the gospel has brought me.
> However, I did not want to do anything
> without your consent;
> it would have been
> forcing your act of kindness,
> which should be spontaneous. (13–14)

So Paul wants Philemon to welcome his slave spontaneously without any pressure from Paul, but Paul pressures him with all these arguments or are they presented more to get Onesimus to go back? In any case Paul not only sends Onesimus back but he is willing to also send some money along to pay anything owed to Philemon. Has not Paul made Onesimus and Philemon an offer they cannot refuse?

III.7.9 And Thus Is a Politics of Love for All

It seems that Paul would be against slavery because in Christ's
love there are no longer masters and slaves but brothers and sisters.
But Paul is not a revolutionary fighting against political institutions.
Rather he is reforming society and culture from within by teaching
that all persons are equal and can love and be loved in equal fashion.
Paul is so certain that everyone should live in *agape* that
he thinks the day of the Lord must come soon when all will live
in heavenly love as he explained to Philemon and Onesimus.
But what is really convincing to Paul and those whom he meets are
not primarily his reasons even though he presents those very
forcefully but rather his living out of *agape* in all its implications.
Paul is primarily an existentialist who gives reasons of the heart
in all the ways he loves and in the very tone and taste of his life.
His being a rationalist and giving all the reasons that he gave
in this letter to Philemon is secondary and supportive of his living.
He can change society because of the power with which he loves
and then because of the power with which he reasons with others.
Paul and the others who lived out the love of Jesus laid the
foundations for the Politics of Love that progressed step by step
in the West and now in our postmodern age is going out to all
who are feeling its social and economic effect in our Global Village.
Paul can even joke and play as he presents his arguments of love
that overcome slavery for the *Bible of Jerusalem* points out
that the word Onesimus means "useful" so Paul is
playing with a pun when he writes:

> He was of no use to you before,
> but now he is useful
> both to you and to me. (11)

A person is more than a useful means to an end but
when that persons is loved and loves that can help bring
about the new Politics of the Kingdom of Love for everybody.

III.8 Paul's Love Letter to the Philippians

III.8.1 Paul's Logic of Reconciliation Bases All

Logic has to do with seeing implications and conclusions that flow out of a basic starting point or premise with consistency. As Paul has written in Romans 5:

> So it is proof of God's own love for us,
> that Christ died for us while we were still sinners.
> How much more can we be sure, therefore,
> that, now that we have been justified
> by his death, we shall be saved
> through him from the retribution of God. (vv. 8–9)

All Paul's faith, hope and love; all his preaching praying and kindness flow out of this most basic premise of his belief. And it is implied that we should love others as God loved us. Thus in 2 Corinthians 5 he again wrote:

> It is all God's work:
> he reconciled us to himself through Christ
> and he gave to us the ministry of reconciliation.
> I mean, God was in Christ
> reconciling the world to himself,
> not holding anyone's fault, against them,
> but entrusting to us the message of reconciliation. (vv. 18–19)

So Paul's most basic belief is that just as God has so loved us that he gave his only begotten Son for us so we are now free to go out and serve others by bringing this message to them. As he puts it in his letter to the Philippians,

> Nothing is to be done out of jealousy or vanity;
> instead, out of humility of mind
> everyone should give preference to others,
> everyone pursuing not selfish interests
> but those of others. (2:3–4)

Paul is in prison as he writes this letter just as he was when he wrote to Philemon and still with Christ he can be joyfully loving.

III.8.2 On Giving Preference to Others as Did Jesus

Here we see the very heart of Kierkegaard's philosophy in *Works of Love* for that is based on preferring others to oneself. Kierkegaard's double movement leap of faith and the connection between all his basic concepts is rooted in Paul's logic of love. Out of love God became flesh and thus loved us more than himself. The humble service of others continued after the incarnation in the way of the cross and the crucifixion in order to serve all others. Paul imitated Jesus in humbly serving others and Kierkegaard built his philosophy of love on the way Paul revealed the God-man to him just as Paul got his start by seeing how Stephen revealed Jesus' love. The logic of Paul's love sets up a base of charity, joy, peace, patience, and kindness which allows Paul even to appreciate being in prison. In 1:12–14 of his letter to the Philippians he says after his greeting of love;

> Now I want you to realize, brothers,
> that the circumstances of my present life
> are helping rather than hindering
> the advance of the gospel.
> My chains in Christ have become well known . . .
> and so most of the brothers in the Lord
> have gained confidence from my chains
> and are getting more and more daring
> in announcing the message without any fear.

The Gospel and the message is the miracle of reconciling love that Jesus preached and practiced and that now Paul preaches and practices. Actions can speak louder that words and just as Paul learned from Stephen so Paul is joyful to be now in chains that the brothers might learn from him that the whole purpose of life is to serve others. Paul might even be able to aid in the conversion of the prison guards as he joyfully loves them in a way they never saw or imagined.

III.8.3 Who as God Emptied Himself

In the beginning of chapter two Paul tells his beloved Philippians that they should:

> Make your own the mind of Christ Jesus. (v. 5)

This is the fundamental principle for the logic of reconciliation. And in quoting a beautiful hymn Paul goes on to tell them just what the mind of Christ Jesus is:

> Who, being in the form of God,
> did not count equality with God
> something to be grasped. (v. 6)

The logic of reconciliation as Paul sees the big picture is that the loving creator brought creatures into being and created humankind in his image and likeness thus giving them freedom. In their pride they used their freedom to try to take the form of God. But that was a rebellion against right order and so to reconcile them once again with God the Son of God while retaining the form of God took on the form of flesh and thus revealed the value of the lowly. This humility in stepping down and becoming a servant in order to love the lowly is the mind of Christ which Paul imitates in prison. Paul thinks that this spirituality of the martyr who witnesses to Jesus' incarnation, crucifixion and resurrection should also be the spirituality of all the brothers and sisters in the Lord Jesus. Jesus was equal with God but he did not grasp on to that for he was willing to become lowly to save the lowly and that revealed that even sinners were involved in a happy fault for without their proud attempt to take on the form of God it would not have happened that Jesus took on the form of a man to save us. No people ever believed that God suffered and out of love would become a slave in order to save slaves but that is what Jesus revealed. That is why this is the greatest story ever told and humankind's highest affirmation because such a love would never occur to humans who always see God as all powerful and beyond all suffering.

III.8.4 By Taking the Form of a Slave

In being all powerful and all loving God is able to empty himself and take on the form of a slave and this self-emptying is the main point that lets reconciliation work for the human in pride wants to take on the form of God but by taking on the form of a slave God shows man how to be like God by humbly willing to be human. In explaining this logic of reconciliation Paul goes on:

> But he emptied himself,
> taking the form of a slave,
> becoming as human beings are. (Phil 2:7)

If humans really want to be God-like they now see how to do that by really wanting to be human-like for that is the way God now is. Paul's letter to the Philippians is one of joyful love which results from the God-man emptying himself and becoming a slave for us. Paul is filled with gratitude for the gift of this great grace which Jesus has revealed by emptying himself and he urges his people to always practice the prayer of gratitude with a great joy. In 4:4–7 he writes:

> Always be joyful, then, in the Lord;
> I repeat, be joyful. The Lord is near.
> Never worry about anything; but tell God
> all your desires of every kind in prayer
> and petition shot through with gratitude,
> and the peace of God which is
> beyond our understanding will guard
> your hearts and your thoughts in Christ Jesus.

All this flows step by step from the first premise of the logic of reconciliation which begins with the mystery of the incarnation. Jesus showed the value of suffering to us as a way of loving others and once we see this and imitate it, all our suffering can be joyful. The *agape* of charity as it is translated in preferring others to self sees even being in prison for the Good News as a cause for great joy.

III.8.5 And by Accepting Death

Paul goes on in the Hymn, at the beginning of chapter two to write:

> and being in every way
> like a human being,
> he was humbler yet,
> even to accepting death,
> death on a cross. (v. 8)

For Paul the logic of Agapeic reconciliation is the logic of the paradox.
This logic of mixed opposites governs the incarnation, crucifixion and
the resurrection in a mystery that the mind would never discover.
Out of love for others the creator brought forth creatures and let
humans be free so that they too like God could be co-creators.
In their freedom and pride they wanted to take on the form of God
so to reconcile them with himself the creator became a creature
and in humility taught them that to be like god they needed humility.
This logic of the incarnation has to do with the Almighty
Creator becoming a humble creature so that humans might take
a pride in their humanity that will let them humbly submit to God.
Now Paul shows how the logic of love becomes humbler yet
in showing how the lover God-man will suffer and die the
worst death possible to teach us how to suffer with love for others.
We like him can love with a proud humility and joyful suffering
as we show a preference for the needs of others that takes us
beyond our own natural, egoistic preference to loving them.
If we come to love God in the God-man with a total adoration
then we will love ourselves more than ever even by loving others.
Paul's logic of mixed opposites is rooted in a love that
empties itself to let others be full and thus becomes fuller.
Our heart is like a glass of beautiful wine and when we let
our enemy drink it we can glory in a heavenly intoxication.
For where there are loving crucifixions there are resurrections.

III.8.6 So That All Beings Should Bend the Knee

After this beautiful Hymn sings of love's incarnation and crucifixion it goes on to sing of the logic of the resurrection:

> And for this God raised him high,
> and gave him the name
> which is above all other names;
> so that all beings
> in the heavens, on earth
> and in the underworld,
> should bend the knee
> at the name of Jesus. (2:9–11)

In chapter three Paul goes on to write of the true way of salvation. Through faith in Christ he has come to know

> him and the power of his resurrection,
> and partake of his sufferings
> by being molded to the pattern of his death,
> striving towards the goal
> of resurrection from the dead. (vv. 10–11)

A loving death with Jesus for others guarantees for Paul a resurrection into eternal life so that even in the underworld the knee should bend in adoration for Jesus and who knows that underworld may not be hell but only a purgation for a while. Belief and hope in the resurrection of all flesh is what ultimately lets Paul take joy in being in prison and in all of his suffering. Just as Jesus taught him of a glorious resurrection that lets suffering be joyful so he wants to teach others of that very logic. The paradox of a love that lets suffering and dying for others give one a greater eternal life completes the logic of taking pride in humility and of taking joy in sorrow with the Lord Jesus. The humility, suffering and death of Jesus lets us adore him and it brings us to a worshipping love beyond natural love.

III.8.7 At the Name of Jesus

Because Jesus obeyed the will of the Father and emptied himself in the humility of the incarnation and the crucifixion God has given him a name which is above all other names so that every person should bend the knee at the name of Jesus and

> every tongue should acknowledge
> Jesus Christ as Lord
> to the glory of God the Father. (2:11)

This Hymn and Paul's ideas about the name of Jesus have to do with the beginnings of the Jesus prayer which can be cultivated as the very essence of all prayer as its adorational focal point. Those who imitate Christ with the spirituality of Paul might have this sacred name whispering in their hearts as they go to sleep at night, as they awaken through the night and in the morn and through the day. The sacred name of Jesus is the focal point of *The Hail Mary* and in its meaning as "savior" it does manifest the essence of the incarnation, the crucifixion, the resurrection and the coming of the Holy Spirit. The Holy Spirit of the risen Lord Jesus inspires us in the Holy Name. Every tongue that does acknowledge Jesus as Lord does give glory to the Father for to glorify is to manifest the unmanifest in its unmanifestness or to let us feel the mystery that remains a mystery. Jesus in his love has revealed that God is love, the very love between the Father and the Son which is the Holy Spirit and the name of Jesus as we pray it with deeper and deeper adoration takes us into God's love. Paul in prison has more time to pray and thus his letters to Philemon and to the Philippians are becoming even more loving than his previous letters because he is living and breathing the name of Jesus. The *Our Father* begins with "hallowed be thy name" and Paul and this early Christian Hymn are praying the same about the name. The name of each person in The Name of the Father and of the Son and of the Holy Spirit becomes in prayer more and more dear.

III.8.8 Who Will Transfigure Our Wretched Body

What Paul has learned from Jesus is that our suffering and death
will come to a glorious conclusion if we but suffer out of love
in union with Jesus for all the other members of his mystical body.
Thus in concluding chapter three Paul writes:

> But our homeland is in heaven
> and it is from there that we
> are expecting a Saviour, the Lord Jesus Christ,
> who will transfigure the wretched body of ours
> into the mould of his glorious body. (vv. 20–21)

The more wretched our body is now if we but suffer with Jesus
the more glorious our resurrected body will be through eternity.
Thus in chapter 4:4–5 Paul continues:

> Always be joyful, then, in the Lord;
> I repeat, be joyful.
> Let your good sense
> be obvious to everybody.

Paul thinks that suffering joyfully out of love is a matter of good
sense for that is what the Stoics following the Buddhists would do.
They would through meditation and the right eight-fold path seek
peace and tranquility in suffering and that would make good sense.
But to actually be joyful out of love is something entirely new
which Paul could well understand as Jesus took him beyond Stoicism.
As Jesus fulfilled Paul's Stoicism he saw how believing in the
suffering and death of Jesus could transform our mind and heart
with the belief that our wretched body could be glorified with Jesus.
Just as Paul imitates Jesus in the joyful suffering of love for others
so he wants all of his converts to make this love obvious to all.
That is the deepest meaning of glory to let the mystery of God's love
be manifest in our attitude, mood, feeling, thoughts, words and deeds.
Belief in an eternal glorious afterlife that begins right here
would not have been possible without the revelation of Christ Jesus.

III.8.9 Into the Mould of His Glorious Body

What Paul wants for his people is the unity of reconciliation.
In his letters he often makes clear the problem of factions and strife.
At the beginning of chapter two he explains the cause of the problem
and its solution so we return to our beginning:

> Nothing is to be done out of jealousy or vanity;
> instead, out of humility of mind
> everyone should give preference to others,
> everyone pursuing not selfish interests
> but those of others. (vv. 3–4)

So the problem has to do with being motivated by jealous self-interest
which will be in vain for it will cause conflict and lack of unity.
Because no man is an island and we are all part of the main to do
something against another is also to do it against the self for we are
all members of Christ's body and hurting the finger is also bad for the toe.
If one member of the body looks out for the health and happiness of
another member of the body then it will be more healthy and happy.
Thus Paul begins chapter two by writing:

> So if in Christ there is anything that will move you,
> any incentive in love,
> any fellowship in the Spirit,
> any warmth or sympathy—I appeal to you,
> make my joy complete
> by being of a single mind,
> one in love, one in heart and one in mind. (vv. 1–2)

What Paul wants most of all is this unity of a single mind
and a single heart in a single love that loves all other loves.
Paul sees all persons as being members of the single body of Christ.
That this body not self destruct in any way but that all build up
each other is what would make Paul's joy complete and let
all of his suffering as united with Christ's suffering be fulfilled.
All bodies united in the Glorious Body of Christ is our goal.

III.9 Paul's New Evidence for the New Love

III.9.1 From Mere Facts to Seven New Kinds of Evidence

Paul wanted to convert all others to believe in and to practice
the new universal love that was revealed by Christ Jesus
in his incarnation, crucifixion, resurrection and the coming
of the Holy Spirit of the Resurrected Jesus to the family of man.
That the Son of God became flesh was an apotheosis for all flesh.
The creator reveals a new love for all creatures by becoming a creature.
This Son of God who became flesh can thus suffer and die out of love.
The death of this God-man reconciles us to himself with justification.
But then the Son of God is resurrected from the dead and that reveals
to us how this living Lord can save us with an eternal life also.
As Paul went out to proclaim the Good News of this divinizing,
reconciling, saving new love he believed that the Holy Spirit
of the Risen Lord Jesus would inspire all persons with this love.
Paul received a special evidence form Stephen and from
the word of the Lord when he was blinded on the way to Damascus
that he might open his eyes and see all with a new evidence.
If we reflect on his seven letters we can see him presenting
seven new kinds of evidence to those whom he meets that they
might come to believe in and to practice this new kind of love.
He uses these seven kinds of evidence in all of his preaching
and in all of his writing, but to analyze them we can pick out
one kind of evidence in each of his seven authentic letters.
Thus we will examine how he moved from the evidence of facts
to (1) a new historical evidence in 1 Thessalonians, (2) a new
exemplary evidence in 1 Corinthians, (3) a new evidence of
emotional cognition in 2 Corinthians, (4) a new evidence of
comparative ethics in Galatians, (5) of comparative anthropology
in Romans, (6) of comparative politics in Philemon, and (7) of
comparative logic in Philippians, which all imply each other.
In the Acts of the Apostles Paul was convinced by this seven-fold
kind of new evidence, then he seeks to make it clear to others.

III.9.2 *The New Historical Evidence of 1 Thessalonians*

In Paul's age there was many a doubting Thomas as there always are
and his task was to give them evidence that went beyond mere facts.
Paul was not an eyewitness of the loving Jesus who gave evidence
of his Divinity even before his death and resurrection and yet he
was able to believe in the historical Jesus whom he had never seen.
Paul's belief and practice were based upon sound historical evidence
and he had to make that available to others so that they could believe
that the incarnation, crucifixion and resurrection each took place
at a certain time and place because of God's love for all of us.
The first evidence that Paul received was from Stephen who in
imitating the example of Jesus became an example for Paul so that
through Stephen Paul could know the new love of the historical Jesus.
Actions speak louder than words so the way Jesus and Stephen
loved was even more important than what they said about love.
All seven types of evidence fit together in that the evidence of
the example is evidence for the historical Jesus and his love.
The story that is told about the love which is exemplified also
takes us back to Jesus and lets us know of his superior kind
of love in its ethical, psychological, political and logical dimensions.
Thus, in his letter to the Thessalonians which gives literary evidence
for the universal love of Jesus Paul becomes an example for his
Thessalonians by loving them as a mother loves her children.
In this first of Paul's letters he reveals what he has been preaching.
It is with the joy of the Holy Spirit that they took the Gospel.
This joy which Paul is always writing about has to do with our
emotional cognition by which we can feel the value hierarchy.
There are the physical loves of affection, the vital loves of *eros*,
the intellectual loves of friendship and the holy love of *agape*.
Our heart has reasons which the mind knows not and can
see the evidence for these kinds of love and see the ethical,
psychological, political and logical superiority of Jesus' *agape*.

III.9.3 The New Exemplary Evidence of 1 Corinthians

That Jesus' love is divinizing, reconciling and saving each of us
is problematized by many severe challenges for as Paul notes
in this letter to the Corinthians we are at war on seven fronts for
there is worrying, alienation, bickering, and infighting within
each (1) person, (2) family, (3) Christian community, among
(4) different Christian communities, and (5) Jews and Romans,
between (6) the forces of good and evil, and (7) God and evil.
If we are really reconciled by Christ's death where is the evidence?
This seven-fold warring is strong evidence against Jesus' love.
It is an obvious set of facts that challenges Paul and all Christians
all the time and in every place and can let the enemy claim that
no divinization or reconciliation has taken place for things are now
only worse in terms of enmity and suffering as a result of Jesus' coming.
So Paul discovers that there are two kinds of evidence or proof:
the Christian and the non-Christian and that the example of Jesus
has turned love upside down in its very logic as that touches
ethics, psychology, politics and every aspect of our various cultures.
Thus at the beginning of this letter Paul writes:

> The language of the cross may be illogical
> to those who are not on the way to salvation
> but those of us who are on the way
> see it as God's power to save. (1:18)

Paul sees that God's foolishness is wiser than human wisdom and
that God's weakness is stronger than human strength and thus
as we suffer by meeting the many challenges of all the alienation
we can joyfully carry our cross with Jesus and also be examples.
Thus in his ode to love in the thirteenth chapter the main
point is to have faith and hope in the unconditional love
for all others and especially for our enemies as we struggle.
In the fifteenth chapter he shows how we can believe in
the resurrection and thus be on the way to our salvation.

III.9.4 The New Emotional Cognition of 2 Corinthians

In 2 Corinthians 5 Paul writes:

> From now onwards, therefore,
> we will not judge anyone
> by the standards of the flesh.
> Even if we did once
> know Christ in the flesh
> that is not how we know him now. (v. 16)

So, now as Christians we have a different way of knowing
for when our heart is converted into a heart of *agape* it knows
no longer as our heart knew before we loved with Jesus' love.
The heart does have its reasons which the mind knows not but
there are many different kinds of heart and the new heart of *agape*
with its logic turned upside down is now going to love suffering
with joy and see all seven types of warring for what they are as
steps along the way of following Christ toward our salvation.
The new heart of *agape* will know and judge all values in a new way.
The new heart knows from the perspective of a faith and a hope
in that universal love which renewed affection, friendship and *eros*
as Paul proclaimed it to his Thessalonians and now his Corinthians.
The new heart knows that the divinization of all flesh by the flesh
of God becoming flesh is both a gift and a task that Paul and
all members of the body of Christ must work out even politically.
The new heart knows that the reconciliation of man with God
is not only a gift of the God-man who died for that, but that it
is also a task so that Paul makes up in his suffering what was lacking
in the suffering of Christ just as we each need to suffer for that.
The new heart knows that the salvation that is revealed to us
through the resurrection of Christ can even be a mystery for Paul.
He thought that the last day would come within his life time.
But now 2000 years later we can still believe in the saving love
that will let all flesh be resurrected whenever God wants it.

III.9.5 The New evidence of Comparative Ethics in Galatians

Paul could compare many hearts that would know with different kinds of emotional cognition and thus have different kinds of ethics and psychology and politics for he knew the Greeks and Romans. He could compare the Platonic, Aristotelian, Stoic, Epicurean, and Skeptical ethics of the Greeks and the Roman schools and yet when he compared them to the new ethics of universal, unconditional love with its joy, peace, patience, kindness, etc., he knew in his heart of hearts that they were but *Praeparatio Evangelica*. He could easily see from the perspective of his heart that the ethics that saw that in Christ there is no longer Jew nor Greek, male nor female, master nor slave was the best ethics. The new logic of this ethics that saw all persons as equal and yet each as unique and each as members of Christ's body would fully believe in human rights, and would not uphold a caste system or any other unfair ethical system. Even a religion and ethics and culture of the law can bring a curse and now that Christ has died for us we need not keep all the details of the law to be saved for he has saved us. The main thing to do is recognize this and to follow his law of love for he has freed us from the old heart of a self-centeredness and self-indulgence and freed us for loving others with a new heart that can be joyful, peaceful, and self-controlled. By becoming a servant or slave for us Christ freed us from our old hearts that were enslaved to the self and he freed us for a new liberty that we might serve others in order to free them. A self-realization ethics is all about becoming free from that slavery to those habits that lead to self-destruction and further bondage. But fulfilling ourselves at the expense of others who are enslaved from the viewpoint of the altruistic ethics of Jesus is highly unethical and Paul like Jesus wants to become their servant. *Agape* can let us suffer for others with a joy that gives them joy.

III.9.6 The New Evidence of Comparative Psychology in Romans

In his letter to the Romans Paul looks deeply into his own inner struggles and in 7:14 he writes:

> I cannot understand my own behavior.
> I fail to carry out the things I want to do
> and find myself doing the very things I hate.

Paul comes up with a new anthropology, or psychology, or theory of the human person as he tries to understand his own inner struggle. By the death of the *sarx*-flesh which Jesus accomplished in his death all flesh is seen as becoming a corpse and in his resurrection we are all raised up as members of the corporate body of Christ. Without getting to the exact terminology and distinguishing the three main attributes Paul is already working with the notion of the person as interpersonal and having equal worth and uniqueness. Once again in his heart of hearts Paul has the emotional cognition into the value of personhood and can see that no other understanding of the human can match the excellence of this view. Paul's belief in the incarnation, crucifixion and resurrection is seeking understanding and as he ponders our divinization, reconciliation and salvation he sees that we are all members of Christ's Body and that the eye can serve the hand with joy just as the feet can serve the eyes and egoism is destructive. Paul sees that all humans all over the face of the earth and all down through the aeons are brothers and sisters in a family and that we are all inheritors of the promise given to Abraham. It is this being members of one body or members of one family that connects with the logic of the cross and makes sense of all of our struggles and even the suffering of Jesus as he was killed by his brothers and sisters and we can joyfully forgive and love all. The new logic of God's folly and weakness that saves us by the cross of Christ can now make sense of our crosses.

III.9.7 The New Evidence of Comparative Politics in Philemon

The *agape* of Christ Jesus which loves all persons equally and
even gives a preference to the other not only has implications
for psychology and ethics but also for politics at all of its levels.
If we take that psychology seriously that seeks to reconcile
the divisions within the heart, mind and soul of each person
and if we take that ethics seriously that builds up an attitude
of love and cares for all persons, creatures, places and things
then we will work for and promote a politics at the local,
the regional, the national and the international and global levels
that will bring about the best health, education and welfare for each.
As Paul argued in *Galatians* once we understand Christian *agape*
there will no longer be divisions between Jew and Greek, between
male and female nor master and slave for inequality passes away.
Here in this letter to *Philemon* Paul is dealing with the question
of slavery for the slave boy, Onesimus, whom he meets in prison,
becomes a Christian and Paul advises him to go back to his master.
It may seem that his politics is here contradicting his ethics.
But here we can better understand the struggle of Christian love
that has constantly been haunting Paul and his fellow Christians.
Christ has become flesh and shown them the worth of all creatures.
The Son has died on the cross and reconciled all with the Father.
He has arisen from the dead and given all the promise of eternal life.
But this only gets the process of divinization, reconciliation
and salvation started and it still needs to be worked out and
implemented through time psychologically, ethically and politically.
Paul cannot just get rid of Greek and Roman slavery over night.
He still needs to follow the law and let *agape* convert others.
If Philemon and Onesimus primarily love each other as
brothers than *agape* can work from the group up and
as others begin to love, the family and social and political
institutions will be changed and thus love must be patient.

III.9.8 The New Evidence of Comparative Logic in Philippians

The Greeks and especially Aristotle developed several kinds
of logic concerning the laws of opposition and the laws of categorical,
hypothetical and modal implication and they applied these laws
of reasoning to physics, metaphysics, psychology, ethics and politics.
But as Paul pointed out at the beginning of 1 Corinthians
a new kind of logic is initiated by the Creator who becomes
a creature and suffers for the creatures as more important than himself.
As we are seeing this new logic for Paul is connected with a new
physics, metaphysics, psychology, ethics, politics and theology.
If we are to imitate the example of Christ Jesus as did Stephen
and as Paul seeks to do then as he writes at Philippians 2:3–4:

> Nothing is to be done out of jealousy or vanity;
> instead, out of humility of mind
> everyone should give preference to others,
> everyone pursuing not selfish interests
> but those of others.

This new logic of mixed opposites rooted in the paradox of the God-man
states that even God can practice humility of mind which does
not fit in with the notion of perfection of any other God or Goddess.
This logic with its new theology claims that:

> The Son of God emptied himself
> taking the form of a slave,
> becoming as human beings are. (2:7)

This notion of *kenosis* or emptying is the heart of the ethics
that is born of *agape* and doesn't seek self-fulfillment but is
an emptying of one's self that others might be fulfilled.
This God who takes the form of a slave and accepts death
is higher than any other God who cannot be humble.
This loving God with his logic of mixed opposites can let
us be joyful in our sorrow and in all of our difficulties by
offering them with the Suffering God-man out of love for others.

III.9.9 It Is Self-Evident That We Should Love Agape

No human being would have every guessed what God revealed to us through his Son's incarnation, crucifixion and resurrection. That the creator so loved us that he became a creature and died for our reconciliation and rose from the dead for our salvation is so contradictory or at least paradoxical that it is unthinkable. But this illogical idea that seems anti-theological, anti-ethical, anti-political and anti-psychological once it is given as a gift of grace can so grace and move us that it becomes self-evident. Paul begins each of his letters with a prayer for his beloved that they might have grace and peace. And this grace is what lets them see the illogical as the most self-evident for once Paul begins to imitate Christ and love others with the love that sacrifices self out of preference for others it brings great peace. Stephen by imitating Jesus made Jesus' love that could suffer with great joy a self-evident blessing for Paul and now Paul takes it as his loving task to make it self-evident for others. A love that can turn any sorrow into joy becomes self-evident in its power through weakness and its wisdom through folly. A love that makes all the conflicts that Paul experienced into the cross of Christ that he can now carry is self-evident. The grace of God that comes to us from others who love us lets us see in them the face of Paul, the face of Stephen, and the face of Jesus and that face makes self-evident its love. For each person who believes and loves with Paul the example of a God who loves others more than self makes that *agape* self-evident to the emotional cognition of their heart of hearts. Imitating Christ with Paul makes self evident that absurd theology of the loving God who becomes a suffering creature for his creatures and that absurd anthropology which sees us as members of Christ's body and that absurd ethics which becomes free from self to be free for others and that absurd politics that loves a slave like a brother.

IV. Personhood

IV.7 To Love and Personhood from Augustine to Aquinas

IV.7.1 The Caritas Synthesis (Grace and Freedom)

St. Augustine's *Confessions* tell the story of how his philosophy
of man, nature and society came to be for his transformation
like that of St. Paul set the direction for the rest of his thinking.
His first religious philosophy was that of the Gnostic Manichaeans
and he justified his robust sexual activity to his mother
by claiming that he was not free to control his sexual passion.
He learned the philosophies of the Epicureans, the Stoics, and
the Skeptics but most of all he came to believe in Platonism.
He also learned from St. Ambrose how to accept the Bible by
coming to appreciate the four ways of interpreting any text,
the literal and the allegorical moral, mystical and typological ways.
He greatly admired the theory and practice of celibacy in Plato
and tried and tried to sublimate his sexual energy into the creative
quest for the beautiful, the good, the true and the holy so that he
could enjoy the happy life in accord with the correct order of love.
He prayed as a Christian: "O Lord, give me chastity; but not yet."
Then finally he heard the voice in the garden: "Take and read!"
He opened the Bible to Paul's letter to the Romans and he read:
"Why do you walk in drunkenness, debauchery and wickedness
when all you have to do is put on the Lord Jesus and be saved?"
At once and from then on he had no trouble with celibacy again.
He was a converted Christian Platonist just as it happened
on Plato's Ladder of Love in the *Symposium* and up and out of
the Cave in the *Republic* and the Lord Jesus did set him free.
Grace freed him and he knew that he could not be free without it.
Against the Manicheans who believed only in determinism
he could now write his *De Libero Arbitrio*, *On the Free Choice
of the Will*, and later against the Pelagians he would have to
argue strenuously as the Doctor of Grace for the gift of grace.
His *Caritas* synthesis of Christian *Agape* and Platonic *Eros*
was not only his practice and theory but that of the Middle Ages.

IV.7.2 Uti et frui (The Problem of Evil and Loving Suffering)

Augustine's motto was:

> *Noverim me! Noverim Te!*
> May I know myself! May I know you!

This petition is a prayer that God will gift him with this grace. Like Socrates he thought it important to know himself, but as a disciplined disciple of Christ he thought it even more important to know, love and serve the Triune God that he might be happy with the Father, Son and Holy Spirit both now and forever. One of his first books was *De Beata Vita, On the Happy Life,* and his was never a simple disinterested love that would sacrifice one's own happiness out of love for God and neighbor. St. Augustine thought of love in terms of *uti et frui* for loving in his practice and theory was useful and enjoyable. In the Tenth Book of *The Confessions*, as he makes his prolonged mystical ascent by advancing from contemplating the external world of creation to the depths of his own conscious and unconscious self—the "abyss" he calls memory, he suddenly realizes that the search for God is the search for happiness and he wonders how humans can do that when their memory provides no experience of the Happy Life. "You have made us for yourself, O God, and our hearts are not at rest until they rest in Thee!" Augustine was convinced that man is made for the infinite and the finite is not enough for loving finite things can be useful, but it is only loving the infinite that will give us that happiness which is *gaudium de veritate* or a joy given by truth. Augustine found that good will is not enough for we need a method and a wisdom which we lack unless God gives it to us. As a Manichaean Augustine knew only the problem of evil which he felt before he was a Christian when his friend died, but after be became a Christian and his son died he knew resurrection joy.

IV.7.3 Two Loves Have Built Two Cities (Christian history)

In his *De Trinitate, On The Trinity*, Book 5, chapters 7–10, Augustine treats the three persons in one substance and reveals a fine knowledge of Aristotle's notion of substance and the nine accidents and he gives reasons for not calling the person a substance. He reveals an insight into the relationality of persons that avoids the rugged individualism of modernity and is nearly postmodern. But Augustine was as interested in society or the communal person as he was the Divine Persons and the human person and thus he wrote his *City of God* in which he developed his new Christian theory of history that arose out of the Christian notion of personhood. Greeks and Jews wrote histories, but from an ethnic point of view, however, as Paul clearly put it, "In Christ there is no longer Jew nor Greek," and thus history for Augustine becomes universal history, the history of all human persons in relation to the three persons of God. Augustine believed that two loves have built two cities for the love of self has built up the City of Man and the love of God has built up *The City of God*, and given his *caritas* synthesis and his relating of love to *uti et frui* he wants to show how all the histories of the cities of men can help to build up the city of God just as Platonism can help to build up Christianity once Platonism moves from the vulgar to the noble which grace can facilitate. The seven days of creation in the first chapter of Genesis allegorically tells us about seven periods of history so that history is universal, periodized, progressive, and with a temporality that has an eternal end given the temporal-eternal God-man. Augustine started the notion of a Christian culture that is based on the God who is the Love between the Divine Persons and thus the concept of human personhood and laws protects their equal dignity, unique singularity and relationality within a history of developing progress for all persons who are members of the Body of Christ whether they believe it or not.

IV.7.4 From St. Benedict to St. Anslem of Canterbury

The monastic cultivation of love and personhood transformed Europe at the end of the Roman Empire from many Barbarian tribes into a Christian agricultural culture with a new law and order. Benedict and his monks and his Sister Scholastica and her nuns lived out the motto of *Ora et Labora, Work and Pray* so successfully that one monastery and convent after another moved across Europe and all the people who became Christian farmers were ever so happy if one of their sons or daughters received a vocation to become a monk or nun and pass on the gift of the Lord which they received. The Benedictines imitated Jesus, Mary and the Apostles with their vows of poverty, celibacy and obedience that they might go and bring the good news of charity, joy, peace and patience to the ends of the earth. They made a virtue of their work and thereby it was sweet. They sang the Divine Praises eight times a day and the great and beautiful Gregorian Chant took on an evolution of its own as the monks and nuns prayed each week and came to memorize the 150 psalms. From the 6th Century to the 12th Century the Monasticism of Benedict and his and Patrick and his became so successful that cities began to flourish and soon the new technology would call forth new kinds of Dominican and Franciscan spirituality to care for the poor who came to the cities to work and often became lost souls. The sexual energy of the Monastics was sublimated as it was for Jesus, Paul, Plato and Augustine that all might come to enjoy love. St. Anselm, a monk and abbot himself, was a vital part of the 12th Century Renaissance and in a Benedictine and yet also Augustinian way he reconciled not only faith and reason, but all of Christian culture in the mix of his atonement and incarnation theologies with the emphasis on atonement. With his Augustinian method of faith seeking understanding and "I believe that I might understand" he developed his ontological argument for God's existence to help all atheists.

IV.7.5 From Pseudo-Dionysius to St. Bernard

In the Dark Ages there was a light shining in the Monasteries
where the manuscripts of antiquity were preserved and studied.
Then the cathedral schools began to flourish and several kinds
of Platonism began to evolve and converse in a creative confluence.
Pseudo-Dionysius was a genius who left a legacy of many
fruitful ideas such as his concept of Negative Theology in terms
of which he could treat the variety of the names of the ineffable God.
Concerning love and personhood he thought of God as pure
and simple *Eros* who extended his action to the last and least
of beings in a Goodness which was self-diffusing first in creation
and then in salvation by drawing all souls back into himself.
The person is a microcosm or a little universe in which all of
existence is contained from God the Holy Source of the Hierarchy
down through the Angels to humans, plants and inorganic matter.
It is man's grace-given-task to rise inward and upward to God
from the lowest to the highest within ourselves through purgation
illumination and unification and there are nine choirs of
Angels who can light and guard, rule and guide us on our
journey to take us through each stage and one to take us out of each stage.
St. Bernard's more than sixty sermons on *The Song of Songs*
which he gave to the holy sisters has a similar pattern to
that of the Neo-Platonists and especially to that of Pseudo-Dionysius.
Song of Solomon begins with the words: "Let him kiss me
with the kisses of his mouth" and every Holy Nun will yearn to be
the Bride of Christ, but what other kisses are there besides of the mouth?
The ten Kisses of the feet in which I kiss the ten toes of his feet
drive out the nine demonic powers from my soul just as the
ten kisses of his hands fill my soul with the nine Angelic powers.
Then I am ready for the kisses of his mouth and yes even those
of the breasts so that then the Baby Jesus can be born within me.

IV.7.6 From John the Scot to Abelard

John the Scot being from Ireland, where they learned Greek, read Pseudo-Dionysius and was influenced by the idea of man as a microcosm which mirrors the macrocosm and John developed his idea of the universe which included all things in an orderly related whole so that each was a mystery reflecting all. Whereas Augustine thought of evil as a lack of what should be and thereby avoided Gnostic, Manichaean tendencies, John the Scot as he thought about the place of matter in the universe came to see it as a force of disorder and the result of sin in the universe. Man had been intended to have a spiritual body only, without any vegetative and animal needs so now it is our task to detach ourselves from the territorial imperative of wealth, sex and power with the practices of poverty, celibacy and holy obedience. Within the conversation of the many medieval voices about man the microcosm and then nature and its hierarchy and then the whole of society in all of its history there were criticisms against the negative views not only of John the Scot but also of Augustine's view of the Fall as crippling all of nature. It was Abelard who bequeathed a wide, positive view to the Scholastic method with his approach of *Sic et non*. He considered each disputed question in terms of arguments both for and against it in terms of the arguments that led up to it. Thus Abelard who is also well known for his famous love letters with his student Eloise developed that method of loving wisdom which the great masters of the 13th Century would follow as they wrote their great summaries of wisdom. Anselm who wrote besides his *Proslogion* and *Monologion* his *Cur Deus Homo Fit?* (Why did God become man?) thereby became one of the founders of the Scholastic Method.

IV.7.7 Charity Is a Habit Created in the Human Soul

St. Augustine and St. Thomas were of two very different temperaments. Augustine was an erotic Platonist and Aquinas a friendly Aristotelian. Thus Augustine and Christian Platonists related charity to *eros* while Thomas and Christian Aristotelians related her more to friendship. In the Disputed Questions for more advanced readers Thomas devotes six questions and sixty-nine articles to the virtue of charity In the *Summa Theologiae* he treats (1) charity in itself, (2) the subject of charity, (3) the object of charity, (4) the order of charity, (5) the principle act of charity, and (6) the precepts of charity. Thomas begins by asking whether charity is something created in the soul or is it the Holy Spirit itself? And while going back often to Augustine and especially *De Trinitate* he shows how it could be thought that just as the soul is the life of the body, so God is the life of the soul, and since God is love then the human person who has charity has the Holy Spirit. Thomas gives twenty-four quotations which go in the direction of claiming that the love in the human soul is the Holy Spirit. Then he argues against that since we are finite beings and since finite beings are created charity must be created in us. Charity is to love God with our whole heart, mind and soul, and to love our neighbor as ourselves and this most of all is a love that is disinterested in that we do not seek first our own interests. Augustine did see love as primarily seeking its own happiness. But after all the great Christian love theorists of the 12th Century Thomas wondered how we could be transformed from a habit of self-interest to a habit in attitude, mood and feeling in which we would really love our neighbor as ourselves and thus our enemy. For Aristotle the intellectual and moral virtues were habits that enabled us to practice virtue with ease and with delight. The fallen human has the habit of a self-interested love that hates the enemy so we need the Holy Spirit to give us charity.

IV.7.8 Charity Is the Most Powerful Virtue

For Aristotle happiness or the complete fulfillment of all we desire is the goal of human life and virtue is the means to that end. Prudence, justice, fortitude and temperance are each a golden mean between two extremes or kinds of vice that will make us unhappy. The intellectual virtues such as science and wisdom are habits of becoming focused on the end and all the means thereto so that in knowing our cosmos we can be free from wandering in chaos. For Thomas the three theological virtues of faith, hope and charity given our fallen nature cannot be attained by our efforts alone. Before the Christian revelation we would only get as far as Aristotle. We could discover that the unmoved mover is our first efficient cause and our last and final cause, but we could not discover that out of love that God created us out of nothing to know, love and serve him and thereby to be happy with him forever. God is the cause of love inasmuch as he generates love in himself and causes it in others as an image of himself. The infused theological virtue of faith gives us the gift to believe this and the theological virtue of hope gives us the task of trusting always in it and those two make possible the theological virtue of charity which is the highest of the virtues or as Paul puts it: "There are faith, hope and charity and the greatest of these is charity" (1 Cor 13:13). For faith lets us believe in charity and hope lets us strive for it while charity is the substance of things believed in and hoped for. So charity is the most powerful of the virtues for as the apex of the theological virtues it even transforms the moral and intellectual virtues by revealing a new kind of happiness and thus new and higher means of pursuing the *Eudaimonia*. Happiness for Aristotle meant to live with good *Daimons* but happiness for Aquinas is to live in the grace of the God of love. Friendship for Aristotle was not a virtue but a bond that the virtuous could share, but for Thomas friendship is a loving virtue.

IV.7.9 Charity Is Complacency and Concern

Father Frederick Crowe, SJ, in his book *Three Thomist Essays*,
has an excellent article on love as complacency and concern
in terms of which he explains Aquinas' two kinds of charity.
If we but think of prayer in its four modes the distinction
stands out as basic between praise and thanksgiving as
complacency and then repentance and petition as forms of concern.
In praising and thanking we are overflowing with happiness
for the goodness of God and of being whereas in repentance and
petition we are concerned to make things better with active striving.
The very being of the God who is love is a being of complacency
in which there is a being pleased with *dicens, verbum et amor*.
Thomas writes that love is distinguished from hope, in this,
that love implies union whereas hope implies a movement.
In God's complacent love there is only the union of the speaking
Father, the spoken Son and the Holy Spirit of love between them.
On God's part there is no need for any hope or striving after.
According to Thomas there are the six transcendentals of
being, oneness, truth, goodness, something and thinghood so that
everything that is is good, true, etc. insofar as it has being.
All being is good so that we can have a complacent love for
everything insofar as we are pleased with its goodness and,
of course, we can also have concern in striving for things
and for ourselves to be better and to reach our full potential.
Even in the three natural loves of affection, friendship
and *eros* there can be a natural gratitude which Thomas
appreciates as a propaedeutic for supernatural complacency.
So Aquinas can have complacency for all persons, places
and things and for all lovers and that is the basis for his
Catholic universalism which can strive with concern for
further actuating potential but which sees all potential
as grounded in an actual being that can be delighted in.

IV.8 To Love and Personhood with the Franciscans

IV.8.1 Francis' Love for Wolf and Sultan

If we think of Franciscan love in terms of Thomistic love
we might say that Francis prayed with concern for complacency.

> Oh Lord, I seek not so much to be loved . . . as to love;
> not so much to be understood . . . as to understand;
> not so much to be forgiven . . . as to forgive.

The poor man of Assisi was seen by so many as revealing
the very love of Jesus for the rule he followed was the
Eight Beatitudes and his Stigmata showed the love of Jesus.
His loving embrace of suffering taught the suffering to love.
But, the love of Francis went out to all of God's creatures,
to Brother Sun and Sister Moon and to the dear wolf of Gubbio.
There was a ferocious wolf living in the woods outside of
a little village and the menfolk were all trying to kill him.
But, St. Francis went out and loved the wolf and the two
became such good friends that the wolf came with the saint
into the small town and all the people began to befriend him too.
After Francis went away the wolf remained with the people
and he was so loving that he reminded them of Saint Francis.
So love and personhood for Francis had to do with loving
all persons especially the most unloved with whom Francis
could identify as he offered his suffering for the suffering poor.
At the time of Francis there were the crusades in which
Christians were trying to take back their sacred sites from
the Moslems and there was no love found between the enemies.
But Francis went out as a lover and not a warrior to Morocco.
There he met and befriended the Sultan and they became
the best of friends with no enmity in any way between them.
Francis could so love any enemy that they would become
dearest friends for they bonded with him just as did Jesus.
Many Franciscans became great and saintly scholars but Francis
knew God more deeply because he loved him more simply.

IV.8.2 Joachim of Fiore's Unlimited Scriptural Seeds

Joachim of Fiore came to know of Francis and his view
of the world changed beginning with a new view of scripture.
Up until the Millennial Turn St. Augustine's theology of history
dominated the culture of Europe but when Joachim thought
of Francis and his approach to love a new view began to dawn.
Augustinian history was apocalyptic, universal, providential, and
periodized and at its center was the apocalyptic, atonement axis.
The Apocalyptic movement which began with Ezekiel during
the Babylonian captivity and developed with Daniel during
the Hellenistic persecution formed the view of Paul, Mark and John.
It is marked by ten traits: (1) universality, (2) cosmic dualism,
(3) chronological dualism, (4) ethical dualism, (5) predestination,
(6) exclusivism, (7) atonement theology, (8) portrait of a violent God,
(9) eschatological preoccupations, and (10) use of symbolic words.
Joachim began to see how Francis was led by a consciousness
that was strongly eschatological though lacking the apocalyptic tone.
This move away from the apocalyptic tone will imply a
revision of all ten traits of the apocalyptic mentality that
are there in the dualism of Augustine's city of man—City of God.
Joachim goes to the interplay between the Hebrew Bible and the New
Testament to begin spelling out how Franciscan love for wolves
and Sultans and for all the creatures of the world must imply
a way of reading scripture beyond Augustine's four-fold way.
Augustine's *Scriptualis Intelligentia* penetrates through
the literal sense to allegorical, typological and analogical meaning.
But the *Figurae Sacramentales* points out how scripture
speaks of Christ and the Anti-Christ in all of its many books.
And in the third place he puts the *multiformes theoriae* for
who can know the ultimate number of seeds which exist?
When persons read scripture and put the two covenants together
new views that all have some legitimacy will sprout forth.

IV.8.3 Bonaventure's New Universalism of Multiformes Theoriae

Joseph Ratzinger (Pope Benedict XVI's) book on Bonaventure's *Theology of History* shows how the Franciscans went beyond Augustine's Apocalyptic history to their new loving nominalism. In his *Concordia Veteris et Novi Testamenti* Joachim of Fiore had already distinguished the threefold type of biblical exegesis. Augustine and his tradition would show how the crossing of the Red Sea was to be understood as a literal, historical event. But it could also have a moral significance and indicate that we should all pass from a negative slavery to a positive freedom. It could also have a mystical meaning and show how our journey can take us from purification to illumination to unification. Fourth, it can be a type of the sacrament of baptism and show how undergoing the water of baptism can save us with sanctifying grace. All of this for the Augustinian tradition has to do with the passage from the earthly city to the City of God in terms of apocalyptic dualism. But as Joachim says and as Bonaventure develops it that event of passing through the Red Sea is a little microcosmic seed that can sprout forth in unlimited, unknowable ways as each future event of history takes place for those who love. The Hebrew Bible and the New Testament are holy histories of ever creative and renewable events that break forth in qualitative leaps. Augustine argued that the incarnational event of the word-made-flesh replaced the circle of history with a new Biblical linear history. But Bonaventure argues that the living word lets new life come forth from all past events and that it can renew all present events. The Bible as Holy History shows how the incarnational event gives the Red Sea event the unlimited futures of *multiformes theoriae*. Scriptural exegesis needs the awareness of a present that makes the past futural and the future present in a loving goodness that goes beyond all apocalyptic, exclusive dualisms and beyond the wrath of a rewarder-punisher God who predestines persons.

IV.8.4 Bonaventure's History and the Worth of the Temporal Order

Augustine and Aquinas had an equity universalism that opened them to the worth of Plato and Aristotle insofar as there was a shared commonality of ideas and values between them and Christianity. But, Bonaventure has moved to a new difference universalism in which with Joachim and Francis he thinks that all that is, even in all of its differences, is to be loved because of the incarnation. Augustine's apocalyptic, atonement universalism coming out of Paul's Letter to the *Romans* saw the predestination of many damned. Aquinas with the complacent love of his incarnation theology while loving the good in every being still stressed eternal values and with his teleology in seeing virtue as a means to an end still stressed temporality as useful for our eternal salvation. Augustine saw Christ and his *City of God* as the end of the six ages of history; but for Bonaventure Christ is the center of the six ages in such a way that his Kingdom will be established on earth. This temporal reality is not only a means to an end but the incarnation has revealed its worth even to the extent that God not only created it out of love but became flesh for it. In developing Joachim's *multiformes theoriae* Bonaventure relates the Old and New Testaments "as tree to tree; as letter to letter; as seed to seed. As a tree comes from a tree, and a letter from a letter so one testament comes from another." And revelation does not end with the trees, seeds and letters of the New Testament, but unknown seeds can come forth and produce new kinds of trees with an evolution of new species and Francis is a new seed like that. With Francis the sixth age of history is being announced when the church militant will give birth to the seventh age of the church triumphant and the Holy City will come down from heaven. The great prophecies of Ezekiel and Isaiah will be fulfilled for salvation will come in the form of a peace upon our earth and the age of redemption will preserve the flesh and temporality.

IV.8.5 Scotus' Move from Multiformes Theoriae to Haecceity

Since Boethius the definition of the person as "an individual substance of a rational nature" held its own down through history. Augustine did stress the relationality of personhood and knew that relation was only accidental for Aristotle, but the emphasis on substance and rationality continued to receive interpretations. But, once the reality of Franciscan love for each individual creature becomes prominent and the concept of *multiformes theoriae* has been clearly worked out Scotus will be ready to develop his concept of *haecceity* or thisness as the principle of individuation. The Latin word for "this" in its maculine, feminine and neuter form is *hic, haec, hoc* so Scotus takes the pronoun *haec* and makes a noun out of it as *haecceitas* meaning thisness. You remember that Aristotle accounted for individuality which Plato disregarded, with his hylemorphic matter form theory. Matter for Aristotelians differentiated this horse from that one. But, how could you differentiate the persons of the Trinity with this principle of matter since they are without matter? Once he understood the concept of the *multiformes* or many formed theories or seeds that let qualitatively new trees, seeds and letters leap forth Scotus knew he had to account for different persons, places and things in terms of forms itself and not only in terms of matter and thus *haecceity* became a principle that could differentiate Divine persons and human persons and even immaterial ideas and volitions. *Haecceity* means that this person is different from that person because while they each have the common form of human person that gives them their equal worth and dignity their very *thisness* is made up of all the relations that make them unique so that everything a person does, thinks or says and anything that happens to them is part of their *haecceity*. A person is an individual relational thisness of a volitional nature.

IV.8.6 Scotus' New Personhood of Haecceity

By moving away from the concept of an individual substance or form differentiated from other substances by matter to the concept of an individual whose form is differentiated by the many forms of the *multiformes theoriae* Scotus had to differentiate himself from Thomas and the Aristotelians as well as Augustine and the Platonists on every issue about love and personhood and their implications for all of theology. As Richard Cross in his excellent book on Duns Scotus shows the concept of *haecceity* brings Scotus to stress more the differences between the three persons of the Trinity rather than stress their unity as was the case with Aquinas. Scotus can stress that Being can be understood in a univocal rather than in an equivocal or analogous sense because it can mean one thing and be differentiated by its many forms. Augustine went in the direction of a double predestination in which the saved and the damned would both be predestined. Thomas worked out theories of Divine foreknowledge that would let both be free to choose their destiny rationally. But Scotus will try to develop a more loving approach to God and try to mitigate predestination with a voluntarism that lets even the unknowing have a freedom based on love. In the concept of the complexity of *haecceity* there has to be in the very definition of the person a stress on our freedom to meaningfully choose out of love and in terms of the most loving possibility rather than stressing our rational nature. So for Scotus all persons are equal in their worth as persons for the form of personhood is the same for each of them. But each person is vastly complex in their uniqueness for every relation they have further differentiates them with the many forms of the *multiformes theoriae* that are beyond knowing but are lovable in the goodness of all their qualities.

IV.8.7 From Multiformes Theoriae to Ockham's nominalism

Another problem Boethius bequeathed to philosophers was that of universals which had to do with the four theories of ultra realism, moderate realism, conceptualism, or nominalism. Words have a universal nature for if we say "green" that word extends to all green things in the universe and Plato would say it primarily refers to the form of "green" in which all things participate and thus things here are not as real as is the form. Aristotle in trying to protect the reality of material things argues for the position of moderate realism and held that universals have a foundation in reality and with the intellect we abstract them. Thus trees are real and the universal idea or form of tree is an idea that we generate in order to understand them. However, Aristotle is a realist and does not think that we simply generate the universal idea as an idealist would. The third position is that of the conceptualist who like Kant does hold that universal ideas are generated by our minds alone. The realists would try to avoid conceptualism because they think it undermines the possibility of truth which they define as a correspondence between our ideas and the things themselves. But the conceptualists argue that truth has to do with coherence between ideas and not correspondence and they are able to explain scientific knowledge successfully in terms of their theory that universal ideas are only concepts in our mind and not things. Nominalism argues that the universal is only a name on our lips and that the universal is not a valid concept or thing in itself because all things are only individuals and not parts of a whole. Nominalism is a skepticism which shows how we can never get a full universal knowledge of any single individual and that is why Ockham became a nominalist that he might protect the complexity of each *haecceity* from being falsely universalized for the *multiformes* are not reducible.

IV.8.8 From Ockham's Nominalism to Luther's Modernity

Of course, Socrates and the Greco-Roman sceptics would have
been nominalists if they had worked out the theory of universals,
and Dogmatists have always sought to avoid nominalism because
they see it as leading to a relativism in both ethics and religion.
But we should remember that Socrates first got ethics going
as a sceptic against the Pre-Socratics and the sophistical relativists.
Ockham's nominalism was the fruit that grew on the Franciscan
tree which had for its roots the love of Francis for all creatures,
and for its trunk the new *multiformes theoriae* of Joachim,
and for its branches Bonaventure's new theology of history
with its anti-apocalyptic concern for our temporal world,
and Scotus' blossoms of haecceity in all their uniqueness,
and finally the fruit of nominalism which came forth with Ockham.
His point would be that the very seeds of his fruit could
give birth to different kinds of trees evolving as new species.
And that is exactly what happened for a very new tree, seed and
letter came forth with Luther and then with each of the modernists.
And in our day at this millennial turn all the postmodernists
as they go back and reclaim the tradition that Luther junked
see themselves as nominalists with a great respect for
contingency and complexity that only nominalism theorizes.
Luther was an Augustinian monk and he well knew
Ockham's nominalism and saw in it a truth that alone
was adequate for our senses and reason give no truth.
Whenever we speak we should not be fooled by our
universal language which is only a name on our lips
and as nominalists we should always warn ourselves
of the inadequacy of reason and the whole philosophical tradition.
Thus Luther opted for scripture alone and against reason.
Nominalism made him a skeptic concerning philosophy
but he could still believe in the revealed word of God as truth.

IV.8.9 From Ockham to Postmodern Nominalism

For the Franciscans from Joachim to Ockham the person is an unique individual of vast complexity in all of its differentiating relations that cannot begin to be fathomed with the conscious mind. In fact all of existence is like this, filled with many seeds, or as the postmodernists would say filled with unlimited voices. Luther as a skeptical nominalist abandoned philosophies and went to scripture alone or to Paul's letter to the *Romans* alone. Paul would say we are saved by faith alone and not by works. Since James says that "faith without works is dead" Luther will treat him in the same way he treated all the philosophers. But once Kierkegaard and Nietzsche, those fine Lutheran postmodern existentialists, come along after Kant and Hegel another pair of fine Lutherans they saw the truth of many perspectives and objective uncertainty so that they, like Joachim and Ockham, could see truth in "the conflict" of interpretations. So Ockham's nominalism was interpreted in two opposite ways insofar as Luther would reason: Reason ends in scepticism and failure alone, therefore, we should follow faith alone. And the postmodernists would say: Nominalism shows the truth of the many perspectival, conflicting voices in dialogue, therefore let's listen to the many voices and reason together. Of course, as with Francis the ultimate criterion for truth has to do with what way is the most loving for all creatures or as Nietzsche would put it with: Humankind's highest affirmation which goes beyond resentment with a Yes and Amen for all of existence" in Kierkegaard's "most passionate inwardness. Again Joachim of Fiore is very prophetic for there can be unlimited interpretations of scripture that only protest against each other as with Luther and his modernists or there can be the truth in the appropriation process of many voices in dialogue on trial with the Jesus of the incarnation.

IV.9 From Love to Justice for Modern Individuals

IV.9.1 From Calvin's Tulip to Hobbes' Homo Homini Lupus

The spirit of modernity, which has given so much to our world today, took hold of Europe most of all with Calvin and his followers. Right in the Lord's Prayer its formula can be found when we pray: "Thy Kingdom come. Thy will be done, on earth as it is in heaven." Calvinists wanted to bring the Kingdom of God's will to earth and God's will for a much better life on earth can be accomplished when the elect or predestined follow the covenant or social contract. The Calvinist's doctrine of double predestination is the tulip doctrine:

T TOTAL DEPRAVITY—all human aspects are corrupted by sin.
U UNCONDITIONAL ELECTION—God elects who will be saved.
L LIMITED ATONEMENT—Christ's works were not for all, but for a limited number.
I IRRESISTIBLE GRACE—God's grace cannot be resisted.
P PERSEVERANCE OF THE SAINTS—People can never fall away: any argument against this is branded as Pelagianism.

Hobbes' social contract can be thought of in terms of Calvin's doctrine of the blessed saved and the cursed damned for since *Homo Homini Lupus*—man is a wolf to man we need a set of laws and a police force to enforce the laws and to protect the wealth of families and of nations from those predestined to be evil. Modernity began with a simple logic for Calvin and Hobbes who thought that if you are one of the elect you will live according to God's law, but the many non-elect necessitate police and armies. Modernity might be thought of as beginning in 1492, when Columbus set sail and began the age of mercantile individualists. Spain, Portugal, and Holland became ruggedly individualist nations, as they built up the wealth of nations with their new sea powers. Soon England came on the scene with her lusty pirate ships and then her own great colonizing fleet allowed the elect to amass wealth by plundering and enslaving the non-elect.

IV.9.2 From Luther's Faith Alone to Hume's Experience Alone

Luther with a brilliant stroke of genius initiated the power and the prosperity of modernity with the focusing of his *Sola Fidei*. By concentrating upon being saved by faith in the atoning work of Christ's cross alone, Lutherans emphasized conservative family and national values without relying on their own works. Faith without the works of love meant faith without the Papacy and the paganism of the hierarchy of the seven holy orders; without monasticism with is poverty, celibacy and obedience; without Marian devotion and the spiritual and corporal works of mercy; without pagan philosophy that corrupted sacred scripture alone. As fiscal conservatives Lutherans ended indulgence money for Rome. As social conservatives with the *Cuius Regio, Eius Religio* Catholic churches could be taken over and such moral laxity as the carnival of the *Drei Tollen Tagen* could be contained within the Catholic Provinces alone without polluting Lutherans. Through the discipline of preaching the law such excellence in every phase of life could be cultivated that there could be *Deutschland uber Alles* in every aspect of German culture. Since Lutherans downplayed working out their eternal salvation with spiritual works they could put their effort into secular works and build up our modern world with health, education and welfare. Luther's move from the Catholic logic of the both-and of the mixed opposites of the Incarnational God-man and the consequent scripture and tradition together with faith and works to his logic of exclusive opposites of either faith or works but not both has been the hallmark of modernity for the last five hundred years. For Hobbes it was matter alone without spirit just as for Hume's ethics it was sentiment alone which intuits right values and motivates us to pursue them without any rational natural law ethic. Faith without works was the slippery slope to secular personhood.

IV.9.3 From Henry VIII's Anglicans to Locke's Democracy

Henry VIII did not use the logic of exclusive opposites with which
Calvin and Luther initiated their modernity models of atonement alone.
Like King David, Muhammad and Brigham Young he was more
concerned with the battle of the sexes, as he sought power alliances
through marriages, than with the battle of all against all or the
battle of one religious culture with another as in the 100 years wars.
Within the Anglican world there can be conversations between
high, middle and low voices that co-operate rather than fight.
In keeping with this Locke with his new social contract sets up
a liberal democracy of executive, legislative and judicial branches
which can act as checks and balances upon each other so that
there cannot be a misuse of power as there can be in a monarchy.
Each male person owning property would have the right to vote.
And so the notion of personhood was beginning to become political.
Before Protestantism and the rise of modernity the kings, nobles
and clergy had the political power and with the *Magna Carta* and
the Franciscan influence of Friar Tuck and Robin Hood the nobles
did get their rights in a written constitution against the king.
But, now with Locke persons are beginning to become much more
equal in their actual rights here and now and while those
without property and women do not have a political voice
there is at least another step in the direction of equal persons.
While Locke's political democracy does begin to make the person
and his property much more valuable in a practical way
he remains a rugged individualist with all the protestants
in their protest against the community of the one Catholic Church.
Henry VIII with his power marriages and Locke with his power
politics were very successful in making England a power-
house among the nations and each rugged individual with the
new democracy could now become healthier, wealthier and wiser.
How is modernity to move from rugged individuals to community?

IV.9.4 From Descartes' Cogito to Leibnitz's Monad

As Descartes went beyond Socratic skepticism and Ockham's nominalism he began by doubting all things with them, but then argued that I have to be in order to doubt so with his *cogito ergo sum*, I think therefore I am, he fallaciously proved that I am a thinking thing by going from thinking to thinking thing. Again Descartes is operating with an exclusivistic logic which leaves him with the problem of how to explain the union of mind as a thinking and body as an extended thing for he separates these things in a way that the tradition from Aristotle to Aquinas never did for body and soul are principles of a thing and not things in themselves. But Descartes like Luther wanted to drop the whole tradition and start afresh and even though he borrows many ideas and never acknowledges them he still got modernity started falsely because he did not understand the difference between the hylemorphic principles of body and soul and two separate things. Leibnitz corrects the rugged individualism of Descartes and Locke. He continues Locke's attitude of benevolent optimism but moves to a communitarianism based on the monads or evolving seeds. Leibnitz recovers the concept of *multiformes theoriae* and thinks of the monads which God created as interrelated and codependent. They are all good and we do live in the best of all possible worlds even though great suffering and death are inevitable evils for each. Leibnitz seeks to end religious wars and move from exclusive opposites to the parallel opposites of matter and spirit co-evolving. He thinks that a leap of faith rather than science can reveal the best solution to the problem of theodicy or the question about whether God can be justified in permitting evil in the world. Science need not exclude faith and it can operate best as subordinate to it for science is motivated to make a better world out of love for all suffering persons and creatures. Leibnitz before Hegel is the hinge between modernity and postmodernity.

IV.9.5 From Wesley's Evangelicals to Smith's Wealth of Nations

In 1740, John Wesley preached his first open air revival sermon
and the Evangelical movement began and in this Calvinism
for the masses any born again Christian could now be saved.
There was a new optimistic spirit in the air and Wesley's new
Methodist movement had a tremendous impact on the social,
economic and political life of the lower classes who before
had been estranged from the Church of England in their misery.
Wesley's Evangelical movement was in no small measure
responsible for the transformation of English society from
a fractured, slave trading aristocracy to a free democracy.
Adam Smith argued that the invisible hand of God could
provide through capitalism a great new wealth for the nations.
The middle class could expand indefinitely as the extremely
wealthy and the extremely poor would dwindle in their numbers.
Wesley did much to recover some of the traditional concepts of love
and personal growth for whereas Luther emphasized the justified man
and Calvin the obedient servant, Wesley focuses on the perfected person.
Modernity began with the rugged individualism of unequal and
non-relational persons with Luther, Calvin and Henry VIII. with
Descartes, Hobbes, Locke and Hume, but by the time we reach
mid-modernity with Leibnitz, Adam Smith and Wesley
the concepts of communal love and persons in relation are
beginning to come forth and some of the tradition is recovered.
Wesley went through a transformation in the way that
Paul, Augustine and Kierkegaard did and which seems to be
lacking in Luther, Calvin and Henry VIII and this enabled
Wesley to know the meaning of reconciling love and personal growth.
In keeping with his recovery of love for all persons he preached
universal salvation, free salvation, full salvation and sure
salvation and thereby went beyond faith without works
and predestination to a heart full of love for all of humankind.

IV.9.6 From Rousseau's Gratitude Alone to Kant's Reason Alone

Rousseau pondered the Social Contract theories of Hobbes and Locke and Leibnitz's approach to the problem of evil with his best of all possible worlds theory and he worked out a new Social Contract theory and a more optimistic approach to the problem of evil. Rousseau argued that humans were essentially without war in hunter-gatherer times but had been corrupted by the great agricultural empires with their constant wars for power and wealth. With his belief in the primacy of goodness Rousseau was even more optimistic than Leibnitz because this is not only the best of all possible worlds, but with our co-operative efforts and a new Social Contract we can all work together for the best actual world. We have a moral law within that can lead us to a new enlightenment. We only need to pray the prayer of praising thanksgiving for repentance and petition are unnecessary since God has given us all the gifts we need and our problems are really tasks that good government and right effort can progressively overcome. Hume with his trust in experience alone awakened Kant from his dogmatic slumber and Kant was so enlightened by Rousseau and Newton that he saw religion within the limits of reason alone. Luther began with faith alone in scripture alone given by grace alone so that he could stand alone and be justified even though he would be *justus et peccator*, justified and yet a fallen sinner. Luther with his exclusive logic which, however, kept the mixed opposites of *justus et peccator*, got rid of the philosophers and so with the same logic they got rid of him by trusting in experience alone and then a religion within the limits of reason alone. Kant thought that with Rousseau's moral law within and with Newton's starry sky above we could know the almighty creator of the starry skies and have the categorical imperative commanding us with no ifs, ands or buts to treat all persons as ends in themselves and never to reduce them to mere things.

IV.9.7 From Kant's Persons to Hegel's Persons in Relation

Kant's ethics was centered on the equal dignity of all persons
for the Categorical Imperative demands of us that we universalize
our maxim when making a decision and ask if all persons
should do what we want to do and if all can then we can too.
We should always treat all persons in accord with their full
and equal worth and never reduce anyone to a mere thing.
Kant's concept of the equal worth of each person expresses
the very core of the Christian culture's custom, law and politics.
But he does disregard the uniqueness of each person and he does
not make explicit the full relationality essential to personhood.
The postmoderns will recover the uniqueness of each person
which was made most explicit by the Franciscans even though
all the Aristotelians were trying to do that and perhaps that is
why Luther was so opposed to anything that was Aristotelian.
Hegel moved away from the Aristotelian metaphysics of
substance and causality to a new metaphysics of the relational
person in progress through the dialectical moments of history.
His famous formula is "I that is we." and with this insight
he brought to an end the rugged individualism of modernity
and which to some degree was rooted in the concept of the person
as "an individual substance of a rational nature" for that
stress on individual substance that made relationality only
an accident had been seen as problematic by Augustine and
was the main reason for Scotus really stressing *haecceity*.
Of course, Leibnitz was already working with the concept
of persons in relation when he thought of the monads as relational.
But modernity is brought to an end by Hegel as he works
out the concept of persons as fully relational and he is
the inspiration for each of the postmoderns to begin working
on their philosophies of a fully loving personhood with all three
structures of equality, uniqueness and relationality worked out.

IV.9.8 From Pentecostal Spirit to Equity Feminism

As modernity continued to unfold the rewarder-punisher
Father of Luther and Calvin gave way to the saving Jesus
of Wesley and the Evangelicals and then to the Holy Spirit
with all of her gifts and fruits to the charismatic Pentecostals.
In our postmodern time after the year 2000 the Evangelicals
are continuing to flourish as are especially the Pentecostals.
But the God of Luther and Calvin who puts most people in hell
doesn't strike anyone anymore as all that loving and love is
beginning to count again especially with the Pentecostal groups.
In many ways the Pentecostals are like the charismatic Franciscans.
Pentecostals are such that charismatic Catholics feel right at home
with them and in fact feel rewarded to praise and learn from them.
Mrs. Aimee Semple McPherson attracted thousands as she
proclaimed the fourfold gospel with every means at her disposal,
her magnetic personality, her great artistic and dramatic gifts
and her ability to utilize even unfavorable publicity to her advantage.
She was so filled with the Holy Spirit that she could turn every bad
trick into a good one and gender inequality into a new equality.
The women's movement began with the Holy Spirit movement
and voting rights in the modern democracies went from men
with property to all men and finally to at least white women.
In premodern Christianity in the west wherever men were
at work there also were women for with Benedict there was
Scholastica, with Francis Clare, with John of the Cross
Teresa of Avila, and later Therese, the little Flower, and Mother Teresa.
The Modern Women's movement was an equity universalism
and stressed with Kant and Hegel that all persons everywhere
both male and female are equal in dignity and should have
equal opportunity for education and for work and for even voting.
Late modernity is preparing the way for the difference feminism
and the difference universalism that will blossom forth in 1968.

IV.9.9 From Pope's Total Goodness to Martin Luther King's Dream

For the first fifteen hundred years of Christianity there had been
the mystery of suffering and the cross was embraced out of love.
But in modernity the logic of exclusive opposites brought back
the problem of evil for the rewarder-punisher God who
predestined persons to be evil and then punished them for eternity
struck many as a God who could not merit the notion of God.
The Epicurean Atomists used the problem of evil against the
existence of a God; for if he were all good and all powerful
how could he permit so much evil in the world since if he
were good but not powerful you could understand evil, but
he would not be God; and if he were powerful but not good
again that would not fit with how humans think of God.
But with Luther and Calvin there was the belief that the wrath
of the rewarder-punisher God was paramount so the problem
of evil had to be answered so that moderns could still believe.
Leibnitz answered the problem of evil by arguing that we live
in the best of all possible worlds and Rousseau argued that the
actual world is better than Leibnitz best possible world because
we humans as empire builders made it evil, but anything
we suffer now can be a challenge to built a better actual world.
Finally, Alexander Pope gave the most optimistic solution:

> All nature is but art, unknown to thee;
> all chance, direction, which thou canst not see,
> all discord, harmony not understood;
> all partial evil, universal good;
> And, spite of pride, in erring reason's spite,
> One truth is clear, whatever is, is right.

And this loving view about the goodness of all persons,
places and things fits right in with the dream of King.
The modern Pentecostal movement arises out of many
rhythms of African origin and today we dance together in the Spirit.

NOTES

1. Søren Kierkegaard, *The Sickness unto Death*, ed. and trans. Howard V. Hong and Edna H. Hong (Princeton, NJ: Princeton University Press, 1980) 77.
2. Søren Kierkegaard, *Works of Love*, ed. and trans. Howard V. Hong and Edna H. Hong (Princeton, NJ: Princeton University Press, 1992) 29.
3. Søren Kierkegaard, *Training in Christianity*, trans. Walter Lowrie (New York: Random House, 2004) 31.

Bibliography

de Sales, St. Francis. *An Introduction to the Devout Life*. Rockford, Ill.: Tan, 1994.
Hegel, G. W. F. *Hegel's Philosophy of Right*. Translated with notes by T. M. Knox. Oxford: Oxford University Press, 1967.
Kierkegaard, Søren. *The Concept of Dread*. Translated by Walter Lowrie. Princeton, NJ: Princeton University Press, 1969.
———. *The Concept of Irony with Continual Reference to Socrates*. Edited and translated by Howard V Hong and Edna H. Hong. Princeton, NJ: Princeton University Press, 1989.
———. *Concluding Unscientific Postscript to Philosophical Fragments Volume 1*. Edited and translated by Howard V. Hong and Edna H. Hong. Princeton, NJ: Princeton University Press, 1992.
———. *Eighteen Upbuilding Discourses*. Edited and translated by Howard V. Hong and Edna H. Hong. Princeton, NJ: Princeton University Press, 1990.
———. *Either/Or*. 2 vols. Edited and translated by Howard V. Hong and Edna H. Hong. Princeton, NJ: Princeton University Press, 1987.
———. *Fear and Trembling*. Edited and translated by Howard V. Hong and Edna H. Hong. Princeton, NJ: Princeton University Press, 1983.
———. *Philosophical Fragments*. Edited and translated by Howard V. Hong and Edna H. Hong. Princeton, NJ: Princeton University Press, 1985.
———. *The Point of View of My Work as an Author*. Edited and translated by Howard V. Hong and Edna H. Hong. Princeton, NJ: Princeton University Press, 1998.
———. *Practice in Christianity*. Edited and translated by Howard V. Hong and Edna H. Hong. Princeton, NJ: Princeton University Press, 1991.
———. *The Sickness unto Death*. Edited and translated by Howard V. Hong and Edna H. Hong. Princeton, NJ: Princeton University Press, 1980.
———. *Søren Kierkegaard's Journals and Papers*. Vols. 1–6. Edited and translated by Howard V. Hong and Edna H. Hong. Bloomington and London: Indiana University Press, 1967–78.
———. *Stages on Life's Way*. Edited and translated by Howard V. Hong and Edna H. Hong. Princeton, NJ: Princeton University Press, 1988.
———. *Training in Christianity*. Edited and translated by Walter Lowrie. New York, N. Y.: Random House Inc., 2004.
———. *Upbuilding Discourses in Various Spirits*. Edited and translated By Howard V. Hong and Edna H. Hong. Princeton, NJ: Princeton University Press, 1993.

———. *Works of Love*. Edited and translated by Howard V. Hong and Edna H. Hong. Princeton, NJ: Princeton University Press, 1992.

Krippner, Stanley. "The Epistemology and Technologies of Shamanic States of Consciousness." *Journal of Consciousness Studies* 7 (2000) 93–118.

Lowrie, Walter. *A Short Life of Kierkegaard*. Princeton, NJ: Princeton University Press, 1942.

www.ingramcontent.com/pod-product-compliance
Lightning Source LLC
Chambersburg PA
CBHW071145300426
44113CB00009B/1091